SYLVIA PLATH
AND THE MYTHOLOGY
OF WOMEN READERS

SYLVIA PLATH
and the Mythology of
Women Readers

JANET BADIA

University of Massachusetts Press
AMHERST AND BOSTON

Copyright © 2011 by University of Massachusetts Press
ALL RIGHTS RESERVED
Printed in the United States of America

LC 2011021552
ISBN 978-1-55849-896-9 (paper); 895-2 (library cloth)

Designed by Steve Dyer
Set in Electra by House of Equations, Inc.
Printed and bound by Thomson-Shore, Inc.

Library of Congress Cataloging-in-Publication Data
Badia, Janet.
Sylvia Plath and the mythology of women readers / Janet Badia.
p. cm.
Includes bibliographical references and index.
ISBN 978-1-55849-896-9 (pbk. : alk. paper) —
ISBN 978-1-55849-895-2 (library cloth : alk. paper)
1. Plath, Sylvia—Appreciation. 2. Women—Books and reading.
3. Feminism in literature. I. Title.
PS3566.L27Z575 2011
811'.54—dc22   2011021552

British Library Cataloguing in Publication data are available.

Excerpts from MONSTER by Robin Morgan,
copyright © 1972 by Robin Morgan.
Used by permission of Random House, Inc.

Quotations from Ted Hughes's published and
unpublished works used by permission of
Faber and Faber Ltd., © The Estate of Ted Hughes.

*For Sylvia Plath and her readers,
especially those who have graced
my classroom over the years.*

Contents

PREFACE

ANYONE HOPING TO WRITE ABOUT SYLVIA PLATH UNDERSTANDS the nature of the path she's undertaken. According to Ted Hughes, it's a rather mad path that often leads the critic to her own "mental breakdown, neurotic collapse, domestic catastrophe," all of which have "saved" him and his family "from several travesties" of literary criticism.[1] Only the most "insensitive" of the critics, he added, succeeds. I must admit, these words echoed in my mind throughout the writing of this book, but they got especially loud during the final stages of the book's production as I set out to secure permissions for the material I wished to quote in making my argument. Like several scholars before me—many of them women, most of them feminist in their perspective—I ran into considerable obstacles as I attempted to acquire permissions.

Following the guidelines outlined on Faber and Faber's website, I sought permission for material written by Ted Hughes (some published, some unpublished) by submitting my request to the estate. At that time, I provided the quoted material in its context, as Faber requested. A month later I was asked to send the entire manuscript electronically, which I immediately did. Five months later, there was still no word from Faber and Faber, despite follow-up e-mails asking for information about the status of my request. I ran into delays trying to get permission for Frieda Hughes's work as well. While her American publishers granted permission within four months of receiving my request, the permissions I needed from abroad did not come so easily. Months were lost right from the start after I made the mistake of sending my request directly to Ms. Hughes, following the instructions I received from her U.K. publisher. After receiving the correct information from her American publisher, I sent off a second request, only to be told after a month had passed that the information I

provided to secure U.S. permissions wouldn't be sufficient to secure the
U.K. permissions. Should I wish to continue with my request, I would
need to submit portions of the manuscript.

When it became clear that I would have to delay the publication of my
book for a second time were I to try again for permission in the one case
or wait to hear from Faber and Faber in the other, I made the decision to
edit my use of quotations to fit within the Library of Congress's guidelines
for fair use in the United States and the British Society of Authorship's
description of fair dealing in the United Kingdom, following a practice
similar to the one Lynda K. Bundtzen adopted in her 2001 book *The
Other "Ariel."* I am indebted to her leadership on this front, especially her
willingness to outline meticulously in the preface to her book her own
rationale for cutting or keeping quotation as she did.

Like Bundtzen, I had hoped to make significant use of unpublished
material, in my case material from letters written by Ted Hughes. Without permission from the estate, I cut down my extensive quotation of this
material. But then, just as the manuscript was about to go into the final
stages of production, I received word from Faber and Faber that it would
grant me permission to use all of the material I wished to include, assuming of course that I could pay the fees associated with the permissions.
Because University of Massachusetts Press had some flexibility in its production schedule, I was able to partially restore material from Hughes's
unpublished letters. Without this material, my argument in chapter 4
would have been significantly hamstrung. After all, the exact words are
everything in a study of rhetoric. And in the end, I am relieved that all of
the time and money invested in my use of Hughes's archives did not go
to waste. While I regret still having to cut some quotation, especially in
my discussions of Ted and Frieda Hughes's poetry, their poems are at least
widely available to readers.

ACKNOWLEDGMENTS

OVER TEN YEARS HAVE PASSED SINCE THE SEEDS FOR THIS book were first planted; I am extremely grateful to those colleagues, friends, students, and onetime strangers who have helped the book on its long way. During the research stage, I benefited from the able assistance of several students and many librarians. Becky Click, Matthew Prochnow, Sara Blevins, and Chris Belcher helped collect and organize the vast collection of book reviews I discuss in chapter 1. In Adelaide, Australia, Emily Cock, who was kind enough to answer a call for research help from a complete stranger, located material unavailable to me here in the United States. I also thank Kathy Shumaker and Emily Chase at Emory University's Manuscripts, Archives, and Rare Book Library; John Wells at Cambridge University; Alan Delozier, director of Special Collections at Seton Hall University; and the interlibrary loan staffs at both Marshall University and Indiana University–Purdue University Fort Wayne.

Throughout the writing stage I benefited from many mentors and friends who kept the book on track and offered helpful but always very kind feedback. At Ohio State University, where a crucial part of this book originated, I thank members of the English Department First Draft Group, as well as my dissertation committee, for encouraging me to explore the relationship between Plath's readership and popular culture. I feel a special debt of gratitude to my frequent collaborator Jennifer Phegley, whose own interest in women readers sparked mine, and to Jeredith Merrin, Georgina Dodge, Marlene Longenecker, and Jim Phelan, whose conversations about my dissertation gave me early direction. At Marshall University, colleagues Kellie Bean, Whitney Douglas, Chris Green, Sherri Smith, and John Young helped me figure out just what portions of my dissertation had to be shed. They were very thorough in their work. I thank them all for the generosity of their feedback and, even more important, for their intellectual stimulation and their love of texts both literary and not. I am especially indebted to Kellie, who read nearly every page of this book in manuscript (in some cases more than once) and whose conversations about feminism have been instrumental to my thinking throughout. I also wish to express my gratitude to Julie Armstrong for keeping me productive over the course of my sabbatical in Florida and for her careful feedback on early drafts of chapters 3 and 4, and to Jo Gill and Anita Helle for supporting my work early on and for helping me locate my place within Plath studies. In the final stages of the project, my editor at University of Massachusetts Press, Brian Halley, offered encouragement and demonstrated considerable patience, both of which helped me plow through the frustrations of dealing with the Plath-Hughes estate

Having begun my career at a university with a heavy teaching load, I am especially grateful for those who made research and writing possible. As chair of the English Department at Marshall University, David Hatfield was instrumental in helping me carve out time for research and find resources for travel. I am grateful as well for the sabbatical I received from Marshall that finally allowed me to build up some momentum on the project. An award from the West Virginia Humanities Council also came along at just the right moment, providing me a summer free from teaching to sit down seriously with my ideas and construct a project I could get excited about. For help with the expense of permissions and other production costs, I thank the College of Arts and Sciences and the Office of Research and External Support at Indiana University–Purdue University Fort Wayne.

And in the end, there are those debts that can never be adequately acknowledged through words. To my beloved cats, for gracing my lap during the many, many hours I spent sitting at a desk while working on this project and for teaching me the value of the small things in life (and for not accidentally deleting crucial material while walking across the keyboard); to Lachlan Whalen, for making every idea in this book better and every day of my life richer; and to Eugene and Mary Jane Badia, my much-missed parents, who, despite the emotional and financial expenses involved, insisted I go to college, which is where I first encountered Sylvia Plath. For this—and much more—I am always grateful.

• • •

Portions of this book appeared earlier in somewhat different forms in the following publications:

"'Dissatisfied, Family-Hating Shrews': Women Readers and the Politics of Plath's Literary Reception," *LIT: Literature Interpretation Theory* 19, no. 2 (April–June 2008): 187–213. © 2008 Taylor & Francis Group. Reprinted by permission of Routledge. http://www.inforworld.com.

"The 'Priestess' and Her 'Cult': Plath's Confessional Poetics and the Mythology of Women Readers," in *The Unraveling Archive: Essays on Sylvia Plath*, ed. Anita Helle (Ann Arbor: University of Michigan Press, 2007), 159–81. © by the University of Michigan 2007. Reprinted with permission of the publisher.

"*The Bell Jar* and Other Prose," in *The Cambridge Companion to Sylvia Plath*, ed. Jo Gill (Cambridge: Cambridge University Press, 2006) 124–38. © Cambridge University Press 2006. Reprinted with permission of the publisher.

"'One of Those People Like Anne Sexton or Sylvia Plath': The Pathological Woman Reader in Literary and Popular Culture," in *Reading Women: Literary Figures and Cultural Icons from the Victorian Age to the Present*, ed. Janet Badia and Jennifer Phegley (Toronto: University of Toronto Press, 2005), 236–54. © University of Toronto Press, Inc., 2005. Reprinted with permission of the publisher.

"There Is No Such Thing as a Death Girl"

Literary Bullying and the Plath Reader

IN 2003 I COMPLETED WORK ON AN ESSAY, "THE 'PRIESTESS' and Her 'Cult': Plath's Confessional Poetics and the Mythology of Women Readers," which later made its way into print in Anita Helle's 2007 collection *The Unraveling Archive: Essays on Sylvia Plath.*[1] Although I had been researching and writing about Plath for several years, this essay marked my first sustained exploration into the topic of Plath's readers. It begins, like chapter 2 of this book, with a brief description of the figure of Kat Stratford, one of the central characters of the 1999 film *10 Things I Hate About You.*[2] Kat caught my attention because on two different occasions in the film she is depicted as a Plath reader; she is even shown sitting in a chair in her family room reading *The Bell Jar.* In my examination of Kat in my essay for *The Unraveling Archive,* I explained my interest in the question of Plath's readership as I saw it embodied by the character of Kat this way: "As a scholar who once devoured Plath's writings in daily doses, I am intrigued by this figure of the Plath reader."[3] At the time of its composition, the statement certainly seemed true enough. A little revelatory perhaps for the stodgy world of literary criticism, but an honest statement of how I saw my relationship to Plath's work. Several years of research and a book later, however, the statement gives me pause. Part of me would like to take it back, or at least footnote it with a disclaimer. I would do so not because the statement now lacks truth, but because it does work I did not intend it to do.

I wrote the statement to convey a literal reality: my interest in Kat Stratford as a cinematic representation of a Plath reader springs at least partially from my recognition of myself in her. That is to say, I find Kat interesting because I see my own early interest in Plath's writing reflected in her image. When I first discovered Plath in a poetry workshop at college ("Tulips" was my introduction to her work), I was struck by the originality of her voice, the authenticity of the emotions her images conveyed, and, perhaps most important to me then, her willingness to explore even the thorniest questions about what it means to be a young woman. I don't remember if I did so immediately thereafter or not, but before too long I sought out her other works. My most vivid memory of myself as a young Plath reader is the Saturday I spent reading *The Bell Jar* on the living room sofa, chuckling at the scene in which Esther tries, rather clumsily and even comically, to strangle herself by wrapping the cord of her mother's robe around her throat and pulling. The following Saturday I reread the novel, launching what would eventually become a singular scholarly interest, one that took me from senior thesis, to numerous graduate seminar papers, to dissertation, to book. In describing myself as one who "devoured Plath's writing in daily doses," I meant to capture this early interest, which, while it has evolved and taken different shapes over the years, has never waned. I am still struck by the originality of Plath's voice, the authenticity of her expressed emotions, and the courage of her interrogations. Yet I do regret the statement, for reasons this entire book is designed to explain. For those looking for a more concise explanation, let me try to synthesize the reasons for my desire for redaction here.

While I meant my statement to reveal the simple truth of my interest in Plath's writings, the research I've conducted over the course of writing this book has revealed to me the troubling overdetermination of the tropes I used to convey that interest. What I didn't fully realize in 2003 was that, by describing my reading of Plath as a process of devouring her writing in daily doses, not only had I offended the limits of alliteration in literary criticism but, more important, I had stepped into the very bog that would become the focus of my research: namely, the reliance of literary and popular culture on tropes meant to disparage Plath's fans, especially the young women readers among them, as uncritical consumers, as Plath addicts, and even as literary cannibals.

Let me clarify. It's not that I was completely unaware of the existence of such tropes as they applied to Plath's work. I had seen them used before, by none less than Sandra Gilbert, who in 1978 published an essay titled "'A Fine White, Flying Myth': Confessions of a Plath Addict."[4] I'm sure I also heard them come from the mouths of people I met who shared my strong interest in Plath's writings. What I was unaware of, rather, is the historicity of such tropes and their participation in a much larger and long-established discourse about women readers of all kinds of literature, a discourse so persuasive it permeates English-speaking and non-English-speaking societies, as well as literary and mainstream cultures; a discourse so entrenched it has lasted (at least) through the eighteenth, nineteenth, and twentieth centuries, and into the twenty-first; a discourse so natural-ized as to appear devoid of its own historicity.

Despite my intentions, my statement about myself as a Plath reader evokes this larger discourse, which might not be such a regrettable result if it weren't for the deeply troubling nature of its history, including its satu-ration with ungenerous, if not intentionally unkind, accounts of women's reading practices and the misogyny that often underwrites those accounts. Indeed, while my use of the tropes of consumption and addiction were chosen to convey my full engagement with Plath's writing as a young undergraduate—an engagement that has become the basis of a career in literary and women's studies—such tropes have been used historically to convey just the opposite: specifically, an uncritical relationship with texts which can have disastrous consequences.

"Who Will Buy This Book?": The Plath Reader and Literary History

The small explosion of scholarship that has taken place since the early 1990s on the subject of women readers, especially readers in the eigh-teenth and nineteenth centuries, provides rich grounds for thinking about the tropes historically associated with women readers and their reading practices. The leading book of this explosion, *The Woman Reader, 1837–1914*, by Kate Flint,[5] provides one of the most comprehensive and thoroughly researched studies of the rhetoric surrounding women readers in the nineteenth century. Concerned primarily with the "rhetoric of reading practices" and its "assumptions about what, when, and how a woman should read,"[6] Flint uncovers the figure of the woman reader as a "discrete category" affecting the "composition, distribution, and marketing of literature" in Britain throughout the nineteenth century.[7] Flint's analysis points to several trends in the discourse about women readers which are relevant to the question of how we talk about Plath's women readers today. The studies of women readers that have followed Flint's provide further context for understanding the similarities between the discourse that surrounds readers today and the discourse that surrounded past generations of readers.

Perhaps the most obvious point from which to begin a discussion is with the key assumption that appears to drive the discourse about women readers in the eighteenth and nineteenth centuries: the assumption that women, thought to be arrested in a state of perpetual adolescence, are "peculiarly susceptible to emotionally provocative [reading] material" and thus are most in need of regulation and prescribed reading material and practices.[8] Given this assumption, it's perhaps not surprising that discussions about women's reading often centered on women's identification with the texts they read. As Jacqueline Pearson explains in her study of women's reading in Britain between 1750 and 1835, "the female intellect was viewed as, like the female body, soft and fragile, with female ego-boundaries dangerously permeable. . . . As a result, women were deemed vulnerable to excessively identificatory reading practices—'this identifying propensity'—which might endanger their fragile sense of rational selfhood."[9] Looking at similar anxieties within American culture during the nineteenth century, Suzanne Ashworth observes that, according to the general discourse about women's reading in the conduct books of the time, "the majority of women habitually read themselves into fallen stances; their habits of reading were thoughtless, intemperate, self-indulgent, and consequently, self-perverting."[10] The result of such widespread assumptions was "an intense, even punishing, scrutiny of the woman reader and the subsequent demarcation of 'appropriate' reading methods, materials, and aims."[11]

Within this broader discourse about women readers, the facet of the conversation that is most relevant to my discussion about Plath's readers is the one that plainly attempts to pathologize women's reading practices by defining them symptomatically, either as signs of illness or as potential causes of it. Concerned with fiction reading in British and American Victorian culture, Catherine Golden illustrates the preoccupation with women readers shared by the "medical authorities" of the time, who linked "excessive and unsupervised reading of popular fiction" to "early menstruation, painful menses, and infertility, as well as nervousness, insanity, and even premature death."[12] And as Kate Flint demonstrates, reading was central to the diagnosis and treatment of hysteria: the wrong reading practices, it was argued, could incline one to the disease, while the right reading could contribute to its cure or prevention.[13]

One finds the traces of these connections between women's reading and women's health in the art produced during this time as well, particularly in paintings. While there appears to be no shortage of paintings from the nineteenth and early twentieth centuries that romanticize women as readers,[14] more than a few depict women readers as dangerously lost, not simply in a book, but in a melancholy state of mind, including Claude Monet's *Meditation (Madame Monet on the Sofa)* (ca. 1871), Hans Heyerdahl's *At the Window* (ca. turn of the century), and David Alison's *Woman Reading by a Window* (ca. early twentieth century), to name just a few. In Monet's painting, for instance, Madame Monet has apparently abandoned her book, which lies closed on her lap, and retreated into isolation and gloomy contemplation. Particularly revealing is the way she gazes into space in the direction of the window (significantly covered by curtains) but seems to withdraw from its light, opting instead for the recesses of the darkness. She appears, in other words, to have separated herself from the light outside and enveloped herself in the shadows. Reinforcing this theme, Madame Monet appears entombed in heavy black clothing, which in turn accentuates the shadows cast upon her face and the dark circles surrounding her eyes. Hers, one supposes, is a gloomy mood, triggered, the painting suggests, by the seductively bright red book that stands out against her darkened body as if calling attention to itself as the cause of her desolation. While the painting offers no explanation for precisely how the book could have had such an impact on Madame Monet's body, rather than simply on her imagination, written discourse about women's reading fills in many of the gaps.

Perhaps the most interesting links between women's bodies and the books women read are to be found in the tropes of food consumption and addiction that become so central to the discourse about women's reading during this period. Understood as a "physical appetite," reading was seen as "supplying the food of the mind,"[15] and as such it was understood to be open to the same hazards as any diet. Moreover, a woman could not necessarily be trusted to consume healthy portions of reading material or to avoid those books ill matched to her constitution, both of which were required lest one risk varying degrees of physical and mental damage. So common were analogies between reading and food consumption that, as Golden notes, even those nineteenth-century critics and book reviewers who relied on them felt compelled to point out their triteness.[16] As a correlative to these tropes of consumption, the trope of addiction offered an equally powerful expression of the perceived dangers of bad reading habits. Novel reading, as numerous scholars have demonstrated in recent years, was especially prone to such fears. Regarded as having the potential to create "drug-like habits of dependence,"[17] not only could novels, especially sensation fiction, produce "intellectual opium-eat[ers]" hooked on reading and therefore negligent of their domestic duties,[18] but they were sure to breed a broader loss of discrimination, rendering women incapable of making even sound moral judgments. In his work on women's reading in eighteenth-century Germany, Stephen Schindler offers a helpful explanation for why tropes of addiction and illness in particular took root so thoroughly in the discourse about women readers. Put simply, to pathologize is to invite prescription and cure.[19]

Not surprisingly, scholars of women's reading, from Flint to Pearson to Golden, connect this discourse about readers to broader fears and anxieties surrounding everything from the politics of revolution in Europe in the late eighteenth century, to the incursion of women writers into the nineteenth-century literary marketplace, to the increase in women's literacy, to changes in women's education, to the women's movements of the nineteenth and early twentieth centuries. In other words, as a body, women readers have served throughout the past few centuries (probably for as long as there have been literate women) as a site of contest, a concrete ground on which those who wished to uphold the status quo could wage their resistance to broader cultural changes.

As I discuss in chapter 1, similar fears and anxieties converge in the 1970s, the decade that just happens to mark not only the height of Plath's popularity as an author but also a significant increase in women writers' access to publishing and a significant growth in women readers' book-buying habits more generally. Once again, women readers, especially those associated with the women's movement and second-wave feminism, become the focus of broader cultural anxieties, often in terms not too far removed from those we see in nineteenth-century discourse. Take, for example, Susan Wood's review of Anne Sexton's *Words for Dr. Y.: Uncollected Poems with Three Stories* (1978) for the *Washington Post Book World,* in which Wood asks and answers an apparently simple question about Sexton's posthumous publication: "Who will buy this book? I think, from hearing them speak at poetry readings and in poetry workshops, it is primarily young girls and women who admire Sexton for all the wrong reasons, making her a martyr to art and feminism; who seem, out of their own needs, to identify with her pathological self-loathing and to romanticize it into heroism. It has very little to do with poetry and it does neither poetry nor Anne Sexton a service."[20] What emerges from Wood's review is a clearly provocative portrait of women readers, one just as concerned as eighteenth- and nineteenth-century discourse was with uncritical consumption, identificatory reading practices, and the harm resulting from both. For Wood, women readers, compelled by their need to turn Sexton into something she ostensibly is not, have become Sexton's biggest liability. They will buy her book, enriching her literary estate, but at what cost to the poet? That is, the question is not whether this book of Sexton's previously uncollected poems will find an audience to justify its publication. The question is whether it will find the *right* audience. Indeed, Wood worries that the book can only find the wrong kind of reader, attracting "primarily young girls and women" who, blinded by illness or feminist ideology, fail to understand how such a work should be properly read or valued and who in the process endanger Sexton's reputation as a serious poet.

This same question drives the review Wood wrote about *Anne Sexton: A Self-Portrait in Letters* (1977) the previous year. Here, too, Wood wastes no time getting to the point she wishes to emphasize, opening anxiously: "These letters have, unfortunately, a built-in readership—not so much those who admire Anne Sexton's poetic achievements as those who, since her suicide in 1974, have perversely worshiped her, as they do Sylvia Plath, as some sort of Sacrificial Priestess of Madness and Art. (For reasons which I won't try to explain, these suicide cultists seem to be predominantly female, though not exclusively so.)"[21] For Wood, women

readers, here troped pejoratively as "suicide cultists" who "perversely worship" Sexton, represent a "built-in readership," a phrase that implies, we
might assume, that they will buy the book regardless of its content and
quality. As we will see in chapter 1, Wood's tropes echo many of those
that define Plath's reception around this same time, a point not lost to
Wood, who makes the connection between the two writers explicit when
she expresses her fears that readers' adoration could transform Sexton, à
la Plath, into a "Priestess" who sacrifices all for the reader.[22] Such a transformation, Wood scolds, will only "present a false picture that obscures
any assessment of what really matters, her poetry." As negative as her view
of Sexton's readership is, however, Wood does not use this construction of
women readers to argue against the publication of Sexton's work, as she
would do a year later in her review of *Words for Dr. Y.* Whereas *Words
for Dr. Y.* provides Wood no opportunity to defend the quality of Sexton's
writing, the publication of Sexton's letters does. This difference in the two
reviews is important because it suggests that Wood's preoccupation with
women readers transcends her literary judgment. That is to say, for Wood
at this stage, it matters little whether Sexton's work merits publication or
not. Women readers have already ruined it. In their directness, Wood's
reviews of Sexton's works provide a stark snapshot of the literary scene of
the 1970s and encapsulate the discourse about women readers that was
central not just to Sexton's reception but to Plath's as well, a discourse
that rather unabashedly constructs women readers as a body of uncritical,
misguided, even pathological readers.

In this book I set out to examine this discourse, tracing its eruptions
and evolutions throughout literary and popular culture in order to demonstrate the significant effect it has had on the production, reception,
and evaluation of Plath's oeuvre. What I question, in other words, is not
the assumption that women readers constitute a large portion of Plath's
audience, but rather how this assumption has evolved into a mythology
about women readers and how this mythology, in turn, has shaped and at
times even sustained Plath studies. I argue, for example, that this mythology of women readers has driven, and continues to drive, the direction
of Plath scholarship, leading to its dismissal of (auto)biographical and
even feminist approaches to her work, as well as its rejection of the label
"confessional"; that it has dictated the terms of Plath's reception by the
literary establishment and by popular media; that it helps to explain the

nearly ubiquitous image of the Plath reader in popular culture, including in films, television shows, and mainstream media coverage; and that it significantly influenced Ted Hughes's and now daughter Frieda Hughes's management of Plath's writings, including their decisions about how to publish her work and whether to grant permission for its use by scholars. In short, I argue that this mythology of women readers has provided the very grounds on which Plath's value as author has been determined.

To illustrate these arguments, I begin in chapter 1 by tracking the preoccupation with women readers that has defined reviews and criticism of Plath's work, focusing closely on the trope of uncritical consumption that critics have attached to Plath's readers and its centrality in the literary establishment's debates about the aesthetic merits of her publications. In the next two chapters I analyze specific examples of the Plath reader, beginning with fictional depictions of young women reading Plath's books in television shows, Hollywood films, and mainstream contemporary novels, and later moving to historical (one might say "real") examples of readers from the fan culture surrounding Plath. When taken together, my examinations of these literary, historical, and cultural constructions of the Plath reader reveal not simply the persistent nature of her association with uncritical (and largely feminist) reading practices, but also the extent to which our collective preoccupation with this figure of a woman reader has constrained and circumscribed discussions of Plath, leading, for example, to reviews and critical approaches to her work that seem to be inspired principally by a (misplaced) desire to protect Plath from readers who do her and her work harm. In the final chapters of the book, I demonstrate some of the practical effects of this preoccupation with readers on Plath's posthumous career, as I turn to Ted and Frieda Hughes's public and private statements about Plath's readers. Focusing on the estate's perception of readers as "dogs" that "devour" Plath's writing and destroy her reputation in the process, I explore a range of evidence, including poems, essays, opinion pieces, and private letters Ted and Frieda Hughes have written on the subject of Plath's audience, some of which I have collected from the Manuscripts, Archives, and Rare Book Library at Emory University, which holds many of Ted Hughes's papers, as well as archives at Cambridge University and the British Library.

This intensive focus on readers throughout this book is interventionist by design, aiming to move Plath studies forward in several much-needed ways. Indeed, what has motivated this project from its inception is my concern that, for the most part, Plath studies has become bogged down in its preoccupation, even obsession, with repairing the damage that has allegedly resulted from the author's association with the label "confessional poetry," with (auto)biographical criticism and reading practices, and with young women readers. Which is not to say that I think these three issues have represented three distinct problems within Plath studies. As I've argued elsewhere, efforts to distance Plath from the label "confessional poetry" and from (auto)biographical modes of interpretation are closely, even inextricably, linked to assumptions—indeed, anxieties—about her audience.[23] While a full review of the history of the label and its connection to (auto)biographical reading practices is beyond the scope of this book, a close look at a few key moments in the history makes clear why the kind of intervention I'm calling for is needed.

Originating with M. L. Rosenthal's 1959 review of Robert Lowell's *Life Studies*, the label "confessional poetry" gained popularity in the 1960s as a description of a particular mode of poetic writing, one defined by its hyperpersonal subject matter and perceived transgressions of poetic decorum, and it is in this form that the label is first applied to Sylvia Plath's poetry in the mid-1960s. In the decades following the initial publication of her work, however, literary critics expanded the label "confessional," creating, I would argue, a more encompassing critical construct that could serve to designate not simply a particular mode of writing but also a particular mode of reading—one that ostensibly exchanges critical judgments of the aesthetic merits of the poetry for what a host of critics have suggested is a kind of spectatorship. As my use of the word "spectatorship" perhaps conveys, what the label "confessional poetry" comes to signify, in other words, are reading practices that are decidedly (auto)biographical and therefore, in many critics' minds, uncritical and subliterary.

While it would be difficult to identify precisely when this evolution of the label "confessional poetry" begins—even Plath's earliest reviewers reveal an excessive preoccupation with issues of readership—the opening pages from the introduction to Judith Kroll's *Chapters in a Mythology*, published in 1976, most clearly convey the shift in focus:

> Among the current classifications in literary criticism, Plath is usually assigned the category "confessional" poet. That view is usually

facilitated by the obviously autobiographical element in her work and by the apparent accessibility of many of her best-known poems, in which the "confessional" surface is sensational enough to divert the reader from seeing deeper meanings. One might even prefer to read many of her poems as one might view the bloodstains at the site of a murder, as residues of real events. . . . The thrill this provides might easily be lessened when the more impersonal dimensions of such poems are considered. But the very accessible confessional aspect of her work is so powerfully affecting that the thought that there might be something more, and quite different in nature, hardly arises.[24]

As this excerpt makes clear, central to Kroll's statement about Plath's status as confessional poet is an assumption about reading practices. Specifically, she suggests that the confessional mode is as much a mode of reading as it is a mode of writing. This mode of reading, or in her words "misreading,"[25] is one that responds to the surface of a poem, to what is immediately "accessible" and most "sensational." So thrilling is this mode of reading that it can cripple or at least distract readers' critical facilities, rendering them unable to see the deeper meanings of Plath's poetry, which for Kroll lie in the complex mythic system articulated by the poet. To remedy the problem, Kroll insists that readers should abandon the preoccupations that encourage and enable such practices, opting instead to "confront [Plath's] work on its own terms, which is to say, as literature."[26]

The importance of Kroll's statements about the nature of confessional poetry is in no way small. In her insistence that readers get back to the work—to legitimate literary concerns, that is—Kroll helps to construct a critical paradigm that, I would argue, set the terms for Plath criticism throughout the 1970s and 1980s. To grasp the pervasiveness of this paradigm, one need only look as far as the book jackets of the critical literature that followed. The synopsis appearing on the jacket of *Sylvia Plath: New Views on the Poetry*, a collection of essays edited by Gary Lane and published in 1979, for example, describes both the project of the book and the climate of the time: "These new essays broaden the perspective of Plath criticism by going beyond the images of Plath as cult figure to discuss Plath the poet. . . . The serious reader, whatever his or her initial opinion of Sylvia Plath, is sure to find that opinion challenged, changed, or deepened."[27] Another example from the same year comes from Jon Rosenblatt's *Sylvia Plath: The Poetry of Initiation*, which, according to the jacket, is a "closely argued study" that "redirects the readers of Sylvia Plath's poetry away from the nonliterary concerns that have swamped Plath criticism and places [its] emphasis on the work itself."[28] Pinpointing just what these "nonliterary concerns" might be, Mary Lynn Broe's 1980 *Protean Poetic: The Poetry of Sylvia Plath* similarly promises not to dwell on the "lurid details of [Plath's] life" in the hope of getting past "the public's fascination with Plath's personality [that has] discouraged critical estimation of the poetry."[29] And, finally, the jacket from Harold Bloom's 1989 collection of essays on the poet brings the issue of autobiography sharply into focus: "Sylvia Plath is often labeled a confessional poet. The events of her turbulent life . . . often seem to overshadow her prose and poetry, making them read like simple autobiography."[30]

The thread that runs through these book jacket synopses—from Rosenblatt's "nonliterary concerns," to Broe's "lurid details of Plath's life," to Bloom's "events of her turbulent life"—obviously echoes Kroll's concern with extratextual "misreadings." What emerges from these collective comments, furthermore, is a less than flattering portrait of Plath's audience: they are readers who have allowed their reading practices to be governed by their preoccupations with Plath's life and death—in other words, they have insistently read Plath's poetry as autobiography—and in doing so, they have failed *as readers*. For most of these critics, moreover, the label "confessional poetry" is so thoroughly entangled with specific subliterary reading practices that the two become almost synonymous, so much so that to discredit one is to discredit the other. And one can see why the entanglement would have such appeal. By suggesting that the measure of a poem's confessionality lies in the act of reading rather than in the act of writing—that is, by attributing the confessional aspects of a poem to the reader rather than the writer—Kroll and the critics that followed could begin the process of rehabilitating Plath's reputation as a so-called serious poet.

While I do not want to discount the value of Kroll's work, I also do not want to ignore the implications, indeed the consequences, of such arguments about confessional poetry and autobiographical reading practices. I want to insist, in fact, that while Kroll and her contemporaries claim to be arguing for the literary merits of Plath's poetry—for it to receive the treatment it deserves as serious literature—they have done so at great cost to Plath's readers. Put another way, I am proposing that in their persistent hand-wringing over reading practices, Kroll and a host of other critics writing in a similar vein not only fetishize the notions of "high art" and "serious literature" but also perpetuate, if not cause, the very damage to Plath they seek to stop by fueling a construction of her audience as deficient, misguided readers.

A glance at the Plath criticism that has been written in the past decade or so reveals the continuation of this mode of thinking about readers' ostensibly uncritical reading practices. In *The Other Sylvia Plath* (2001), one of the more widely admired book-length critical studies about Plath,[31] Tracy Brain, for example, describes her project as one that seeks "to reveal [Plath's] poems as often being about subjects much larger than one woman's autobiography."[32] Explaining the motives behind this goal, Brain continues:

> There is much unkindness, not to mention little value and reliability, in using poetry and fiction as evidence for Plath's supposed anger toward her husband or parents or female rivals; or, at the opposite extreme, as proof of her presumed victimhood. To treat Plath's writing in this way is to belittle her work, for the implication of such an exercise is that Sylvia Plath was too unimaginative to make anything up, or too self-obsessed to consider anything of larger historical or cultural importance. . . . Many [readers] do not notice that they are being cheated, for the fascination with the personal too often interferes with any serious attentiveness to the writing, thereby limiting the ways of responding to and appreciating it.[33]

As this passage makes clear, Brain, like Kroll, dismisses autobiographical reading practices as "misreadings" that interfere with "any serious attentiveness to the writing" and argues instead for readings that attend to the "technical proficiency of [Plath's] poetry."[34] To underscore the seriousness of her concern, she goes on to construct Plath's audience as misguided readers who are so intent on applying biographical details to the poetry— so possessed of a "fascination with the personal"—that they fail to realize they've been "cheated" out of a richer reading experience.[35]

A similar construction of Plath's readers is evident in an essay by Amy Rea for the *Readerville Journal*. Appearing in February 2003, in an issue intended to commemorate the fortieth anniversary of Plath's death, the essay, "Reclaiming Plath," pays homage to the poet and attempts to debunk the myths surrounding her readers. In fact, the stated aim of the essay is to challenge the stereotypical image of the Plath reader as a woman "hung up on death," to make it "OK to like Plath minus an obsession with death."[36] While Rea seeks to show that Plath's fans are "many and various" and thus do not conform to a stereotype, a goal one can certainly respect, she does so in a way that effectively undermines her purported objective. For Rea, certain ways of reading Plath's writing—and therefore certain kinds of readers—are inherently less valuable than others. As she argues, "labeling the work as strictly confessional strips it of its mythic qualities and detracts from the very disciplined intellectual approach Plath brought to her work."[37] In arguing this point, Rea clearly echoes Brain's rhetoric of "technical proficiency." She also echoes Brain's worries that autobiographical readings "belittle" the work by denying the imagination and effort that go into writing good poetry. In the end, then, Rea's "reclaiming" of Plath serves only to replicate—and, I would add, reinforce—the paternalistic anxieties about women readers that pervade Plath criticism, anxieties that emerge most fully at the close of Rea's essay, where she predicts: "With each new generation of young readers who find themselves fascinated with her death, there will be a revival of Plath as suicide icon. But those readers will also age and gain perspective from their own life experiences, and they'll inevitably come to see a more complex Plath— the accomplished and talented poet."[38]

While it is true that neither Brain nor Rea specifically identifies the readers each wishes to critique as women, Brain's indictment of Plath's "many" readers certainly implicates women, long regarded as Plath's primary audience. More important, I would argue that the implication of gender is always already there. All it requires is a little history to bring it into the light—not only history in the shape of the long-established discourse about women readers that I have already outlined but also the history of the discourse about Plath's women readers that I seek to unfold over the course of the following chapters. As both histories make clear, uncritical reading practices have long been associated—and continue to be associated—with women readers, whether Brain and Rea mean to evoke the association or not. Until attention is paid to these histories, I think Plath studies will remain bogged down by its excessive worry over the reading practices of Plath's general audience and its concomitant need to shut down certain approaches to her work, rather than encourage the diversity of interpretations surely made possible by the impressive nature of Plath's body of writings.

To pull us from this bog, I begin by challenging what I see as the most damaging assumption made by Plath criticism today, an assumption made not about Plath's readers but about Plath's texts, specifically the assumption that we can (and should) resolve differences between how Plath's unschooled readers approach her work and how literary critics want them to approach her work simply by appealing to the texts themselves. As everyone from Kroll to Brain to Rea and many critics in between have insisted, if readers would just attend to the written page, if they would just approach Plath's writings as pure works of literature untainted by the discourse surrounding the author, then a true understanding and appreciation of Plath could be brought to light. It's time, I think, that we see such appeals within Plath studies to a liberated and determining literary work for what they, in effect, are: literary bullying.

As Tony Bennett has written, "the concept of the 'text itself' is produced and has effects as an essentially rhetorical device used to enhance the claims of a particular ideology of reading." While "it provides the means by which a new reading seeks to clear a space for itself and to displace the cultural power of prevailing readings,"[39] its result does not encourage an understanding of the text as polysemous, for as Bennett puts it elsewhere, "the attribution of any authority to the 'text itself' has the effect of bullying other readings not just off the field of battle but out of existence entirely." Thus, "dismissed as 'untutored readings,' as distortions [or] misunderstandings, [these other readings] are located as part of a history of incomprehension rather than as readings which . . . deserve to be understood on their own terms."[40] Such bullying within Plath studies, even when conducted under the guise of clearing space for new readings, strikes me as unnecessary, if not counterproductive. And of course, such bullying within Plath studies, whether intentional or not, is more than a little ironic. Having suffered under the constraints placed on them by the Plath estate's efforts to control interpretations of her work by withholding copyright permissions (by literally withholding the text itself), Plath critics seek to exercise a similar control over interpretations of her work, a control grounded, à la Ted Hughes, in their claims of having privileged access to the text itself. It is this grasp for hermeneutic control that ought to worry us, rather than the reading practices that provoke it, for as Bennett notes, "texts are kept alive only at the price of being always other than 'just themselves.'"[41]

Working from these assumptions, I seek throughout this book to resist the ideology that underwrites the vast majority of the Plath scholarship that is published today; this ideology insists that the only responsible way to discuss Plath is through a close reading and explication of her literary texts. I understand that this ideology is reactionary in many ways, that it springs at least partially from a desire among scholars to reverse entrenched modes of reading that have ostensibly hurt Plath's reputation or left her work "underread," to borrow Christina Britzolakis's word.[42] But as I discuss later on, we fret unnecessarily, and worse, our fretting only compounds the problem it seeks to cure. In place of fretting, we need to recognize that there are many ways of valuing Plath as author, and the first step toward appreciating these different approaches is to understand where our prejudices against certain ways of understanding her originate. For this reason, my focus throughout this book is not the discussion and analysis of Plath's writings but rather, exclusively, the history and evolution of the discourse surrounding Plath's readers. I say this, of course, fully anticipating that my own work will be seen as relegating Plath's work to the margins, of making "nonliterary" concerns the primary impetus of Plath scholarship yet again, and thus of jeopardizing her reputation even further. I obviously do not share a fear of such dangers.

Shamelessly unconcerned with the texts themselves, then, I approach Plath throughout this book primarily from two theoretical directions, cultural studies and reception theory, which together provide the grounds for examining texts and issues previously overlooked by Plath scholars. While previous biographers and scholars have treated the question of Plath's reception, focusing on whether works were received well or not or examining in depth a small selection of reviews, my book sheds new light on the reception of her work by conducting a close analysis of the larger body of reviews and uncovering the anxieties about women readers that give shape to the literary judgments. It also illuminates the deep relevance of other primary texts that, at first glance, may seem tangential, including films and television shows that have made use of the image of the Plath reader, Ted Hughes's opinion pieces and personal letters, and a wide variety of texts written by fans on Plath's behalf, from Robin Morgan's poem about Hughes's "murder" of Plath, to newspaper editorials protesting the state of her gravesite, to online fan sites like the Sylvia Plath Forum. In looking at such an array of decidedly unliterary texts, I hope to add to the more traditional biographical, textual, and psychological approaches to Plath and her work that have dominated Plath studies thus far, inviting us in the process to think further about the intersections between the popular and the literary—intersections Plath herself deeply engaged throughout her own career as a writer. What I hope emerges from this approach are the seeds of a conversation that might change the very ways Plath and her readers are discussed and valued.

"I'm a Death Girl, and They Need Me": *Imagining Plath's Women Readers*

Central to this book is an image: an image of a young woman reading Plath's work, an image not at all unlike the portrait I offer of myself as a young reader of *The Bell Jar* at the start of this introduction. It's an image that ought to be familiar to anyone in touch with popular culture from the past few decades. Having made numerous cameo appearances in films, television shows, and literary texts, including *The Gilmore Girls*, *Natural Born Killers*, *The Simpsons*, *Family Guy*, Sherman Alexie's *Ten Little Indians*, Sue Grafton's *U Is for Undertow*, and Alice Sebold's *The Lovely Bones*, the Plath reader is an inescapable image. It has even served as the foundation for an entire novel, Meg Wolitzer's 1982 *Sleepwalking*, which centers on a cohort of three female Swarthmore students, Naomi, Laura, and Claire, who are obsessed, respectively, with Plath, Sexton, and a fictional Plath- and Sexton-like poet named Lucy Ascher, who published terribly bleak "death landscapes" before killing herself at the age of twenty-four. Known on their campus as the "death girls," this particular collection of young women readers exemplifies the terms by which literary and popular culture has come to understand Plath's, as well as Sexton's, readership, and in doing so it offers a useful starting point for thinking about the nature and implications of our cultural discourse.

The prologue to the novel establishes these terms from the outset, opening with a depiction of the women's all-night death talks, complete with candles and the recitation of Plath, Sexton, and Ascher poems, during which "they talked about death as if it were a country in Europe" from which they "could simply fly home bearing rolls of color film and tourist anecdotes."[43] Underscoring the women's distorted view of death, the novel depicts their nighttime poetry reading as a near-"religious experience," so hypnotic in its effect that it was "as though they were being lulled into an easy trance" (6). Furthermore, these ritual poetry readings are the center of the young women's lives; everything else, writes Wolitzer, was just time that had to be passed until "the sun came down over the trees and the death girls started to wake, to come to life" (6). Recognizing this obsession with death in one another, Naomi, Laura, and Claire "had banded together, apparently drawn to each other by the lure of some secret signal as unintelligible to everyone else as the pitch of a dog whistle is to human beings" (6). Even their bodies betray their oddity. When they laugh, they are "joyless," and as the narrator tells us, they "could easily be identified from several yards away by the clash of a winter-white face with a perennial black turtleneck" (6, 3). Not surprisingly, they are the objects of jokes among their classmates, who regard the three women as living in "some dream world" of "depressing women's poetry" (4).

While the novel at times complicates the image established so thoroughly in the prologue (in Claire's case providing motivation for her obsession with Ascher's bleak poetry by recounting her teenage brother's death), it certainly doesn't seem interested in challenging the reader's expectations. For the most part, the image of the three women that emerges from the prologue carries through the entire novel. From start to finish, they are depicted as dark and humorless. Even "bright-eyed" Julian (21), Claire's boyfriend and the character who serves as the emblem of normality throughout the novel, can't recall a time when he actually saw "one of them smile"; as he puts it, "their faces just weren't cut out for it" (10). Even more relevant, their dark, humorless personalities are depicted as inextricably linked to their reading practices. In recounting to Julian her parents' concern over her engrossment in Lucy Ascher's poems, Claire describes the impossibility of stopping. In the narrator's words, "she simply could not close the book; she was drawn to it with a pull she had never felt before" (15). Underscoring the idea of reading as addiction, Claire tells Julian: "I used to read those poems the minute I woke up. The night before, I would select a poem to be read in the morning, and I would put the book on my night table. . . . When I woke up I would slowly remember the poem waiting for me, and I would open the book and read it lying there in my bed, barely awake. I didn't even get up to brush my teeth or pee or anything but just read the poem through, and it really made me feel good" (15–16). Similarly, when Claire's mother confronts her about that "thing you have for that woman poet," Claire screams internally, "It is not a thing! . . . It is everything; it is my life." So profound is the effect of Ascher on Claire that, according to the narrator, "the earth split apart for Claire when she first read Lucy Ascher" (43).

As this collection of passages suggests, the young women's interest in Plath's, Sexton's, and Ascher's poetry transcends the boundaries of reading. Just reading their chosen author's books is not enough; their obsessions are so complete that they must attempt to insert themselves into what remains of their author's life. In Naomi's case, it involves voyeuristically watching Plath's surviving mother come and go from her house; in Laura's case, it involves kneeling at Sexton's gravestone; and in Claire's case, it involves becoming a housekeeper for Lucy Ascher's grieving parents. As these actions portend, their reading of poetry, if not already so at the outset, quickly becomes pathologized. We learn, for example, that Naomi's reading of *The Bell Jar* in high school sent her into a sleepless "manic stupor" (98). As she puts it while retelling the experience to Julian:

> When I was in high school, I read the book and it really shook me up. I was valedictorian of my class and a National Merit Scholar, and I suddenly realized that all the awards and prizes I'd been racking up meant absolutely nothing. Zilch. I'd been pushing ahead of everybody for years, like Plath, and I saw that none of it would mean anything in the long run, that I would die like everyone else. . . . I was very tempted to go to Smith—that's where Sylvia went—but part of me was scared. I thought if I went there, I might be following in her footsteps or something. . . . I thought I might go off the deep end. (173–74)

While Naomi seems to have avoided the pitfall, eventually giving up being a death girl by the novel's end, Laura (the Sexton reader throughout the novel) ends up in the exact position Naomi feared. When we last hear of her, she is seeing a psychiatrist, taking Valium, and "[lying] around all day, depressed" (172). Claire appears to escape such a fate largely, if not entirely, because of Julian's intervention. Concerned for her well-being when he learns of Claire's stay at the Ascher house, Julian sets out to "retrieve" her. When he arrives there, Claire tries to explain to Julian why she feels she should stay. "I'm very important to [the Aschers]," she says. "I'm a death girl, and they need me." Julian persuades her to leave by effectively crushing her illusion. He tells Claire: "There is no such thing as a death girl. . . . Death girls don't exist." To make his point, he lets her know what has been going on with Naomi, who he says is "on the verge of giving up being a death girl," and Laura, who has "become very withdrawn and troubled," as if to represent the only two possible outcomes for Claire (207).

As this scene between Julian and Claire well illustrates, Julian's intervention, combined with Claire's return home, first to her parents and then to college, compel us to view Claire's status as a death girl critically, which in turn means viewing her behavior and reading practices as abnormal and unhealthy. While she has suffered loss in her short life, she has used literature inappropriately, in this case to languish in her grief. Put another way, her reading practices are presented as a sign of deep psychological problems related to her inability to cope or grieve appropriately. Without personal traumas that explain their own misguided reading habits, Naomi and Laura come across more simply as plain old naïve readers, ones unprepared for the fallout on their well-being of such self-indulgent reading practices. Their fates are no less didactic than Claire's, however. While Laura's fate is left ambiguous at the novel's end, it's clear that she has at least sought psychiatric help for her behavior and appears to have abandoned her interest in living as a death girl. Naomi too has abandoned the death girls, an abandonment embodied in her decision to grow out the bleached blond locks she wore in imitation of Plath, suggesting, of course, that while she's growing out her hair, she's also outgrowing the kind of self-indulgent reading habits that have defined the death girls.

On the one hand, the death girls, as their name suggests, are clearly meant to evoke a stereotype. When the novel's narrator first puts forward the image of a band of death-obsessed girls who have been "lured" together by a sound audible only to themselves and who accent their sun-deprived skin with black turtlenecks, it is meant not simply to draw laughs but to elicit, in highly economical terms, a particular response from readers, a nod of recognition, a "yes, I know the type." Yet one is reluctant to view the image as a simple stereotype, for this band of death girls sustains an entire novel—and by most accounts, a successful one. That level of centrality and characterization is an unlikely role for a mere stereotype to fulfill, which suggests that there is a compelling mimetic element to the death girls, and thus that they share an uneasy relationship with reality, at least reality *as we think we know it.* Simply dismissing the image of the death girls as a stereotype allows us to skirt much too easily the difficult question of the relationship of the stereotype to the knowledge and experience we bring to the novel as readers.

The fact that the Plath reader appears to exist simultaneously as both actual reader and mere stereotype makes her an intriguing subject of study, of course. But it also places those of us who wish to study her in a methodological quandary, for how does one approach a subject that hovers somewhere between reality and fantasy? How does one make claims about a subject that can't quite be located, a subject that is tangible and historical even as it is circumscribed by stereotype and cliché? For starters, we recognize that the figure of the Plath reader is a discursive phenomenon; Plath readers, even embodied ones like myself, exist only through the language and texts that constitute them. Yet this approach will take us only so far, for we must still account for what happens to her as discourse; we must account, for instance, for the way the discourse is reified, accepted as reality, and perpetuated largely because it seems so self-evident. To begin this process, I propose that we approach the issue of the construction of Plath's readership as a mythology. Indeed, I have offered an examination of the death girls of *Sleepwalking* because the three characters encapsulate so well the degree to which Plath's readership, largely assumed to overlap with Sexton's readership, has evolved from real audience into a cultural and literary mythology. In using the term, I do not mean to evoke the legendary (i.e., mythic) status of this figure of the Plath reader, though the issue is relevant to my examination; nor do I mean to suggest automatically that the narrative of the reader presented by texts like *Sleepwalking* is based on false beliefs, though that question too is relevant.[44] Rather, my use of the term draws specifically on the early work of Roland Barthes, whose ideas about the relationship between myth, history, and language allow us to understand more clearly the process through which an image of a group of college-age readers could develop into the reservoir of signification it has become.

As Barthes conceives of it, myth operates at the level of second-order signification: it is a "metalanguage," a "second language, *in which* one speaks about" the sign of the first-order linguistic system.[45] In this first-order system, according to Ferdinand de Saussure's well-known formulation, the sign results from the combination of a signifier and a signified: the combination of sound and letters in a linguistic representation (the signifier) and the concept they aim to demarcate (the signified). In Barthes's expansion of Saussure's linguistic system, the sign of the first-order system becomes the signifier in a second-order system and, now imbued with new meaning, develops into a wholly different sign, a process Barthes calls "signification."[46] In this system the signifier once again combines with a signified, but here the relationship between signifier and signified is a radical departure from the one they shared in the first-order system. While their relationship in the first-order system is always arbitrary (the ascription of meaning is simply by convention), their relationship in the second-order system is never so. It is, in fact, motivated by intention, and its intention or function is to distort. In short, myth takes the original sign which had been self-sufficient, impoverishes it of meaning, and turns it into a repository of new meaning. Even as it accomplishes this transformation, however, it also appears devoid of the history which has produced it. That is, it naturalizes that which has been condensed into the new signified and thus transforms history into nature. In this way it looks neutral and innocent rather than ideologically laden. Myth, as Barthes puts it, is "what-goes-without saying."[47]

When I speak of the mythology of women readers, I am referring, in part at least, to the subjection of the woman reader to this second-level system of signification. Accordingly, what most interests me throughout this book are the ways we talk about the Plath reader (in other words, the metalanguage that constitutes her) even as our culture's understanding of her "goes-without-saying." If we return to *Sleepwalking*, for example, part of what allows us to understand the death girls as more than mere stereotype is the very naturalization of the image, particularly how it comes to stand in for real readers. They appear authentic characters precisely because the myth they embody has been naturalized and internalized by literary and popular culture. Indeed, literary and popular culture understands the Plath reader as always already a myth constituted by those qualities that need not be named even as they are continually referenced:

her uncritical reading practices, her precarious mental health, and of course her gender.

In asking that we reexamine our assumptions about Plath's readers, I do not mean to suggest that we cannot make distinctions between different ways of reading. I certainly do not find every single articulation of what Plath's writing might mean convincing.[48] My argument is meant, rather, to suggest that the pervasiveness of an exaggerated and distorted rhetoric about these readers tells us far less about Plath's audience and the value or meanings of Plath's writing than about the patriarchal ideologies that enable the rhetoric and make us blind to its implications, ideologies that allow the very women readers who have bought Plath's books and propelled her success to be turned, ironically, into agents of harm. As we've already glimpsed in Susan Wood's review of Sexton's work, and as I discuss in chapter 1, it's widely assumed that by the early 1970s women readers, and the ostensibly unliterary reading practices they've been associated with, represented a major liability to Plath; critic after critic believed that they had caused significant damage to her reputation, potentially relegating her forever to the position of mere cult figure. Yet with no evidence offered to support such claims, one is left to wonder just what shape such damage took or just how, exactly, readers did Plath a disservice, to borrow a popular word from Plath's reception. In what ways is the damage tangible? In book sales? In the literary awards bestowed on Plath? In the amount of literary criticism about her work that has been published? In her inclusion in anthologies and classroom instruction? Given Plath's indisputable success in these areas, I doubt we will find evidence of damage by looking in any of these directions. The absence of any clear answer to just how readers have damaged Plath suggests to me that the perception of damage is largely, if not entirely, apocryphal. In fact, I would go even further and suggest that damage to Plath's reputation as far as readers are concerned is limited to that which occurs at the moment when the idea of damage is articulated by the reviewer. In other words, any damage caused is discursively produced, the result of the hand-wringing over readers that has gone on in print. To wit, readers' (ostensible) damage to Plath is what everyone talks about, even as it goes-without-saying.

As the totality of this book shows, this willingness among critics and the media to accept the discourse about readers and the disservice they do to Plath as if it were apparent and coherent proves far more dangerous than anything Plath's readers can do, which is why it's crucial that we work to understand the process through which the Plath reader is made to signify what she does. Directing our attention to history is the first step toward that understanding, for as Barthes himself would tell us, mythology accomplishes its illusion of apparentness and coherence through its suppression of history. To remedy this suppression, I turn in chapter 1 to what is perhaps the most significant episode in the voided history: the initial reception of Plath's work by the literary establishment in the 1960s and 1970s.

CHAPTER 1

"Dissatisfied, Family-Hating Shrews"

Women Readers and the Politics of Plath's Literary Reception

THE LITERARY RECEPTION OF PLATH'S WRITING HAS BEEN
summarized by at least a few scholars and biographers over the years,
including Linda Wagner-Martin and Paul Alexander.[1] These summaries
are invaluable to readers looking for either an overview of how Plath's
work has been generally valued within the literary establishment, an indication of whether her individual works were received warmly or not, or
some insight into how Plath may have felt about the few reviews that were
written in her lifetime. While I focus on the reception history of Plath's
work in this chapter, I do not offer simply another summary of her reception. Rather, I set out to examine the anxieties about women readers that
permeate the vast collection of reviews written about Plath's work and to
situate these anxieties not only within the context of Plath's career but,
just as important, within the broader discourse about gender and reading
that has shaped literary culture over the past few decades.[2]

As I demonstrate in this chapter, anxieties about women readers have
driven (indeed continue to drive) critical assessments of Plath's oeuvre,
giving shape to everything from the language critics use when describing
the work under review to the judgments they reach about its quality and
literary worth. For some critics, Plath's popularity with women readers
represents an obstacle to a serious consideration of her work, a distraction
that must be dealt with lest it continue to divert attention away from the

brilliance of her poetry. For less admiring critics, Plath's popularity with women readers is all the evidence that is needed to make a case for the *lack* of brilliance in her work; after all, these critics imply, if so many women like it, how good can it be, especially given women's notoriously uncritical reading habits and undiscriminating consumption of such "low" cultural productions as soap operas? While arriving at different conclusions, both arguments situate women readers at the forefront of the debate about the value of Plath's writing, and with alarming implications.

Given Plath's undeniable popularity with women, it's perhaps not surprising that this particular group of readers has found itself the object of critics' attention. And to those familiar with the history of genres commonly regarded as "lowbrow" or simply "popular," it's not even surprising that women readers have become central to arguments about the aesthetic merits of Plath's writing, especially to arguments that aim to discredit it. We need only remember how the reputations of certain genres, including the allegedly "lowbrow" genres of the contemporary romance novel and the nineteenth-century sensation novel, have suffered from their close association with women readers throughout literary history. What is surprising in the case of Plath's reception is the degree to which the association is so ingrained that it can be easily overlooked or simply discounted as insignificant. This is especially true of those reviews of Plath's work in which references to women readers are made so casually, even humorously, that as we read the reviews, we are made to feel as though we're merely in on a joke the reviewer has made, rather than witnessing the reproduction of an invidious discourse. Such oversights are especially likely to occur when reviews are looked at selectively, without the entire reception history in view, say, while a reader simply pages through a magazine or journal, which, I would guess, is how most readers encounter book reviews. When we look at the larger collection of reviews, in contrast, the *pattern* of the references to women readers from review to review begins to emerge, making each reference impossible to ignore and giving the collective references added significance. And the significance of what exactly is said about women readers also becomes clear. For instance, a casual reference to Plath's readers as "devotees" in one review might seem innocent enough, but when we look at the term "devotee" alongside some of the other, more obviously disparaging terms critics have used to describe her readers—including "hounds,"[3] "necrophilia[cs],"[4] and "shrews"[5]—the implications of a term like "devotee" become more obviously significant.

It is with this fuller picture in mind that I proceed in this chapter. Indeed, throughout my research I have aimed to be as comprehensive as possible in my examination of the reviews, basing the argument of this chapter on the hundreds of reviews written in response to Plath's many publications over the past five decades. Throughout my discussion of this vast collection of book reviews, too, I have aimed to be as comprehensive as possible, so much so that I may well risk alienating my readers with the repetitive feeling of the evidence I present. But the point of this chapter, I suggest from the outset, lies precisely *in* the repetitiveness of the discourse across the large volume of reviews. That is to say, the repetition in this chapter is deliberate, and its purpose is to underscore the pervasiveness and persistence of the discourse about Plath's women readers and thereby make the argument for its significance. What might stand out in particular is the way the discourse traverses different formats and venues, from local to national newspapers, from mainstream magazines to highbrow literary journals, and from American periodicals to publications abroad.

To move us toward a better understanding of this discourse, I focus most of my attention, some might say myopically, on the rhetoric of the reviews, zeroing in on examples of rhetoric that seem either visibly or obscurely relevant to the question of how critics have understood Plath's women readers. In doing so, I identify a mode of understanding and talking about Plath's audience that evolves over the course of her reception into a distinct institutionalized discourse about women readers, one that repeatedly determines the literary judgments rendered in the reviews themselves and that continues to shape our understanding of who reads Plath's work, how they read it, and for what reasons. To provide focus to my examination, I spend most of this chapter discussing the circulation of this discourse throughout Plath's reception in the 1970s and early 1980s, concentrating especially on the shifts that occur during this period that appear to be motivated less by the question of the aesthetic quality of Plath's work than by critics' patronizing and even misogynistic attitude toward women readers.

While more than a few critics are shockingly explicit and direct in how they express this attitude, often attacking women readers quite plainly as

uncritical consumers prone to poor judgment and psychological problems, most are more subtle, veiling their concerns about women readers
behind an array of tropes and anecdotes, some more original than others.
To those who have read Steven Mailloux's work on the cultural rhetoric of
reception, my concern with tropes and anecdotes will sound familiar. In
many ways, in fact, I am conducting an examination of Plath's reception
that aims, in a fashion similar to Mailloux's "rhetorical hermeneutics," to
discover "how particular tropes, arguments, and narratives contribute to
historical acts of interpreting."[6] Such an examination makes several key
assumptions about the nature of literary reviews. First, it assumes that, as
historical acts of interpretation, reviews can, in Mailloux's words, "be read
within the rhetorical context of their production and reception."[7] Second,
it assumes that interpretation functions "as a politically interested act of
persuasion" and thus that "claims for reading are always direct attempts
to affect power relations through coercion or persuasion."[8] Third, it assumes that reviews are not ever just transparent and objective statements
about the literary or aesthetic quality of a work; indeed, it assumes that
the tropes used to discuss the act of reading tell us something important
not simply about literary culture but about broader cultural politics and
ideologies.[9] And last, it assumes that the tropes, arguments, and narratives
of "specialized professional discourse" (like that of literary reviews) can,
to borrow Mailloux's words again, "migrate" to and from "different sites
within a cultural conversation."[10] If we understand reception along these
lines, then the importance of studying not just individual reviews but
the entire reception history of a literary work becomes clear, as does the
importance of studying a particular author's reception within its broader
cultural network.

At the same time as I work from this set of assumptions regarding the
cultural rhetoric of literary reception, I am also aware that Plath's reception is laden with the complex history of the discourse about women's
reading, a history which teaches us that the tropes and narratives used to
describe reading acts "migrate" not merely from "different sites within
a cultural conversation" but from different conversations *across* historical periods. To reiterate the terms I outlined in the introduction, then,
studying the role of women readers in Plath's reception requires both
synchronic *and* diachronic analysis; it requires us to consider how critics'
views of the Plath reader have both *everything* and *nothing* to do with

Plath.[11] For this reason I aim throughout this chapter not only to position Plath's reception within the discourse about women readers circulating broadly in the 1960s and 1970s but also to highlight those facets of the discourse that reflect the anxieties about women readers that have shaped literary culture over the past three centuries at least, including those anxieties I summarized in my introduction. Before turning to this question of women readers, however, I offer a brief overview of Plath's early publications and their general reception for those less familiar with her career.

Plath in the 1960s and Early 1970s: The Initial Reception

At the time of her death in 1963, Sylvia Plath had achieved what might best be described as a respectable reputation as a poet, though hardly one commensurate with the success she had desired throughout much of her adult life, and certainly not one that presaged the level of success that would come in the years after her death as the full extent of her talents unfolded. Following several years of sometimes successful but (for the over-achiever Plath) often frustrating attempts to place her poems in leading magazines, her first book of poetry, *The Colossus and Other Poems*, was picked up by Heinemann and released in England in October 1960. The book received mostly minor notices in British periodicals, many barely a full paragraph in length.[12] Those few magazines and newspapers that took the time to review the book more fully—*Critical Quarterly, Time and Tide, London Magazine,* and the *Observer*—responded to it with what I would characterize as qualified enthusiasm.[13] In his review for the *Observer*, A. Alvarez, a critic who just a few years later would champion *Ariel*, characteristically summed up Plath's poetic abilities this way: "The Colossus needs none of the usual throat-clearing qualifications, to wit: 'impressive, considering, of course, it is a *first* volume by a *young* (excuse me) *American* poet*ess*.' . . . She simply writes good poetry. . . . She is not, of course, unwaveringly good."[14] While undoubtedly disappointed by the book's reception, Plath continued to seek out an American publisher for *The Colossus*. In the summer of 1961 she found one in Knopf, which released the book in the United States the following spring. Unfortunately for Plath, the reception *The Colossus* saw in the United States proved even less momentous than in England. In the months that followed its publication in the United States, the book was the subject of only a handful of reviews in such periodicals as the *Herald Tribune*, the *Christian Science Monitor*, and the *Kenyon Review*. While the reviews were uniformly positive, they were also brief, most as brief as a single paragraph.

Perhaps because the reception of *The Colossus* failed to match her ambitions for her poetry, Plath devoted much of her writing time in early 1961 to her novel *The Bell Jar*. Having contracted for publication in October 1961, Heinemann released the novel in England under the pseudonym Victoria Lucas on January 14, 1963, just a month before Plath's death. Coinciding with rejections from American publishers to whom she had sent the novel months earlier, *The Bell Jar* arrived on England's literary scene to a reception nearly as unremarkable as the one *The Colossus* had received. Approximately a dozen and a half magazines and newspapers, many of them local, reviewed the novel.[15] A few early reviewers seemed to agree that *The Bell Jar* was a promising, even "clever first novel," as Robert Taubman put it in his review for the *New Statesman*.[16] One even called it a "brilliant and moving book."[17] But generally speaking, praise for the novel was not so enthusiastic. Simon Raven's review for the *Spectator*, for example, finds *The Bell Jar* to be an appropriately "unpleasant, competent, and often very funny novel" but advises readers "to stick to home produce" since Lucas is "by no means as unpleasant, competent, or funny as her English counterpart, Miss Jennifer Dawson."[18] Of course, it is likely true that Plath fared no worse than most first-time novelists (or in the case of the publication of *The Colossus*, for that matter, most first-time poets).

As the early reception of *The Colossus* and *The Bell Jar* suggests, most readers caught their initial glimpse of Plath's talents only after her death, first through the notices and tributes that immediately followed, many of which included selections from her poetry, and later that same year through the publication of her work in the *Critical Quarterly*, the *Atlantic Monthly*, the *New Yorker*, *Encounter*, and *The Review*.[19] The news of Plath's untimely death, appearing next to previously unseen poems such as "Edge," must certainly have grabbed readers' attention, generating new interest in her work and shaping her reputation as a poet. Still, as instrumental as these tributes and publications were to the visibility of her work, Plath's was not a meteoric rise to fame fueled, as some have suggested, simply by the tragedy of her suicide.[20] Rather, her reputation as a writer and an icon grew gradually over the decade as her work was slowly made available to the reading public. In fact, more than two years passed between her death and the publication of a new volume of her poetry.

When editions of *Ariel* were finally published—one by Faber and Faber in England in March 1965 and a second by Harper and Row in the United States a year later—the book received notable attention and was the subject of more than forty reviews, many in prominent literary and popular venues, including a few in mainstream American magazines such as *Newsweek* and *Time* (the latter even reprinted "Daddy" as part of its review).[21] As if trying to match the hyperbolic construction of Plath offered by Robert Lowell's preface to the American edition of the book,[22] many of the critics reviewing *Ariel* seemed less interested in offering literary judgments about the quality of the poetry than in advancing their own extreme metaphorizations of the poet herself. Take, for example, this statement from a *Time* magazine review of *Ariel* in 1966: "*Daddy* was merely the first jet of flame from a literary dragon who in the last months of her life breathed a burning river of bale across the literary landscape."[23] Or this one from a *Newsweek* review of *Ariel* the same year: "The general effect of the book is that of a symphony of death and dissolution, scored in language so full of blood and brain that it seems to burst and spatter the reader with the plasma of life."[24] While reviews like these seem to eschew, in effect, the question of literary judgment—after all, is it good or bad to be a literary dragon? to spatter the reader with blood and brain?—others cut unambiguously to the question. Some reviewers directly take up the interpretative difficulties posed by *Ariel*. As Alan Ross puts it, "This is not the sort of book discussable, at this stage anyway, in normal critical terms."[25] Others, in contrast, were more than eager to take up the very discussion Ross found impossible, seizing the opportunity to argue that the reception of *Ariel* thus far had "been generous to a fault."[26] Dan Jaffe, in his review of *Ariel* for the *Saturday Review* in 1966, formulates the issue this way: "All of us, I hope, mourn the despair and early immolation of so gifted a writer; but we need to ask whether the poems justify the accolades. I don't believe they do."[27] Two years later in his 1968 review of *Ariel* for the *Sewanee Review*, Robert Stilwell offers an even less sensitive assessment of the poetry: "I should guess that *Ariel* will linger as a very specialized and rather subterranean book of poems, that A.M. theses will be written on it (doubtless several are already under way), and that it will not, finally, add a major dimension to the poetry of the 1960s."[28]

As these comments suggest, with the release of *Ariel*, literary critics became almost singularly preoccupied with the question of Plath's success—success propelled notably by the book's vast appeal among general readers. Indeed, while reviewers often revealed an ambivalence about *Ariel*, especially when examining its relationship to Plath's suicide, general readers embraced the book. In its review of the American edition of *Ariel*, *Time* magazine noted that in just ten months, the book had sold fifteen thousand copies in England, "almost as many as a bestselling novel."[29] And according to Plath biographer Paul Alexander, the book continued to sell in unprecedented numbers, totaling more than a half-million copies after two decades in print, a remarkable figure for a book of poetry.[30]

With so many new Plath readers on the scene, the demand for an American edition of *The Bell Jar* ballooned in the 1960s. As Frances McCullough remarks in her foreword to the twenty-fifth anniversary edition of *The Bell Jar*, before its United States publication in 1971, "at least two bookstores in New York carried [bootlegged copies of] the book and sold it briskly."[31] When the novel was finally released in the United States, it attracted a vast audience, making its way immediately onto the *New York Times* best-seller list, where it stayed for twenty-four weeks.[32] Neither the eight-year delay in the novel's U.S. publication, nor the novel's small, tepid reception in Britain, first in 1963 and again upon its rerelease under Plath's own name in 1966, could suppress readers' demand for Plath's only published novel.

If the number of reviews of the 1971 edition is any indication, the literary establishment appeared equally eager to get their hands on a copy of the novel. At least three dozen periodicals reviewed *The Bell Jar*, from popular magazines such as *Time* and *Newsweek*, to more literary journals such as the *Hudson Review* and the *Virginia Quarterly*, to city papers such as the *Charlotte Observer* and the *New Orleans Times-Picayune*. This time around the reception was warmer, though not unequivocally so. Exemplifying the level of praise present in the positive reviews, Lucy Rosenthal calls it an "uncommonly fine piece of work,"[33] and Robert Taylor calls it "brilliantly authentic."[34] But while some reviewers praised the novel unambiguously, others seem compelled to measure it against either Plath's reputation or her poetry, often to conclude that the novel comes up short in both cases. As Linda Pratt puts it in her review for *Prairie Schooner*, *The Bell Jar* is a "small novel distinguished primarily by those occasional images which find their proper expression in the poems."[35] Even those critics who found the novel compelling seem to have felt obliged to measure it against its reputation, as Clarence Peterson does in his review for the *Washington Post Book World,* when he notes that the novel is "well-worth its fame on merit alone."[36]

Whether critics liked the works or not, the significant commercial success of both *Ariel* and *The Bell Jar* marked Plath as one of the most notable authors of her time and signaled the beginning of what several critics have referred to as her reign as the "priestess" of contemporary poetry.[37] Bolstering her visibility, the release of *The Bell Jar* in the United States was quickly followed by the publication in England of two more volumes of her poetry, *Crossing the Water* in May 1971 and *Winter Trees* in September of the same year. While delayed in the United States, both books were available to American readers by September 1972. Not surprisingly, *Crossing the Water* and *Winter Trees* sold exceptionally well, in both England and the United States, and as Paul Alexander notes, they were even featured as selections of the *Saturday Review* Book Club and the Book-of-the-Month Club, respectively.[38] They were also widely reviewed, especially in the United States. Sometimes jointly discussed within the same article, the two works collectively were the subject of at least four dozen reviews, and just as with the United States edition of *The Bell Jar,* the magazines and newspapers reviewing the works ranged from popular magazines, to literary journals, to national and local newspapers. But unlike *The Bell Jar, Crossing the Water* and *Winter Trees* received an overwhelmingly positive reception. In fact, the most common complaint heard throughout the reception of the two works involves the Plath estate's decision to publish the works separately rather than simply bring out a definitive collection of all of Plath's poetry.

By the early 1970s, then, Plath had arrived full force on the literary scene. Just as important, she had achieved the kind of commercial and critical success that had driven her throughout much of her career as a writer, success fueled in no small part by the women's movement. Well under way by the late 1960s, the movement paved the way for Plath's posthumous career, kicking open doors for women writers by creating a publishing culture more welcoming of women's literature and a reading culture eager for texts that spoke to women's concerns. That Plath's works would emerge in print at the height of these changes all but ensured her appeal to women readers, especially feminist readers, who saw in her narrative many parallels to their own struggles and who quickly adopted her as an iconic woman writer.

To appreciate Plath's evolution into a feminist icon, one need only look through the earliest issues of *Ms.* magazine, the defining publication of the women's movement, which debuted in the spring of 1972. The cover of the preview issue of *Ms.* announces its featured contents, including, in the words of the headline, "Sylvia Plath's Last Major Work," which, one discovers upon opening the pages, is actually "Three Women: A Poem in Three Voices" from the then forthcoming volume *Winter Trees.*[39] If the 1972 issue hadn't predated the publication of *The Journals of Sylvia Plath*, one might even conclude that the cover image for the preview issue was inspired by Plath. Just as Plath revealed her fear of a "life of conflict, of balancing children, sonnets, love and dirty dishes,"[40] the cover features an illustration of a pregnant woman who, while wearing a traditional American-style dress, appears to be modeled after a Hindu goddess. In this case, each of the goddess's eight arms holds a different symbol of the complex lives women lead: an iron, a steering wheel, a mirror, a phone, a clock, a duster, a frying pan, and a typewriter. Just a few months later, in the September issue of the magazine, Plath was once again a featured topic on the cover, which this time promised to deliver "Sylvia Plath Demystified," a reference to an article on Plath included in the issue's contents.[41]

Whatever one concludes about the relationship between Plath's own ideologies and those held by feminism,[42] there can be no doubt that the women's movement of the 1960s and 1970s played a significant part in the formation of her reputation and success as a writer, both directly by promoting her work and indirectly by creating a receptive audience for it. Not surprisingly perhaps, for many critics Plath's status as an icon of the women's movement only further reinforced their perception of her as "priestess," establishing in turn the all too popular image of her audience as a "cult," or to use Frances McCullough's label from her foreword to *The Bell Jar*, as "Plath groupies."[43] Given this particular coalescence of Plath's commercial success and her rise to the status of a women's movement icon, it seems hardly a coincidence that in the literary reviews from this same time, Plath's women readers, especially feminist ones, were in the forefront of critics' minds. In any case, a clear portrait of Plath's reader-

ship had emerged by the 1970s, if not earlier: her readers were perceived
to be young (implicitly white) women who—by transforming Plath's writing into a reflection of their own pathology and/or feminist ideology—had
misunderstood not simply the tragedy of her situation but the work itself.[44]

Plath in the 1970s and 1980s: *The Women's Movement and the Mythology of the Plath Reader*

In his 1976 review of Sylvia Plath's *Letters Home* for the *Observer*, literary
critic A. Alvarez begins his assessment of the work in question by observ-
ing Plath's recent appointment as, in his words, the "patron saint of the
feminists."[45] The observation seems casual enough until the end of the
review, when Alvarez lets loose the following invective at Plath's readers:
"I wonder," he writes, "what [Plath] would think now when all her wildest
ambitions have been posthumously fulfilled: her 'potboiler' 'The Bell Jar,'
an international best-seller . . . ; her name and example a cult for every
young would-be writer with the blues; her cause taken up by precisely
those dissatisfied, family-hating shrews she herself satirized in her poem
'Lesbos.'" It's the kind of success, he concludes, that "would break her
heart all over again." Even without too much scrutiny, Alvarez's comments construct a rather startling image of Sylvia Plath's readers: they are
unhappy young women who have identified with Plath despite her clear
rejection of their identities, politics, and pathologies. Put another way, the
women buying Plath's books—and feeding what Alvarez calls "the whole
noisy, million-dollar razzmatazz"—are poor readers who have failed to
recognize Plath's disparagement of their own kind in her poetry.

I begin this section with this snapshot from Alvarez in part because it
illustrates so well how women readers, especially feminist ones, figured in
the literary reception of Plath's work, but also because it invites us to pay
particular attention to the historicity of the arguments that get made about
Plath's readers, a historicity embodied in this case in Alvarez's dismissal
of Plath's women readers as "dissatisfied, family-hating shrews." Indeed,
it is hardly a coincidence that the construction of women readers put forward by critics like Alvarez emerges alongside the broader cultural backlash taking place against the women's movement in the late 1960s and
1970s, as I think Alvarez's particular brand of invective makes abundantly
clear. Before turning to individual reviews of Plath's work, then, I want to

provide a brief overview of that backlash against the movement, as well as introduce some of the rhetoric defining feminism in the cultural imagination at the height of the backlash, focusing especially on the rhetoric surrounding the circulation and reception of feminist ideas and texts.

In speaking about the women's movement, I am referring of course to what was commonly known in the 1970s as "women's lib," a mass social movement organized largely by young women beginning in the mid-1960s. To advance its agenda, the women's movement relied primarily on a series of well-conceived protests (among its most notable, the protest of the Miss America pageant in Atlantic City in 1968) and the creation of feminist media outlets, including magazines, newspapers, and presses. As Rosalyn Baxandall and Linda Gordon report in their introduction to the movement, over five hundred feminist magazines and newspapers existed in the United States by the mid-1970s, including the flagship magazine Ms.[46] The creation of feminist media outlets did little, however, to help the women's movement construct its own agenda or control its own publicity. By the late 1960s, the movement had become the object of mainstream media coverage, which propelled it onto the larger cultural radar and thus opened it up to the larger cultural imagination. According to Ruth Rosen, this coverage by mainstream media, including articles in magazines such as Time and Newsweek and televised reports on the evening news, turned the concept of "women's liberation" into a diluted and often misunderstood "household phrase."[47] The coverage also played a significant part in the backlash against the movement, institutionalizing, among other things, much of the rhetoric that has come to define the stereotype of the feminist. Susan J. Douglas argues that it was the mainstream media of the 1970s, in fact, that gave us the stereotype of feminists as "shrill, overly aggressive, man-hating, ball-busting, selfish, hairy, extremist, deliberately unattractive women with absolutely no sense of humor who see sexism at every turn."[48] While Douglas's description may strike some as over-the-top, an examination of the news stories of the time quickly reveals the grounds for her pithy synopsis. For my purposes here, I focus on several related tropes that stand out in the media coverage of the women's movement in the 1960s and 1970s, beginning with those that are present in one of the first major news stories about the movement in a national mainstream publication.

Appearing in a November 1969 issue of *Time*, the story describes feminists interchangeably as "angry young women" who have been looked upon skeptically by "most middle-aged or older women," or worse yet as "young girls," "violent in mood," who try to "repel other women rather than attract them."[49] While *Time*'s fixation on the youthfulness of the feminists in question arguably reflects the true demographics of the movement, it also reveals the cultural anxieties provoked by feminist activism. It's telling, for example, that *young* women represent an especially pernicious threat, for they, by virtue one presumes of their immaturity, become, according to the *Time* reporter, "fertile ground for the seeds of discontent."[50] Far from being innocent, such metaphors create an unflattering portrait of feminists, painting the youngest ones as passive receptors of discontent and the presumably more experienced ones as colonizers who plant their ideologies in these young girls' heads and thus take advantage, it would seem, of the gullibility of youth. This unflattering portrait is evident in the other tropes used in the *Time* article as well, including its description of the various feminist groups across the nation as "cells, which constantly split and multiply in a sort of mitosis,"[51] a trope that curiously depicts feminism as a movement that threatens to grow even as it appears completely out of the control of the feminists themselves, as if it were a cancer. Not surprisingly, the articles that would follow the *Time* story echo the sentiment. In *Newsweek* a few months later, for example, a reporter claims that "women's lib groups have multiplied like freaked-out amebas."[52] In other articles, the women of the movement are "rabid";[53] they are "naïve and ignorant" and full of "self-hatred";[54] they are "sick, silly creatures."[55]

The larger portrait of the feminist that emerges from these few but revealing examples from mainstream media is unmistakable. The women of the movement are young, impressionable, uncritical consumers of ideas they fail to understand; they are followers caught up in emotions they cannot control and brainwashed by cult leaders who inspire membership through mystical forms of persuasion. According to the literary and social critic Irving Howe, feminists also tend to be very bad readers, the inevitable result of their uncritical consumption of ideas more generally. Indeed, one of the most fascinating links between the women's movement and Sylvia Plath's reception in particular is Howe, who in little over a year publishes an essay on Plath inspired by the publication of *Crossing the Water* and a lengthy review of Kate Millett's *Sexual Politics* (1970), one of the seminal texts of the women's movement. While Plath's latest publication and Millett's polemic appear to have little in common, both provoke from Howe the same disparaging rhetoric about readers and their reading habits.

Throughout his 1970 review of *Sexual Politics*, Howe's construction of Millett resembles the feminist stereotype I outlined earlier and makes use of similar tropes suggestive of uncritical consumption. She is "a little girl who knows nothing about life" and who is "driven by some ideological demon"; yet, even with such significant shortcomings, she has managed to attract "followers," largely because they too are possessed by a "quasi-religious hunger."[56] For Howe, moreover, these deficiencies in Millett are first and foremost the result of her bad reading habits. While she claims to base her argument in *Sexual Politics* on her reading of important works in Western philosophy, science, and literature, her approach to these works is "ill-informed" and without "intellectual sophistication."[57] As he puts it, "she simply will not read with care."[58] Nor is Millett a sole perpetrator of careless reading, for as Howe is quick to point out, with all its flaws, *Sexual Politics* "will impress those unable or disinclined to read with care."[59]

Relying on similarly condescending depictions of Millett and her readers, an article in the *New York Times* in August 1970 describes Millett as a "heroine of the world of instant culture" and "high priestess of the current feminist wave."[60] Echoing the *New York Times*, a feature article in *Time* magazine just a few months later refers to Millett as the "high priestess of the Women's Liberation Movement" and *Sexual Politics* as its "bible." The article goes on to catalog the complaints critics have waged against Millet and the women's movement in general, paraphrasing the "provocative" questions Helen Lawrenson had raised in an earlier *Esquire* piece about the nature of feminists: "Can the feminists think clearly? Do they know anything about biology? What about their maturity?"[61] As this collection of comments about Millett and her readers suggests, critics were generally unapologetic in their disparaging treatment of women readers and writers, especially those characterized as "feminist."

Even a cursory glance at literary reviews from the 1970s reveals the extent to which social changes such as the women's movement—and the anxieties these changes inspired—were shaping the literary landscape, particularly when it came to whose work was published and read. In fact, as the reviews of the early 1970s suggest again and again, the era that saw the Civil Rights Act passed also saw more women finding publishers for their writing and more readers discovering and buying their work. Of course, this expansion was not to everyone's liking, especially when it came to poetry. In the opening of his 1973 review of poetry by John Berryman, Anne Sexton, Maxine Kumin, and others, Seldon Rodman voices his concern with the growth this way: "Never has there been so much interest in reading and writing poetry, and never have publishers spent so much money publishing it—with almost total disregard for quality."[62] More explicit in his attack on readers, Howard Sergeant makes the following complaint in his 1971 review of a wide range of new poetry: "To judge by the extraordinary interest shown by the younger generation in poetry readings these days, it might well be argued that poetry is in a healthier state than ever before. Yet . . . the new audience appears to be an undiscriminating one, demanding a certain type of poetry and tending to reduce poets to the basic level of performers."[63] Lest one wonder just how Sergeant's and Rodman's complaints pertain to the women's movement, I offer one last excerpt well worth its length, this one from Pearl Bell's 1975 review of works by Sexton, Adrienne Rich, and John Ashbery:

> Surveying the tower of recently published volumes of poetry, I was almost tempted to conclude that there is today a vastly enlarged public for the work of serious poets. Not only are the number and variety of new poetry books a cause for wonder; some publishers have even adopted the admirably practical idea of issuing them simultaneously in hard-cover for libraries and in paper for everyone else, a boon to poets and readers alike.
>
> Alas, upon closer inspection it turns out that the collections being so ardently devoured by the common reader just now seem mainly to be those either of feminists read for their message, not their talent, or of confessional writers esteemed more for their sensational private lives than, such as it may be, for their art.[64]

What emerges from this collection of excerpts are anxieties, not only about the "certain type of poetry" being published, but also about the kinds of readers and reading practices such publications invite.

These anxieties are frequently confounding, as in the case of Bell's re-view, where they are shaped by conflicting attitudes toward the "common reader." While Bell celebrates the accessibility of poetry made possible by the shift to paperbacks, she also laments the consequence of that accessi-bility: namely, that the "common reader" might choose to like the wrong kinds of books. Despite such contradictions, certain points do emerge rather clearly from Bell's review. First, though the gender of the readers remains unspecified, one can certainly assume, given her identification of the poets benefiting from the "boon" as "feminists," that she's particularly concerned here with women readers, especially young women readers. Moreover, the implication of Bell's comments in total are that "feminist poets" are not "serious poets," nor is their poetry really "art," a point made evident by Bell's insertion of the belittling phrase "such as it may be."[65] Such artistic failure is not entirely the poets' own fault, however, since their weakness seems to lie as much in how their writing is read as in any inherent flaws it might have. To convey this point, Bell, like Irving Howe, relies on the trope of consumption to make her point. The readers she imagines "ardently devour" poetry, unable to tell the difference between art and sensationalism, between art and mere "message." Or to put it in Howard Sergeant's plainer words, they are "undiscriminating" readers.

Like Howe's response to *Sexual Politics*, Bell's review can offer us a glimpse into the larger literary landscape of the period, revealing in par-ticular the literary establishment's concern with the public's—especially women's—book-buying and reading habits. As I am about to show, such concerns with just how books are read and by whom erupt again and again throughout Plath's reception, and their connections to the women's movement take many forms, from the direct—such as when Plath's read-ers are consciously labeled "fanatical feminists"[66]—to the indirect, such as in the case of Irving Howe.

Just as he did in his review of Millett's *Sexual Politics*, Howe wastes no time getting to his assessment of those who he thinks will buy *Crossing the Water*. He begins, in fact, to define these readers as early as the opening paragraph of the essay when he proclaims: "A glamour of fatality hangs over the name of Sylvia Plath. . . . It is a legend that solicits our desires for a heroism of sickness that can serve as emblem of the age, and many young readers take in Sylvia Plath's vibrations of despair as if they were the soul's own oxygen."[67] Central to Howe's characterization of Plath's "young readers" is a trope of consumption, for just as Howe transforms Plath from serious poet into glamour girl and, to borrow his words from later in the review, an "authentic priestess,"[68] he also transforms her "young readers" from serious readers into cult followers. Plath, no longer perceived as a poet, puts out life-sustaining "vibrations" that are taken in, not read, by those who admire her. In other words, for Howe, the very act of reading and the critical faculty it involves have been supplanted by a mystical process of consumption that leaves the young intellectually and emotionally crippled, one presumes, by the lack of real oxygen.

Furthermore, it is with this suggestion of mystical consumption that we begin to see the two parallel concerns that run throughout Howe's essay: his concern with Plath's exaggerated status as a poet—he later calls her "an interesting *minor* poet"[69]—and his concern with the absence of critical reading practices responsible for the exaggeration.[70] This link between his two concerns is crystallized when later in the essay he dismisses Plath's admirers altogether, arguing that "one must be infatuated with the Plath legend to ignore" the weaknesses of the poetry.[71] Such statements suggest that Howe, despite his own admission at the beginning of the essay that to do so would be "unjust," allows his own "irritation with her devotees to spill over into [his] response to her work."[72]

The similarities between Howe's depiction of Plath's "devotees" throughout his essay on Plath and his depiction of Kate Millett's "admirers" throughout his review of *Sexual Politics* suggest a broader concern with the circulation and reception of women's writing, one emblematic of the backlash taking place against feminism and the commercial success of feminist writing in the early 1970s. As important as these connections between Plath's success and the feminist movement are, however, I do not mean to suggest that Plath's reception simply mimics the reception of other feminist writers during this time. While an icon in the world of the women's movement, by the 1970s Plath was also, of course, an important figure in the literary world of contemporary poetry—two worlds with decidedly different values, for as Susan Rosenbaum points out, the poetry establishment of the 1960s and 1970s, despite women's progress, was "largely male-dominated, in terms of editors, judges, and published poets," a reality Plath not only recognized but also to a large degree internalized.[73] And as Jacqueline Rose observes, many of those writing about Plath from within this male literary establishment, to say nothing about those editing and publishing her work, seemed intent on "enshrining her unequivocally in the domain of high art."[74] Feminists' adoption of Plath as icon, to say nothing of the commercial success it propelled, presented a particular obstacle for those in this male literary establishment who wished to advocate for Plath's work: not only were feminists thought to privilege political interests over aesthetic ones, but also their association with Plath drew attention to her interest in popular or "low" forms of culture, an interest reflected in *The Bell Jar* and other prose she wrote for women's magazines before finding her "real" voice as a poet. Plath's reception thus produces just the right alchemy of anxieties for the literary establishment, for as Rose puts it, "the dangers of femininity and the dangers of mass culture stand in the most intimate and isomorphic relationship to each other."[75] It seems fair to conclude, then, that it's precisely this tension between the two bodies vying to make her *their* icon—and the larger undetermined meaning of her reputation at the time—that gives particular shape to the anxieties. Put more simply, I am suggesting that Plath's writing and its audience became such contested sites in large part because feminists were not the only ones with a vested interest in her writing during this time.

To return to the timeline of her reception, the release of *The Bell Jar* in the United States ("low prose") and the publication of *Crossing the Water* and *Winter Trees* ("high art") all at the same time created just the right moment for critics to exert influence over the debate. Not only did these three publications offer plenty of occasions for reviews, but they also gave eager critics the opportunity to see whether Plath's remaining poetry would live up to *Ariel*, the work that had made her reputation thus far, and to see whether her only completed novel would live up to the poetry. In fact, despite the six-year lag between the publication of *Ariel* and the release of *Crossing the Water* and *Winter Trees*, it's unusual to find a review of Plath's newest publications that fails to make comparisons to *Ariel*, a sure indication of the expectations and anticipation shaping the reception of *The Bell Jar*, *Crossing the Water*, and *Winter Trees* as a result of *Ariel's* success. In addition, for many critics writing at this time, the release of three works in close proximity was read, for the most part accurately, as a sign of Plath's significant commercial success as an author. Preoccupied with the implications of this success, critics seemed compelled to ask, was

Plath's work deserving, one way or another, of the kind of success it had achieved, especially among women readers?

This preoccupation leads in the 1970s to a distinct shift in how Plath's work is reviewed. Perhaps the most obvious sign of this shift lies in the evolution of "cult" rhetoric within Plath reviews between the reception of *Ariel* and the reception of *Winter Trees*. In reviews of *Ariel* in the mid-1960s, few critics even took notice of the cult phenomenon emerging around Plath, and when they did, the shape of the cult was left ambiguously defined. For example, in a 1966 review revealingly titled "Sylvia Plath: The Cult and the Poems," Melvin Maddocks only speculates that Plath "may become a minor cult,"[76] while in the same year Gene Baro concludes in his review that Plath "straightaway became the object of a literary cult" after her suicide in 1963.[77] Although they disagree about whether the cult exists full-blown already or still lies on the horizon, Maddocks's and Baro's descriptions of the "Plath cult" suggest that it is much less a group of general readers than a camp of those critics who have championed and, in Maddocks's and Baro's eyes, exaggerated the quality of Plath's poetry since her death.

In the reception of *The Bell Jar*, *Crossing the Water*, and *Winter Trees*, in contrast, not only has cult rhetoric become more prevalent, but the cult itself is given a more definable shape as well, often through language fraught with judgment. For example, Stephen Philbrick calls Plath the "idol of a death cult,"[78] while Paul West describes her audience as a "cult which finds her a seraphic cosmic victim, a self-elected St. Joan of the post-natal clinic, whose every word is loaded with unimpeachable witness."[79] But it is Marjorie Perloff who captures the preoccupation with the Plath cult best when she opens her review of *Crossing the Water* and *Winter Trees* with this snapshot: "During the past year or so, Sylvia Plath has become a true cult figure. At this writing, the Savile Book Shop in Georgetown, D.C., has a huge window display in which copies of *The Colossus*, *The Bell Jar*, *Ariel*, and *Crossing the Water* encircle a large photograph of Sylvia Plath, which rests against a copy of A. Alvarez's *The Savage God: A Study of Suicide*, that ultimate tribute to Sylvia Plath as our Extremist Poet par excellence."[80] For a critic like Perloff who felt that the accolades bestowed on Plath's work during this time were well earned, the identification of Plath as a cult figure was one to be overcome, for only then could her work receive the serious treatment it deserved. But for many critics who did not share Perloff's final assessment of the work, the designation of Plath as a cult poet fit all too well, as a return to West's review demonstrates. While the object of his review is *Crossing the Water*, the existence of the Plath cult seems to compel him to comment on the recently published American edition of *The Bell Jar*. West concludes that the novel "is hardly as well written as her weakest poems" and then complains, "yet the cult touts it, extols it."[81]

Implicit in West's characterization of the Plath cult is a judgment, not simply about the quality of the novel but about the quality of those reading it: the Plath cult consists, for West, of readers so blinded by the impetus to worship that they are unable to distinguish between good and bad writing. West is not alone in his judgment. In his review of *The Bell Jar* for the *New York Times Book Review*, Richard Locke calls the novel an "underground talisman" and then curiously complains, "Hardly the stuff of a best-seller. But there it is, number four this week,"[82] as if, oddly enough, best-sellers weren't by definition popular books. Furthering this widespread perception about the lack of critical judgment among Plath's audience, again and again throughout reviews from this time the language used to describe readers strips them of their very status as readers. From one review to another, Plath's readers take the shape of "worshipers,"[83] "admirers,"[84] "band-wagon camp followers,"[85] "voyeurs,"[86] "pursuers,"[87] and even "baying packs of autograph hounds."[88] In similar fashion, the act of reading is also transformed. For Webster Schott, "you don't read these poems. You inhale them";[89] for Jill Baumgaertner, readers "greedily accept [Plath's life] and feast on it" in the act of "a rather strange communion," as if her poetry were "her blood, seeping slowly and then finally gushing forth to splash the reader with something that cannot be removed";[90] and for Jan Gordon, readers are spiritual participants in an act of "communal worship."[91] While none of these critics came out as plainly as Howard Sergeant did when he called the younger generation of poetry readers an "undiscriminating one," they clearly articulate the same concern about the quality of the reading act, for in each of these examples, the act of reading is figured not as an intellectual activity but as an emotional or even a physical one: it's an inhalation, a feast, a spiritual communion. Significantly, the most common explanations for why Plath's readers are especially susceptible to such tendencies implicate their mental health: either they suffer from a "desperate self-absorption and concomitant fascination with themes of sickness and death"[92] or, as Schott argues, they are "young people" with "limited experience" who thus "need literature to help them feel bad."[93]

On the one hand, one could argue that such statements merely reflect the ways Plath's work challenged the status quo of the literary establishment, especially its entrenched relationship, even in the 1970s, to New Criticism and the high modernist tradition that sought to create a small, elite audience. In other words, one could argue that such statements reflect the broader anxieties circulating at this time about the canon and the apparently evolving audience for literature. Or on the other hand, one could argue that they represent critics' attempts to match Plath's own hyperbolic tendencies and discourse about audience—an audience memorably imagined in the poem "Lady Lazarus" as a "peanut-crunching crowd."[94] Yet the tenor of the comments by Plath reviewers—a tenor suggested not only by the hyperbole and metaphor they use but also by the note of accusation involved in such figurations of the reading act as those I just discussed—must certainly lead us to look for a deeper explanation for the anxieties. That deeper explanation becomes more clearly visible in those reviews that take the time to speculate or make assertions about the gender of Plath's audience, especially those that, for the first time in the reception of Plath's work, evoke the women's movement in discussing Plath and her audience. Among the first to do so is A. Alvarez's 1971 review of *Crossing the Water* and *Winter Trees*, in which he observes with some trepidation that, while Plath's cult has already "grown enormously," the potential audience promises to be even more "vast" now that "she looks like being taken up as an early martyr for Women's Lib."[95] By the time James Finn Cotter reviews the American edition of *Winter Trees* in 1973, Plath's identity as an "embattled heroine of the Women's Liberation Movement" appears firmly in place.[96]

While Alvarez's and Cotter's remarks might appear casual enough (at least alongside the invective we know Alvarez is capable of), other critics seem eager to offer a more defined, indeed judgmental, portrait of this newly identified "Women's Lib" audience. In his 1972 review of *Winter Trees*, Jan Gordon, for instance, argues that Plath's ever-changing or "protean identity raises the whole question of the poet's popularity, particularly among those women sensitive to the demands for liberation,"[97] insinuating that the identification of Plath as a feminist erroneously fixes her identity in a way the author herself rejected. While less concerned with the question of Plath's relationship to feminism, Melvin Maddocks is just as eager to point out the faults of her readers, arguing in his review of *The Bell Jar* for the *Christian Science Monitor* that "modern readers tend to feed ghoulishly on other people's madness. Mental illness has become a bit too glamorous to bystanders—the ultimate badge of artistic sensitivity. Perhaps Plath readers should keep in mind that while living in 'the rarefied atmosphere under a bell jar,' what Sylvia Plath wanted, above all, was to *get out*."[98]

As condescending as these male critics are toward Plath's readers, theirs is not necessarily the harshest rhetoric circulating at this time. Far more dismissive in some ways is the portrait Helen Dudar offers in her review of *The Bell Jar* for the *New York Post*. The review opens:

> If you tuned into the novel early, you got a cooperative aunt to buy it for you on her trip to England in 1964. A while later, you found your way to the two book stores in New York that imported the $1.75 paperback and acquired one before they ran out of the latest shipment. You feel slightly superior to the late-arrivals who read it only last month in the American edition. But for those who respond to it with the same intensity the book evoked from you, what you feel most of all is kinship. . . .
>
> People who never buy anything but paperback editions own the Plath hardback. There is known to exist at least one bright young secretary—suggesting the existence of others—who gave up her psychiatrist after the doctor had read "The Bell Jar" and told her he couldn't see how it applied to her at all. All summer long, Fran McCullough, who is the Harper & Row Plath editor, found herself resisting heart-felt pleas and offers of bribes from followers who wanted advance copies of the new Plath poetry collection, "Crossing the Water," due shortly. . . .
>
> To the most fervent of Plath fans, she is simply Sylvia; and the involvement in her life and death is often obsessive.[99]

While Dudar certainly captures the culture of anticipation surrounding the U.S. publication of *The Bell Jar* at the time, her attempts to illuminate the reasons behind the anticipation—or to explain the pursuit of what she coins "Plathism"[100]—rely on the same troubling tropes that are by now so familiar. Readers of *The Bell Jar*, whom she at one point directly identifies as "several generations of young and over-30 readers, many of them women,"[101] are morbid, obsessive, and generally neurotic, all signs she neatly reduces to their suddenly serious book-buying habits, which are reflected in this case in the way their love for the novel has led them to purchase a hardback book for the first time. Lest we doubt this portrait of the Plath reader, Dudar also offers firsthand accounts by several students who ostensibly attest to the validity of her portrayal, including one from a Northwestern University student who recalls a time in school when the "whole class went bonkers" upon receiving a handout of Plath's poetry from the professor and another from a Radcliffe graduate who, according to Dudar, "read it because all her college friends were hooked on it."[102] Of course, the phrases "went bonkers" and "hooked on" feed the perception of Plath's readers as crazy junkies whose madness is infectious. While it's true that the first phrase is a direct quotation from one of the readers herself, a fact that might indeed suggest grounds for Dudar's construction of the reader, it's clear that Dudar selects these students' accounts because they reinforce the dismissive and belittling construction of Plath's audience that pervades the review from its opening snapshot of the reader of *The Bell Jar* to her closing point about the "fan-club atmosphere" surrounding Plath.[103]

While the harsh tone of the rhetoric about Plath's readers throughout the reception of *The Bell Jar*, *Crossing the Water*, and *Winter Trees* is impossible to overlook, it is in the reception of *Letters Home* in the mid-1970s that the rhetoric about women readers reaches its height and achieves its most explicit forms. Present are the typical, and by this time perhaps expected, constructions of Plath's audience and their reading practices. Seldom described as readers, they are identified instead through tropes of adoration and uncritical consumption: they are "devotees,"[104] "followers,"[105] "worshipers,"[106] and even practitioners of "cannibalism, or necrophilia."[107] As a corollary, Plath becomes "the multiform saint of depressives, angries, and Laingian romances";[108] "the martyred high priestess of contemporary poetry";[109] "the goddess of a cult."[110] In addition to the pervasiveness of these common tropes, what one notices in the reception of *Letters Home* is the way references to women readers become nearly as common as references to the more generic Plath cult, as if the establishment and identification of the women's movement finally allowed critics to define the constitution of the Plath cult more clearly. In any case, it's apparent that by 1976 direct connections are drawn between the Plath cult and feminist readers, as Carol Bere demonstrates in her review of *Letters Home* when she writes: "The Sylvia Plath cult has proliferated. . . . To a great extent the myth has been fed by feminist fuel."[111]

While Bere's statement is, relatively speaking, innocuous enough, the simple identification of Plath as feminist icon gives way in reviews from this same time to an intensified rhetoric regarding women readers. Take, for example, the shift from Alvarez's review of *Crossing the Water* and *Winter Trees* to his review of *Letters Home*, both of which I've already mentioned. While in 1971 Alvarez worries about the effect Plath's newly emerging status as feminist icon might have on publication decisions, by 1976 Plath's status as "a cult figure and patron saint of the feminists" provokes the misogynistic depiction of Plath's readers as "dissatisfied, family-hating shrews" with which I opened this chapter. While in the reception of Plath's earlier publications the Plath cult seemed nebulously defined through the lowbrow associations of the term "cult" itself, Alvarez leaves little room for misinterpretation in his new construction of Plath's readers.

This shift toward a more patronizing and even misogynistic attitude toward women readers can be tracked throughout the reception of *Letters Home*, but where I think it is most revealing is in those reviews that turn women readers into sites of comic expression. Anthony Thwaite's and Jill Neville's reviews are the two most notable examples of this phenomenon. Thwaite, for instance, describes how he "once spent most of a painful afternoon trying to persuade a girl of 20 or so, who had fallen under an obsessive Plath spell and who was writing consummate pieces of Plath pastiche, that it was not a necessary part of the pattern for her to kill herself."[112] With similar condescension, Neville opens her review with the following portrait of a Plath reader: "Many an uneasy husband is [*sic*] Sydney, New York, London notes his wife's eyes widen and become glaucous, almost erotic, at the mention of Plath's name. What is the magnetic pull, the heady vertigo of this particular poet and her suicide." This "love she inspires," continues Neville, "has a necrophiliac ardour. Many of her admirers, like James Dean's fans[,] react more to the romantic-agony inherent in the myth than to the art itself."[113]

No doubt Thwaite and Neville expect their readers to snicker at their portraits of Plath's women readers and the embarrassed husbands and indulgent male professors who graciously suffer for the sake of their misled wives and students. Whether one finds humor in such constructions or not, such quips certainly come at the expense of women readers. Indeed, the very tropes on which these jokes rely are ones that clearly aim to mock and trivialize women readers for their apparent gullibility, particularly the ease with which they fall victim to "spells" and "magnetic pulls." Throughout the reception of Plath's work, such tropes are not unusual. From *Ariel* forward, Plath's work is often described as "enchant[ing]"[114] and "spellbinding,"[115] usually with the intention of underscoring the power of Plath's writing. But as Thwaite's and Neville's reviews demonstrate, the reception of *Letters Home* shifts the focus of such tropes away from the power of Plath's writing to the weakness of women readers: so feeble are their critical faculties in the face of Plath's writing that they simply cannot overcome their desire or hunger for her work. As my discussion perhaps suggests, the shift in the trope from the power of Plath's writing to the gullibility or susceptibility of her readers is a confounding one, for it attempts to construct women readers both as victims of Plath's unusually powerful spells (that is, they simply can't help themselves) and as investors in or active constructors of their own bad reading practices. Are they bad readers because they have fallen under Plath's spells? Or are they victims of Plath's spells because they were always already bad readers? For most critics it likely doesn't matter, just as long as we all recognize Plath's readers as uncritical consumers who fail to interpret or judge her work correctly.

For many critics, *Letters Home*, of all of Plath's publications, represents a unique opportunity to deliver this judgment on the reader, which is apparent in one of the other trends that defines much of the reception of the book: namely, the argument by critics that *Letters Home*, specifically the image it paints of Plath as a "sunny young woman,"[116] reveals just how wrong women readers have been in viewing her as an early feminist icon. Geoffrey Wolff argues, for example, that "feminists who have used her autobiographical novel, *The Bell Jar*, as a tract and her suicide as an enactment of protest against her martyrdom by males will not recognize their saint in these letters."[117] Wolff's use of the word "used" instead of "read" is telling, of course, for it implies that feminists have adopted the book for a particular purpose—and thus effectively misused the novel—rather than attended to its textual meanings. In similar fashion, Erica Jong laments how "Plath's message was muddied by the feminist political current of the time and also by the myth that sprang up out of her suicide."[118] While not explicitly identifying the Plath reader as female, the comments made by other reviewers express a similar concern with the apparent lack of critical judgment involved in readings of Plath's work, such as Maureen Howard's remark that "cultists have over-simplified and pinned on her their label of victim,"[119] or Stephen Trombley's claim that without help from recent criticism, "few readers would be adequately equipped to make sense of the contradictions, the gaps, the inconsistencies that arise" with the publication of *Letters Home*.[120]

One need not look long to find an explanation for the shift with the reception of *Letters Home* to an even more emboldened and dismissive tone toward women readers, especially feminist ones. As comments like Wolff's demonstrate, many critics resented the adoption by the women's movement of Plath as icon and seized the opportunity presented by the decidedly unfeminist content of *Letters Home* to debunk the construction of Plath as feminist. In fact, some critics saw the publication of the letters as a calculated attempt on the part of Aurelia Plath to "extricate" Plath from her "legend,"[121] or at the very least as a revelation likely to, in effect, "give the lie, with circumstantial absoluteness, to those who have seen Sylvia Plath as a pioneer, or founder-member, of women's liberation."[122] In either case, it's clear that many critics used the reception of *Letters Home* to express their frustrations over the perceived damage readers had caused to Plath's reputation, both directly by "using" Plath for their own purposes and indirectly by motivating in the first place the publication of books of questionable value like *Letters Home*.[123]

Indeed, more so than with any other Plath publication, what one encounters again and again in the reception of *Letters Home* is a frustration among critics with the publication of Plath's work—a frustration often taken out on readers. In their separate reviews, Hugh Haughton and Carol Bere, for example, express their fear that the publication of *Letters Home* will diminish the seriousness with which Plath's poetry is taken, a poetry that, in Bere's words, "deserves more."[124] Speaking more plainly, Larry McMurty asserts that "the impulse to publish ought to have been discouraged" and complains that "it will be a long time before we have finished having the worst of her."[125] But it is Doris Eder who encapsulates the frustration among critics when she laments the future of Plath's posthumous career now that it looks as if Aurelia Plath has been able to publish a book in order to "profit from her late daughter's cult or, more likely, to set forth her own view of Sylvia, an intimate corrective to the image cherished by her worshipers."[126] Eder writes: "Her cult is still going strong. We are and will continue to be glutted with books about her. . . . I wish profoundly that this woman might be permitted to rest in peace. The peanut-crunching crowd has fingered her relics enough."[127]

The mixed metaphors of Eder's characterization of Plath's readers and their bad reading habits—they figure here as both the "peanut-crunching crowd" who stand to be "glutted" by Plath's books and as "worshipers" who desire to "finger her relics"—collapse two of the central tropes that define the construction of the uncritical reader so central to the reception of Plath's work: the reader as gluttonous consumer and the reader as spiritual worshiper. Because these two tropes are so central to the way readers figure in the critical imagination, it's worth pausing a moment to consider their implications beyond the more obvious negation of critical reading practices. What one might notice, for example, is how Plath's writing is made to figure as a body in both metaphors, either as an object consumed like food (whether as part of a mundane diet or holy communion) or as an object transformed, even spoiled, by unwelcome touch, voyeurism, or adoration. It's difficult in a post-Foucauldian world not to see masked in such metaphors our larger cultural preoccupation with turning the body into the site of social control—of regulation, normalization, and improvement. And notice here that it's the critic who imagines Plath's writing as a body for the reader, which leaves the impression that it's precisely the critics' struggle for control that is made manifest in the metaphors. If Plath's writing is understood as body, then it too can be disciplined and opened to new and improved ways of reading. That these new and improved ways are implicitly in opposition to the kind of *gluttonous* readings practiced by women readers makes the imagery even more resonant. As Susan Bordo shows in her work on the disciplining of women's bodies through the discourse surrounding food, "female hunger . . . is depicted as needful of containment and control, and female eating is seen as a furtive, shameful, illicit act."[128] And, she goes on to note, depictions of the female appetite are seldom about just food. While Bordo is speaking specifically about the marketing of food to women in contemporary advertisements, I think Plath's reception uses the trope of female hunger in similar ways. Female readers troped as gluttons or gourmands are readers who must be contained and controlled, lest their desire or urge ultimately ends in the destruction of the object consumed, which may be Plath or which may be the enterprise of poetry itself, depending on the particular perspective of the critic.

In pointing out these implications here, however, I do not mean simply to lump Doris Eder in with all the other critics who have deployed the tropes of food and relics. More than a mere encapsulation of these tropes, Eder's review suggests some of the motives shaping such grasps for control, as well as the stakes involved in the reviews of Plath's work. Unlike the complaints of many of her contemporaries, who seem motivated simply by their annoyance with Plath's popularity among general readers, Eder's concern about the value of this latest Plath publication appears to be driven by a fear of what lies ahead in Plath's posthumous literary career. What ill-chosen work will be published next, she seems to ask, and what will its effect on her reputation be? As my discussion of the larger collection of reviews demonstrates, Eder's protective concern about Plath's literary reputation is not an idiosyncratic one. Nor is it specific to the reception of *Letters Home*. It also pervades reviews of Plath's next publication two years later, *Johnny Panic and the Bible of Dreams and Other Prose Writings*.

As the publication of *Johnny Panic* in England in 1977 makes clear, the question of how Plath's prose writing might affect her literary reputation becomes central to the reception of her work. Published in a slightly different edition in the United States in 1979, *Johnny Panic and the Bible of Dreams* includes a small selection of the more than seventy stories Plath had written in the decade before her death, as well as examples of her journalism and narrative sketches excerpted from her journals. Given Ted Hughes's own admission in the introduction to the collection that some pieces contain "obvious weakness,"[129] it's not at all surprising that most reviewers also found the collection to be generally lacking in literary quality. Perhaps because their own jobs as reviewers had been preempted by Hughes's disclaimers about the quality of the work included, many reviewers zeroed in on the question implied in the disclaimers themselves:

with the collection's flaws so readily apparent, who exactly would want to buy the book?[130]

While some reviewers conceded that the book would have value to Plath scholars, many assumed that its main audience would be Plath "devotees,"[131] those who, in Kay Dick's words, "will find little to criticize"[132] and therefore will be quick to digest what Carol Bere calls the latest "chunk of Plathiana . . . available for popular consumption."[133] Others, however, couldn't even imagine this much of a readership. As Simon Blow writes, "even Plath addicts cannot have grown so indiscriminate as to swallow these writings whole."[134] Of course, the rhetoric surrounding Plath's readers in these reviews is nothing new, which is exactly why I find it so interesting. Just as they were in the reception of *The Bell Jar*, *Crossing the Water*, *Winter Trees*, and *Letters Home*, her readers are seen as uncritical consumers or "cultists" who traffic or "deal in the legend of Sylvia Plath," who "buy" the "myths and mystifications" with little or no regard for how they damage Plath in the process, how they "do her actual career—her dedication to craft and her precocious artistic commitment—something of a disservice."[135] They also still figure predominantly as "feminists," who are in this case not only "fascinated by madness and suicide," as Katha Pollitt writes,[136] but also so immersed in that fascination that they seem ill equipped to handle any work from Plath that doesn't conform to their narrow conception of her as a feminist writer.

Given Hughes's own disclaimers about *Johnny Panic and the Bible of Dreams*, the questions raised about its value as a publication may well seem fair. Yet it would be a mistake to think that the discourse about Plath's readers at this stage can be justified or explained by a legitimate concern about the handling of Plath's estate, just as it would be a mistake to expect that the discourse would simply go away if or when the estate returned to publishing supposedly less questionable work from Plath's oeuvre. Far from going away, the discourse about readers only grows more and more entrenched, having the appearance at times of a perfunctory gesture.

Indeed, throughout the reception of Plath's *Collected Poems* (1981) in the early 1980s, nearly every review makes some kind of reference to readers, usually women readers. Many of these references are made with a degree of self-consciousness which suggests that the disparaging rhetoric has become all too familiar by this time, especially to the critics themselves.

Christopher Reid observes, for example, that "it is sometimes alleged that her work attracts aficionados not so much of poetry as of personality: connoisseurs of morbid states of mind; feminists keen to see their grievances projected in dramatic form; those who are thrilled by the idea of suicide; soul-mate egoists and the like."[137] For the most part, however, references to readers simply maintain the trope of uncritical consumption that had characterized the reception of Plath's earlier works. For instance, Susan Fromberg Schaeffer writes, "To many people, Plath is only a literary version of Marilyn Monroe or Judy Garland: doomed, tragic, sensational in outline, and somehow unsavory,"[138] while Dave Smith echoes the sentiment and even the syntax: "For many readers Sylvia Plath is still the phosphorescent ingenue of contemporary American poetry, not a woman who would be now on the edge of fifty."[139] Similarly, Tom Clark laments the confessional aspects of Plath's poetry, for it is those aspects, he argues, that have regrettably turned her poetry into "a posthumous spectacle for popular consumption" and an object of "largely uncritical mass attention."[140] Even when Clark backs away from the trope of consumption, he still depicts readers as less than serious, much as Helen Dudar did in 1971. As Clark puts it in his reflection on Plath's earlier success, *Ariel* "sold 270,000 copies, many of them to people who hadn't previously bought a poetry book, and who haven't bought one since."[141] In his own reflection on *Ariel*, Denis Donoghue echoes Clark's construction of the reader as a bad consumer, arguing that *Ariel* was received "as if it were a bracelet of bright hair about the bone, a relic more than a book,"[142] all to the detriment of other readings of the work. The other facets of these tired tropes of reading are repeated as well. Helen Vendler casts the relationship between Plath and her readers as one of symbiosis, noting that "an electric current jumped between 'Ariel' and a large (mostly female) set of readers."[143] And in a manner reminiscent of Anthony Thwaite's and Jill Neville's reviews of *Letters Home*, William Pritchard clearly aims to ridicule the young female reader in particular: "Too many readers, younger ones especially, approached these later poems with religious awe as if 'Sylvia' . . . were to be treated in a manner befitting Jesus Christ; it was she who died for our sins—so the distressed young student might feel, especially if female."[144]

That reviewers finally had the opportunity to review a work with clear merit obviously did not do away with their desire to belittle and dismiss Plath's readers. In fact, it may have merely given them new purpose, highlighting precisely what readers and their bad reading habits had allegedly jeopardized. For critics like Tom Clark, Steven Ratiner, and the unnamed reviewer at *Virginia Quarterly Review*, readers—or, more specifically, their obsession with the Plath myth, their feminist "battle cries,"[145] and Plath's subsequent "feminist martyrology"[146]—had obscured the value of the writing itself. With the publication of the *Collected Poems*, however, that value, such critics argued, could once again come to the forefront. Moreover, the collection had the power to bring readers back from the brink by forcing them to return to the poetry, rather than spurious interests. That is to say, *Collected Poems* would now enable readers to "see more clearly than before," as Michael Hulse puts it, and thus would be the "corrective to many myths and misunderstandings" surrounding Plath.[147]

While it seems clear from the context of such comments that critics like Hulse are speaking about the reading practices of general readers, the reception of *Collected Poems* marks a small but significant shift in the reception of Plath's work by book reviewers as the reading practices and critical discourse of the critics themselves come under scrutiny in the reviews. Helen Chasin's review marks this turn most clearly. Taking up both *Collected Poems* and the newly published *Journals* (1982), Chasin sees the two new publications as an occasion to review recent Plath criticism. Writing specifically about both general readers and literary critics, Chasin complains: "The Plath phenomenon has everyone going in circles. It engenders a profound confusion of the art with the biography, of textual analysis with postmortems and autopsies. It results in serious misreadings. While Plath's poetry is at times difficult, the misreadings don't attach to its obscurities but rather to the readers' blind spots and allergies." Speaking specifically about *The Journals*, she adds, "and unfortunately the material which might be expected to counteract all this misguided critical industry turns out to be more of the same."[148]

Of course, Chasin's choice of metaphor—the depiction of critics and readers "going in circles"—and her concern with their "misreadings" reiterate much that we have already seen in the reception of Plath's work, but for Chasin it is the "misguided critical industry," rather than the general reading public, which is mostly to blame for the confusion in reading practices she observes. In fact, Chasin becomes one of the first critics to challenge explicitly much of the rhetoric that had by this point swirled about Plath and her readers. As she puts it: "The critical consensus is

that Plath was something else [than a poet]: a conduit, a vessel, a sybil, a
priestess, a prophetess, a fury pursued by furies. A witch, a bitch, a kvetch.
A lunatic, a fever case, a case of possession, a hysterical bleeder who got
poems the way she got her period. Or not much of a talent at all, but an
icon for a cult of overwrought females and fem-symps. Plath herself is
neither the agent of all this hoopla nor the victim."[149] Yet, even as Chasin
seems critical of the common rhetoric used to describe Plath and by ex-
tension her readers, her assertion near the end of the review that "there's
an audience—not all of whom are crunching peanuts" still replicates the
rhetoric surrounding readers at this time, suggesting that she too can approach the problem only by distinguishing true readers like herself from
pseudo-readers, whoever they might be.[150] That Chasin ultimately finds
value in the Collected Poems while deeming The Journals a mere "propaganda job" only underscores this replication.[151] That is to say, if the Collected Poems had the potential to rescue readers from themselves—and
Plath from her readers—The Journals would just as quickly foreclose that
potential insofar as it would encourage the same "serious misreadings"
that had already emerged from the critical industry and general readers.

Chasin's depiction of The Journals as a work likely to lead Plath's readers further astray is a sure sign that little about critics' perceptions of
Plath's readers had changed come the publication of The Journals. While
it may be true that fewer critics voice a preoccupation with Plath's readers or "cult" when discussing The Journals, those that do are still likely
to rely on the all too common tropes. In Quill and Quire, Paul Stuewe,
for example, represents the Plath reader as an uncritical sponge when he
complains that The Journals will no doubt be "absorbed" by "the Plath
market" despite its being of "minimal literary value."[152] Taking a different avenue but arriving at a similar conclusion, in her review for the
New Leader Phoebe Pettingell locates "the source of [Plath's] immediate
appeal to many readers (especially women)" in Plath's "almost mystical
process of regeneration," which has led women to "identify with the el-
emental emotions she expressed."[153] In addition to replicating the image
of the Plath reader as simply emotional and identificatory in her reading
practices, Pettingell suggests that such shortcomings have led Plath's readers to miss the irony of her poetry, specifically her construction of "Saint
Sylvia/Bitch Goddess, a figure first mockingly created by her, then seized
upon with deadly earnestness by her worshippers."[154] Not to be outdone,

Kathy Field Stephen offers an even harsher portrait of those who would be interested in *The Journals*, one which suggests that their shortcomings lie less in the approach they take to Plath's writing than in their sheer laziness. As she puts it, while "the journals obviously lack the characteristic compression of Plath's poetry," they "may ultimately become the way a wider public—unwilling to puzzle out her many difficult poems—will come to understand and appreciate Sylvia Plath."[155] In short, the rhetoric used to describe Plath's general readers throughout the reception of *The Journals* replicates the image of them as a confused, incapable, and misled bunch. If anything has changed, it's critics' willingness to conclude that readers aren't simply missing vital reading skills; they are also willfully negligent and lazy.

Plath's Recent Reception: Readers in the Aftermath

Surprisingly, this particular portrait of the Plath reader hasn't altogether improved in the years that have passed since the publication of *The Journals* in the early 1980s, as the reception of *The Unabridged Journals of Sylvia Plath, 1950–1962* (2000) and *Ariel: The Restored Edition* (2004) has shown. While the disparaging rhetoric about women readers isn't nearly as widespread in the response to these two more recent works as it had been in the reception of those works published in the 1970s and 1980s, one doesn't have to strain hard to hear its echoes. For starters, one encounters yet again the common tropes and arguments that have been attached to women readers, including those that ridicule Plath's feminist readers in particular.

For example, as if nearly twenty years hadn't passed between the two editions of Plath's journals, in her review of *The Unabridged Journals* Joyce Carol Oates, before dismissing "Plath's elevation in the 1970s as feminist martyr and icon" as "comically incongruous with her hatred of the female sex," notes that "uncritical admirers of Plath will find much here that is fascinating," while "other readers"—one presumes better readers—"may find much that is fascinating and repellent in equal measure."[156] In her review of *The Unabridged Journals*, Cynthia Ozick makes a similar case, describing how Plath has "become all things to all men, and especially to all women," and then later lamenting Plath's transformation into an "object of confusion and misunderstanding and mistake."[157] In language

almost as harsh as any we see in the 1970s and 1980s, she goes on to claim
that readers and their approaches to the journals—from "min[ing] the
journals for Plath's despairs and exhilarations" to "read[ing] the journals
backward from Plath's suicide in the hope of finding clues to it"—are all
simply "bogus."[158] For her, "there are the poems and only the poems."[159]
Given that Ozick and Oates represent a generation of critics steeped in
the disparaging rhetoric of the previous decades, perhaps one shouldn't
be surprised to encounter more of the same in their reviews. But a look at
the wider body of reviews shows even the new generation of critics and reviewers poised to take up the rhetoric. In her review of the British edition
of the unabridged journals, Christina Britzolakis approaches the question
of the book's value from the same assumptions about its readers as Kathy
Field Stephen had when reviewing the earlier edition of the journals
back in 1982, calling the unabridged edition "a useful corrective to lazy
tendencies to see [Plath's] poems as a 'confessional' suicide note."[160] As
if in chorus with Britzolakis's view of the book as a corrective to (or cure
for) poor reading practices, the reviewer for the *Library Journal* opens by
announcing that "Plath's admirers should prepare themselves for another
dose of her bitter medicine."[161]

This focus on whether new editions of Plath's work could somehow
serve as cures for bad reading habits feeds the reception of *Ariel: The Restored Edition* as well, which is perhaps not so surprising, given that this
edition has itself been frequently regarded as a corrective to the originally
published *Ariel*, one that might finally lead us to, as one critic puts it,
"the real Plath."[162] In *American Book Review*, Anthony Cuda suggests that
Frieda Hughes's foreword to the new edition will serve as an especially
effective remedy, so much so that it might even leave readers "startled"
by what they will discover there.[163] Barbara Hoffert shares a similar view
of the edition's transforming possibilities. She suggests, in fact, that the
publication of the book was designed, at least in part, to bring just such
a transformation about. As evidence she offers a quote from David Semanki, the editor then in charge of Plath's work at HarperCollins: "There
are so many Plath fanatics out there, and this is another way of focusing
on Plath's work, not biography."[164]

Not surprisingly, given the patterns we have already seen in Plath's
reception, while most reviewers conclude that both *The Unabridged Journals* and *Ariel: The Restored Edition* have the potential to remedy poor

reading practices, others remain unconvinced of the books' prospects for
bringing about such a change. In Lee Upton's view, "obsessions" are simply so great that "it is unlikely that the restored version will put to rest
some readers' wish to possess an iconic image of the author."[165] In her
review for the *New Republic*, Zoë Heller similarly concludes that the
new edition of the journals will "only aggravate the problem" of readers'
tendencies to view Plath's poetry through her death and thus "thicken the
obfuscating cult around the writer."[166] Interestingly, though both Upton
and Heller arrive at a conclusion about the books' value different from
those of Hoffert, Cuda, and the others, their assessments of Plath's books
are no less driven by a perception of readers' uncritical habits. What
matters is not the value that can (or cannot) be found in the publication
itself, but rather the publication's potential for combating or, alternatively,
exacerbating uncritical reading practices.

While reviews from the past decade or so largely abstain from the
more disparaging rhetoric of the 1970s and 1980s, sparing us overt attacks
on women readers, they bring only minor consolation, especially when
one considers that scale likely matters here. One wonders, for instance,
if we would find the kind of intensified rhetoric that was so common
in reviews from the previous decades in the reception of Plath's more
recent publications had the books received more attention or been more
widely reviewed than they were. Given that the disparagement of Plath's
readers often seems to escalate as attention to Plath increases, this seems
a fair question to ask. In any case, while overt attacks on women readers
are less common in more recent reviews of Plath's work, assumptions
about her audience appear to have changed very little. Moreover, these
assumptions tap into the same anxieties that have surrounded women
readers throughout Plath's reception, if not the same disparaging rhetoric that has been historically associated with women readers, especially
throughout the eighteenth and nineteenth centuries. As the scholarship
on the history of women readers frequently demonstrates, large-scale
social changes—like the revolution in Europe in the late eighteenth century and the incursion of women writers into the literary marketplace in
the nineteenth century—have often been accompanied by a heightened
concern with women readers, a concern that has led those self-charged
with the regulation of literary culture to cast women's reading in the
most unfavorable terms: as addiction, as disease, as a dangerous activity

begging for someone's intervention lest it wreak havoc on both reader and society. Although its persistence into the last decades of the twentieth century and the first decade or so of the twenty-first century might have seemed unimaginable, the phenomenon has been plainly present in Plath's reception since the early 1970s, when the backlash against the women's movement appears to have made it permissible (yet again) to be as disparaging toward women readers as one likes. Perhaps the relative absence of the more overtly misogynistic rhetoric in the reviews of Plath's more recent publications is a sign that attitudes toward women readers are starting to progress, that the language empowered by the backlash against feminism in the 1970s and 1980s is beginning to lose its hold. Or perhaps women readers are as likely to incite our anxieties as ever. As I discuss in the next chapter, maybe the anxieties do not dissipate so much as they simply emerge in a different location.

CHAPTER 2

"Oh, You Are Dark"

The Plath Reader
in Popular Culture

LOOSELY BASED ON SHAKESPEARE'S *Taming of the Shrew*, the film *10 Things I Hate About You* (1999) tells the story of Kat Stratford, a darkly cynical and socially outcast teenager who has renounced dating after losing her virginity to the untrustworthy boy now pursuing her younger sister Bianca.[1] Having completely and contemptuously rejected the conventional high school scene, Kat is despised by her peers at Padua High and frequently referred to as a "heinous bitch." While it is certainly true that Kat occasionally behaves badly—on one occasion she purposely smashes her own patchworked muscle car into her former boyfriend's sporty new convertible—she is hardly the Midol-deprived, "mewling, rampallian wretch" her peers and teachers make her out to be. Quite to the contrary, Kat sees herself more as a nonconformist who locates her self-worth in her rejection of both conventional high school life and the patriarchal order that surrounds her. Emphasizing the potential merit of this aspect of Kat's character, the film portrays Padua High's student body as a collection of absurd cliques (a student can be a "cowboy," a "future MBA," or a "coffee kid," for example) and the adult males in Kat's life as oppressive, controlling figures. Most notably there is Kat's father, whose initial "house rule" forbids the two sisters to date, and Mr. Morgan, the English teacher who routinely sends Kat to the principal's office for "terrorizing" his class, including once after she challenges the omission of important women writers in his lectures.[2] But even as the film presents Kat as a nonconformist above the rigid boundaries that shape her peers and her family, it typecasts her in another way. Seething sarcasm, grungily dressed, and a fan of riot grrl music, she is a millennial version of the angry feminist intellectual, or at least one in the making.

The reason for my portrait of Kat Stratford at the opening of this chapter is simple: as I noted in the introduction, she is a Plath reader. Indeed it is Sylvia Plath, among other feminist writers, whom Kat wishes to see added to Mr. Morgan's syllabus. Underscoring this initial allusion to the poet, the film also offers a revealing look at Kat as she sits in a family room chair reading Plath's best-selling novel *The Bell Jar*. To call attention to the scene of Kat reading, the camera carefully pans through the front window of the Stratford home, resting directly on Kat and centering deliberately in its frame the open cover of *The Bell Jar*. To those viewers who recognize the novel Kat holds in her hands, the implication of the scene is unmistakable: all we need to know about Kat to prepare us for her current behavior in school and at home can be encapsulated by a single scene that, in Hollywood shorthand, figures her as the quintessential Plath reader.

As a scholar of Plath's writing and the history of women's reading, I am intrigued by this popular figure of the Plath reader. How exactly did a young woman reading one of the most influential best-sellers of the second half of the twentieth century come to signify so much in a Hollywood movie? And as signifier, what cultural attitudes does her presence express about Sylvia Plath, her work, and her readers, and how are these attitudes connected to the anxieties about women readers that have shaped the literary reception of Plath's work? Does this image of the Plath reader merely reproduce the discourse about readers from the reception, or does the image transform that discourse in some way? Put more simply, does this image offer a story different from the one told by literary critics, or is it all more of the same? Admittedly, these questions assume first that there is a connection between Plath's reception and this particular figure of a woman reader and second that the connection is worth the attention of literary and cultural critics. In fact, one of the aims of my examination of Kat Stratford is to reveal not simply the connections between her image and the discourse of Plath's reception but also the overdetermining nature of those connections. To begin, I consider how the image of Kat read-

ing is made meaningful only in discourse which has already organized
her representation and shaped what can be said about it. Furthermore,
by relying on the idea of overdetermination here, I mean to suggest an
understanding of the discourse surrounding Plath's readers that moves us
away from the assumption that representations like Kat merely reflect the
nature of real readers, as if the discourse were simply mirroring the image
of real readers or as if real readers were the single determination of the
discourse. The idea of overdetermination works against such oversimpli-
fications, requiring that we recognize a web of multiple, inseparable, and
complexly interrelated determinations shaping the discourse. In looking
closely at Kat, and her many film and television counterparts, in light of
the discourse I examined in chapter 1, we can see just how mutually con-
stitutive conversations about Plath's readers in literary and popular culture have been. Whether the Plath reader is presented through an image
in a film or an anecdote in a book review, the story that is told about her
unfolds in much the same way and with similar effect. The significance
of this story is perhaps nowhere more apparent than in the images from
film and television I take up here, all of which feature a young woman
who reads Sylvia Plath's work. A close examination of these images in
their contexts—particularly the ways they trivialize and even pathologize
young women's reading—shows just how pervasive and entrenched the
cultural anxieties surrounding Plath and her women readers are.

Of course the image of the young Plath reader is hardly new, even in
Hollywood. In many ways, Kat Stratford is merely an updated version of
the image Woody Allen evokes in his 1977 film *Annie Hall* when Allen's
character, Alvy, with *Ariel* in hand, describes Plath as an "interesting poetess whose tragic suicide was misinterpreted as romantic by the college girl
mentality."[3] While Kat herself would likely balk at comparisons between
herself and the young reader Alvy has in mind, the path between *Annie
Hall* and Kat is not a hard one to follow, especially when the path includes
more developed images of the "college girl mentality" to which Alvy
glibly refers.[4] The phrase can't help but bring to mind, for example, the
stereotypical Swarthmore "death girls" who inhabit Meg Wolitzer's *Sleepwalking*, the novel that opens my discussion of Plath's women readers in
the introduction.[5] Indeed, when we see Kat curled up in a chair holding
her anniversary edition of *The Bell Jar*, it is difficult not to impose a death
girl–esque aura of depression and darkness on her, especially since she

is so effectively foiled by her sister Bianca. Often dressed, appropriately, in white, Bianca is at bottom everything Kat is not: she is perky, popular, and for the most part superficial. Contrasted so sharply with Kat, Bianca foregrounds the darkness, one might say melancholy, that lingers over Kat from the film's opening scene, when the blare of her Joan Jett music drowns out the pop song coming from the car stereo of a group of popular, Bianca-like girls. Not only do scenes like this one prepare us for the moment of Kat reading, but also they shape our response to that moment when it does come by inviting us to see her as dark and depressed. The film, in fact, counts on us to recognize this aura of darkness and depression around her. It hopes we do, I would argue, because only then can we accept the transformation of Kat from boy-hater to love-driven teen that is central to the film's conclusion as a romantic comedy. To ensure this response, then, the film constructs Kat as a Plath reader who not only reads the author's work but actually mirrors the widely accepted public image of the poet herself: the abandoned daughter,[6] the woman scorned by male betrayal, and the intellectual who haughtily desires to be above it all. As significant as these similarities are, the most revealing image of Kat as a reflection of Plath comes toward the film's end, when, in a gesture toward the film's title, Kat recites a poem she has written for her literature class. The poem, addressed to her new boyfriend, Patrick, after she discovers he has been paid to date her, catalogs all the things she hates about him, reveals the betrayal she feels, and all the while discloses her desire still to be with him. It is a confessional poem modeled as much after Plath's poetry as after the Shakespearean sonnet Kat was assigned to imitate, and it appears to owe its existence not to Kat's innate creativity but to a boy who inspires the very emotions the poem catalogs. In other words, it would seem that Patrick plays Ted Hughes to Kat's Sylvia Plath.

As I hope this portrait of her shows, Kat Stratford serves as a particularly revealing example of a pathologized woman reader: a woman whose reading practices are defined symptomatically, which is to say, either as a sign of illness or as a potential cause of it. Such pathologization reflects broad cultural anxieties concerning what women read, how they read, and what effects their reading habits might have, either on themselves or on the culture at large. As I discussed in the introduction, throughout the history of women's reading such anxieties have often rendered women "bad readers" in dire need of protection from the corrupting influence of certain kinds of literature and, concomitantly, from their own gullibility. For the most part, Kat is no exception to this image. Toward the climax of the film, for example, Kat is asked to the prom by Patrick and is thus placed in a situation in which she must "read" his motives for dating her. The moment is especially important because it marks for the first time Kat's doubts about Patrick's motives. Oblivious to the fact that Patrick is being paid to date her by the two boys scheming for Bianca's attention, Kat simply cannot understand why he wants to go to the prom, a symbol for her of the same high school scene she and Patrick have rejected.[7] But she does decide finally to accompany him to the dance, and when his initial financial motives are exposed at the prom, Kat leaves in tears, a victim of both the plot hatched by the young men and her own "misreading" of Patrick. Reinforcing this image of Kat as a poor reader, her misjudgment of Patrick echoes a series of previous misjudgments on her part, including her peer-pressured decision to lose her virginity to the arrogant, self-absorbed Joey Donner. The film suggests, in other words, not only that Kat misreads situations but also that her misreading has left her in an unhappy, if not altogether depressed, state.

To better demonstrate the anxieties often embedded in such pathologized constructions, I want to move on now to another image of a Plath reader, one many of my readers will probably be surprised to discover. Mallory (née Wilson) Knox, the violent murderer and companion to Mickey Knox in *Natural Born Killers* (1994), is also depicted as a Plath reader, as we learn in one of the early scenes of the film.[8] Just moments before the violence erupts in the Wilson family home, the film offers us a glimpse of Mallory sleeping while an open copy of *The Bell Jar* rests facedown beside her on the bed. A close look at the scene reveals that the book's appearance is unusual insofar as its front and back covers both prominently feature the title, suggesting the possibility that a particular edition was selected to ensure the book's identification, or even (and I think more likely) that the image of the book has been manipulated altogether. Just as calculated is the scene's placement within the film. As if to prepare us for Mallory's participation in the violent murder of her parents and the subsequent killing spree she embarks upon, Mallory's reading precipitates her plunge into violence and thus works to signal her pathology, just as Kat's reading prepares us for her subsequent behavior toward boys, her feminist sympathies, and her overall depressed state. In Mallory's case, however, the pathology is far more insidious, pointing not toward typically rebellious teenage behavior but to severe psychosis: Mallory, the film makes clear, is not simply a natural born killer but a young woman psychically corrupted—and turned into a murderer—by an abusive father, a neglectful mother, and a culture that glorifies violence and degrades women, to say nothing of the various media she consumes, including, one might speculate, the books she reads.

The film further underscores her disturbed nature during Mickey and Mallory's encounter with a Native American elder and his young grandson. In the scene, the four characters sit around a fire in a hogan while the grandfather and grandson exchange thoughts about Mickey and Mallory in their native tongue. During the conversation, the grandson inquires about Mallory, asking the grandfather pointedly, "Is she crazy?" to which the elder replies, "She has sad sickness . . . [she is] lost in the world of ghosts." Literally highlighting this exchange, the words "she crazy?" are projected across Mallory's chest as the grandfather speaks, according to the film's convention of interpolating extratextual images and words into the visual field of the screen. Of course, the question projected is a rhetorical one, as the truncating of the word "is" conveys. Mallory is indeed crazy, at least as crazy as the culture that produced her. Given the preponderance of evidence favoring such a diagnosis, one might wonder, then, why it matters that Mallory is framed with *The Bell Jar*.

I would insist that it matters a great deal, for while the presence of *The Bell Jar* on Mallory's bed may tell us little about her violence, it speaks volumes about the iconicity of Plath and her women readers. In particular, I would posit a perhaps surprising correlation between the film's depiction of the public and its depiction of Mallory as reader. As those who have seen the film know, central to *Natural Born Killers* is a critique of the mass culture's romanticization of Mickey and Mallory as celebrity murderers. They may be sick people, but they are no less revered by adoring fans who appear at various points throughout the film sporting "I Love Mickey and Mallory" T-shirts and holding signs that read "Murder Me Mickey!" The film argues, in other words, that Mickey and Mallory are the products of a culture of uncritical consumers who recklessly transform murderers into pop culture icons.

Given the film's emphasis on uncritical consumption, the depiction of Mallory reading *The Bell Jar* begins to appear far less gratuitous than it at first seems. Like Mickey and the public that adores him for his violence, Mallory cannot critically separate herself from the violence that has surrounded her throughout her life and thus is presented as a poor reader. One could even argue that the film depicts Mallory with *The Bell Jar* in order to turn her into another example of an uncritical consumer, in this case one whose bad taste and judgments are reflected not only in her reading material but also in the poetry she periodically composes for Mickey's ears. If we follow this line of thinking, *The Bell Jar* comes to stand in for Plath, who, like Mickey and Mallory, serves the film as yet another example of a pop phenomenon who has been propelled into iconicity by a public who, in her particular case, cannot distinguish between sensational autobiography and legitimate literature and thus wrongly romanticize her suicide and her work.

While far removed from each other on the spectrum of bad behavior, the characters Mallory and Kat emerge from the same anxieties. In one brief scene (devoid, interestingly enough, of any speech on their part), each woman asks to be diagnosed as sick and assessed as an uncritical consumer of "bad" literature. That the diagnosis and assessment are elicited through *The Bell Jar*, of all of Plath's publications, makes the anxieties that are present all the more interesting. Certainly one reason for the novel's selection is its recognizability; it is after all Plath's most commercially successful publication. At the same time, the fact that *The Bell Jar* is widely regarded as adolescent literature that appeals to young girls rather than grown women also helps explain its selection. In this way, the presence of *The Bell Jar* in the films underscores the relative immaturity of both women, establishing them as young readers who presumably suffer from inexperience and naïveté. It serves, in other words, to infantilize them, a process made especially clear in *Natural Born Killers*, as subsequent scenes in the film depict Mallory bouncing like a child on the front seat of Mickey's car and tossing a doll off a bridge before marrying Mickey and finally becoming "a woman."

To demonstrate this process of infantilization more fully, I want to shift briefly to an example of a non-cinematic Plath reader. Carol Anshaw's novel *Seven Moves* (1996) depicts a woman reading *The Bell Jar* in a fashion that underscores the book's association with juvenilia and thus pathologizes the idea of a grown woman reading the novel.[9] The scene occurs early in the novel after Taylor Heyes mysteriously disappears and

Chris Snow, the novel's central character and Taylor's lesbian lover, goes looking for a photo of her to give to investigators on the case. The photo Chris takes from the refrigerator door captures Taylor in a chair reading a book during what Chris always thought to be a happy period in Taylor's life. Chris's memory of the moment is altered, however, when she realizes on looking at the photo again that the book in Taylor's hands is *The Bell Jar*. As the narrator remarks: "Now, Chris notices that in the photo Taylor is holding a copy of *The Bell Jar*, and she thinks, who over the age of nineteen would be reading Sylvia Plath? Everywhere now she is looking for some dark cast to Taylor's soul which she might have missed, or not wanted to see."[10] Of course, the moment establishes Taylor as the quintessential Plath reader, one whose previously unnoticed propensity for darkness and depression becomes evident through her reading of *The Bell Jar* and whose previously inexplicable behaviors—in Taylor's case her desire to use "codes only [Chris and she would] understand," to get "matching tattoos," to participate in a "blood ritual," and to write "terrible poems" about the lover she "lost her mind over"—begin to make sense in light of her reading material.[11]

A sign of uncritical consumption, disturbed pathologies, inexperience, and naïveté: Has the cover of any other book—or any scene of a young woman reading—ever conveyed such a loaded and complicated story? Can a cover alone even convey all that? Indeed, it's probably more accurate to regard the image of *The Bell Jar* in both *Natural Born Killers* and *10 Things I Hate About You* as the moment that activates the story about the Plath reader rather than simply encapsulating it. As my discussion of the two films suggests, what makes Kat and Mallory such compelling examples of the Plath reader is the way the films' understanding of both women depends on and then perpetuates a discourse about the Plath reader that is inseparable from the history of women readers and feminism in particular.

"Every Woman Adores a Fascist / The Boot in the Face"

So far in this chapter I've been concerned mostly with the correlations between what and how women read and the apparent pathologies they embody. But as the history of women's reading has taught us, it would be more accurate to examine the image of the Plath reader not simply as a correlation between two anxieties but as a triangulation of three inter-related cultural concerns: a concern with reading habits, with women's health, and with feminism. As I discussed in chapter 1, the women's move-ment of the 1970s and the image of the feminist reader figure centrally in the reception of Plath's work within the literary establishment, giving shape to everything from the judgments critics reach about the value of Plath's work to the discourse they adopt when speaking about her read-ers. Feminism figures no less centrally in the image of the Plath reader in popular culture. Anxieties about young women readers, their health, and their relationship to feminism appear to migrate, more or less intact, between the literary establishment's reception of Plath's work and popular culture. We see them in Mallory, whose impulse toward revenge against her father becomes the foundation of her lethal empowerment, and we see them in Kat, whose feminist politics pour out during her confronta-tions with Mr. Morgan over the lack of women writers in the curriculum of her English class.

Significantly, both moments are closely tied to the scene of reading, and both are played for comedy that comes mostly at the expense of our two young women readers. In *10 Things I Hate About You*, Kat's contempt for and rejection of patriarchal society is served up for laughter in one of the very first scenes of the film, which, in addition to containing Kat's critique of Mr. Morgan's syllabus, depicts in-class repartee between Kat, Mr. Morgan, and other students from the class. The witty exchange be-gins when one of Kat's classmates responds to the teacher's invitation for discussion about *The Sun Also Rises* by calling Hemingway a "romantic." Dripping contempt, Kat responds to the comment by calling Hemingway "an abusive, alcoholic misogynist." When a late-arriving student inter-rupts the discussion to ask what he missed, Kat snarkily answers, "The oppressive, patriarchal values that dictate our education." Pointing to the irony of Kat's own position as a privileged white woman attending an af-fluent school, Mr. Morgan, an African American man ostensibly in touch with his urban roots, sarcastically thanks Kat for her point of view, espe-cially, he notes, in light of "how difficult it must be for [her] to overcome years of upper-middle-class, suburban oppression." While Mr. Morgan may deserve credit for exposing one of the ironies of Kat's disaffection (her rejection of her family's wealth and materialism, for example, ends when her father agrees to pay for her to go to her top-choice college, Sarah

Lawrence), his retort to Kat's complaint effectively ridicules her and her legitimate feminist critique of the education system.

In *Natural Born Killers* the comedy emerges in a far less conventional manner. Indeed there is little that is naturally funny about the scene in which Mallory walks away from *The Bell Jar* and begins her murderous spree, yet the entire scene is scored to classic cartoon music and Bugs Bunny–type sound effects. While those early cartoons of course have their own relation to violence, the score is still hard to reconcile not only with the murders about to be committed but also with what we just learned during the prior flashback to Mallory's family: most notably that Mallory's father has been sexually molesting her. Paralleling the use of cartoonish music in the murder scene, another flashback scene (the one in which we first meet Mallory's family) is fashioned after a classic television sitcom, right down to its use of laughter and applause tracks. Despite the sitcom treatment, the scene unfolds a tragic narrative of abuse clearly designed to prepare us for Mickey and Mallory's murderous rage, which at bottom is an outlet for revenge, as Mickey pays back Mallory's father for putting him in jail for auto theft, while Mallory avenges the years of abuse. But unlike Mickey's vengeance, Mallory's is tinged with self-empowerment. When helping to drown her already beaten father in a fish tank, she pummels him with the same vitriol and sexual innuendo with which he once be-rated her: "You stupid bitch, you will shut up, you will eat your food. . . . Are you clean? Are you sloppy and wet?" While the scene marks the first moment of empowerment for Mallory, the moment is undercut—and, significantly, rendered "silly," in the words of director Oliver Stone—by the cartoonish music that scores the entire scene of Mallory and Mickey's confrontation with her father, just as the earlier revelation of sexual abuse is rendered trivial by the sitcom structure through which it is told.[12] While the audience might not laugh at the scene of Mallory's empowerment in the same way that we are meant to laugh at Kat's rebellion against Mr. Morgan, both scenes turn women into comedic objects, and as a result, both fail in equal measure to take women's empowerment—and, one might add, women's reading as a source of that empowerment—seriously.

Given the less than serious treatment granted the Plath reader in film, perhaps one shouldn't be at all surprised to encounter a Plath reader as the butt of the joke in a television sitcom. Yet when a friend pointed me to one in the early 1990s sitcom *The Fresh Prince of Bel Air*, even I was more than a little surprised. After all, the show is a situation comedy about an urban black male teenager named Will who has been transplanted from a neighborhood in West Philadelphia to the Bel Air section of Los Angeles, where he now lives with his well-heeled aunt and uncle (the Bankses) and attends Bel Air Academy, a private all-boys school. Hardly the recipe for a cameo from a Plath reader. Yet despite the unlikely setup of the show, the episode that features our Plath reader plays out along similar lines, with two notable exceptions: this Plath reader is a young black woman, and the text she reads is not *The Bell Jar* but rather "Daddy."[13] Before assuming that the diversity evident in this Plath reader's race might signify a larger change in the narrative, one should remember the context of the show: one of its comedic tropes from season to season is the way the Banks family, especially teenage son Carlton, continually challenge Will's assumptions about what it means to be black.

We first meet Christina Johnson when Will encounters her at a Poetry Club meeting, during which she recites an excerpt from Plath's poem. Long before the encounter itself, the scene has been set up for laughs by the events that have brought Will to the club in the first place. Pressured by his aunt and uncle to get involved in extracurricular activities or get a job, Will sets out to find an activity. As he loafs in the school hallway plainly bored with the endeavor, Will looks up to discover a group of girls from Bel Air Academy's sister school on their way to a meeting of the Poetry Club. As Will is quick to notice, the girls sport bobby socks and provocatively short Catholic schoolgirl uniform skirts (the kind you tend to see in films, television, and music videos). Other than the faculty adviser and now Will, the girls are the only members of the club. Will is especially smitten with the club leader, Christina, who opens the meeting with what she calls "a reading of 'Daddy' by Sylvia Plath," but which might more precisely be called a melodramatic rendering of a short passage from the poem:

Panzer-man, panzer-man, O You—

Not God but a swastika
So black no sky could squeak through.
Every woman adores a Fascist,
The boot in the face, the brute
Brute heart of a brute like you.

I say melodramatic rendering, for what we witness is hardly your average poetry reading. Christina, who immediately before and after her reading oozes a strange mixture of saccharine innocence and flirtation, transforms upon her performance of "Daddy" into an angry militant feminist who barks the lines as if she were yelling out orders to an infantry platoon. It's a performance that leaves Will aghast. His bug-eyed stupor is only momentary, of course, and when Christina offers the coda, "Sylvia Plath killed herself shortly after writing this poem," before reassuming her flirtatious smile and taking her seat, Will quickly counters, "Yo, if she didn't, her daddy would've," and then nervously laughs at himself. Responding to Will's interjection, the young woman sitting at the desk in front of him looks back over her shoulder and with scornfully squinted eyes demands, "*Who* are you?"

In all the scene lasts barely more than a minute, yet it sets the stage for the entire episode, which centers largely on Will's quest to impress Christina by adopting her interest in poetry. As it turns out, impressing Christina proves not so hard to do, for as she notes to Will at the Poetry Club meeting, hearing poetry read by a "deep, sensual, masculine voice" moves her profoundly. With this handy bit of information, Will agrees to contribute to the meeting by reading a poem himself. Having brought nothing to share, of course, he decides to make up a poem on the spot, which he presents as a work by the East L.A. poet Rafael de la Ghetto. For inspiration, he looks about the room until he notices the clock on the wall. Having found his inspiration, he begins the poem he calls "Tick, Tock, Clock," a hip-hop style seduction poem. His performance is met by "oohs" and wild applause from the young women, who, clearly stunned by Will's poem, shake their heads in pleased disbelief. Christina is especially impressed and quickly goes to Will to praise his reading. Though it's obvious to the television audience that Will knows nothing about poetry—in the same scene, he mistakes Christina's use of the word "metaphor" for a reference to an illegal drug—Christina gushes to Will that she thinks his reading was "brilliant" and is even erotically turned on by it, telling him that her "body just quivers, crying out for more" when she hears de la Ghetto's work.

From here the episode unfolds like a comedy of errors, as Will is pressed into producing the nonexistent de la Ghetto for a public reading at the school after Christina makes a persuasive, and unabashedly sexual, plea to Will. As one would expect, Will's plan to have someone impersonate de la Ghetto at the reading backfires when the family's butler Geoffrey fails to stay in character during his performance as the poet and is finally revealed as a sham. One might think that Christina's duping would end there, but it doesn't. When Christina confronts Will about the lie, she is interrupted by another de la Ghetto impersonator, this time in the form of Will's friend Jazz, who swoops in to take advantage of Will's loss. Skeptical at first, Christina challenges this new de la Ghetto's authenticity—after all, she asks, where are his afro and dashiki?—but she quickly abandons her doubts after Jazz recites a poem to her, a poem every bit as bad as "Tick, Tock, Clock," if not worse. Apparently blind to bad poetry and convinced that Jazz is de la Ghetto, she exits the scene arm in arm with Jazz, leaving Will to stew in his frustration.

As I hope this brief synopsis of the episode suggests, I do not think that we're supposed to have a lot of confidence in Christina's judgment. Despite the insistence of Will's Aunt Viv that girls like poetry "because girls think with their brains," there is little in the episode to suggest that Aunt Viv has it right in Christina's case. While Christina knows how to manipulate and flirt to get what she wants, she remains profoundly gullible throughout the episode. And just as important for my argument here, she is as easily duped by bad poetry as she is by Will's deceit. Which brings us back, finally, to the scene in which Christina recites the passage from "Daddy." Looking back on the scene of reading in light of her persistent gullibility, one can't help but wonder if the foibles of her personality aren't of a piece with her performance of Plath's poem.

On the one hand, of course, the moment of her reading is simply fodder for the audience's laughter, especially as we watch Will grapple to reconcile Christina's lovely image with her militant performance of "Daddy." Approaching the scene of reading in this way fits squarely with the episode's recurring concern with appearances and reality. Things, the episode tells us again and again, are not always what they seem. But this view has its limits, especially since it would lead us to believe that the authentic Christina—the one Will discovers in the Poetry Club—is the militant feminist she becomes upon her recitation of "Daddy." Clearly Christina is not a militant feminist; even Will knows this much, which is one reason why the scene is funny. At the same time that we laugh at Will's response, however, we must also recognize that the object of laughter is as much Christina as it is Will. Even before Will's reaction to her performance becomes apparent, the in-studio audience laughs at Christina's rendition of the poem, and rightly so. There is something plainly comical about the discrepancy between Christina's personality, even the little bit of it we've seen up to this point in the episode, and her performance. It suggests, among other things, that she doesn't really understand the poem she recites, or even that she's aping the delivery of the poem that she thinks is expected. Either way, like so many young women readers before her, Christina is rendered silly by her uncritical consumption of the text she reads. If "silly" seems too strong a word, consider all the ways she becomes the butt of the joke throughout the episode, from the scene of her performance, to her adoration for "Tick, Tock, Clock," to her continued belief in de la Ghetto's existence. Moreover, immediately following the scene of Christina's final duping by Jazz, the camera cuts to a shot of the exterior of the Banks family's house, from which boisterous laughter emerges. When it cuts again to a shot of the interior, we see that the object of all the laughter is Will's rehashing of the events at the poetry reading for his family. While much of the laugher is directed at Will's imitation of Geoffrey's performance, the moment when we hear the laughter in the house without knowing its object leads the viewer to think that the laughter is directed at the idea of Christina's final seduction. And as it turns out, some of it is, since the family does eventually get around to laughing at Jazz's use of Will's poem and the de la Ghetto cover to seduce Christina.

The results of the various impersonations aren't the only subject from which the family draws amusement. Just as silly, it would seem, is poetry itself. Despite the fact that Aunt Viv is a literature teacher, and despite the inclusion of her moving reading of Amiri Baraka's poem "Three Modes of History and Culture," the scenes that take up the subject of poetry throughout the episode present poetry as a silly endeavor. It's just not something to be taken seriously, which is perhaps never more apparent than in the final minute of the episode, when, following Aunt Viv's reading of Baraka's poem, the camera cuts to Will, who, breaking the fourth wall, offers a message to the television audience: "If you'd like to learn more about poetry, you can reach us at—*Psych!* We just kiddin'. Good night, y'all." Even though Aunt Viv's reading of the poem is immediately undermined by Will's bogus public service announcement, we are at least led to view her reading as an authentic performance, in direct contrast to Christina's reading of "Daddy." Aunt Viv clearly understands and appropriately appreciates the poem she's reading, which adds an interesting layer to the question of how race impacts the depiction of Christina as Plath reader. One might conclude, for example, that Christina's performance of Plath is inauthentic not only because of the farcical nature of her delivery but also because she's not meant to like Plath's writing in the first place. Just as Carlton's "whiteness" (which encompasses everything from his nerdiness to his preppy dress to his conservative Republican politics) gets mocked repeatedly by Will, Christina's performance of Plath can be seen as a performance of a white militant feminist identity that is rendered inauthentic by the rest of the plot.

In any case, while poetry appears to matter a great deal to Aunt Viv, her interest is laughed off, if not roundly dismissed, with the inclusion of the bogus PSA. It's a dismissal with far-reaching implications, given the episode's insistence that poetry is, above all, a feminine pursuit. It's connected to love, seduction, and basically anything domestic. As Jazz responds when he learns that Will is writing a poem for his Poetry Club: "Poem? Then what you goin' do? Bake some cookies? Hem a dress?" Even Will, the new convert to poetry, finds little value in the project. He's just "doing it to get the girl," he tells Jazz.

Yet even as the episode genders an interest in poetry as female, poetry apparently lies outside the purview of young women. With the exception of Aunt Viv, women are just too silly to understand it or to appreciate good poets when they encounter them. And of course, with the exception of the faculty member who advises the Poetry Club and Geoffrey (who happens to be a domestic worker himself), when men do take up poetry, it is merely a tool for seducing (that is, duping) young women. Herein lies the key, I think, to why "Daddy" fits so well into the episode. "Daddy" isn't so much a direct clue to Christina's character as it is an opportunity for the show to highlight just how uncritical of ideas and texts women ostensibly can be and therefore just how easily they are seduced by them. As prelude to a series of events that exposes Christina's naïveté and poor judgment, her performance of "Daddy" seems designed to prove to us just how shallow and intellectually unsophisticated her character is, which might explain why Christina is made to read the particular lines from "Daddy" that she does. Frequently cited as evidence for just how wrong feminists have been in their adoption of Plath as feminist icon, this particular passage offers us the opportunity not only to see Christina acting out of character, which is central to the comedy of the scene, but also to witness how silly feminism itself can be. For many literary critics, the idea that "every woman adores a fascist" is simply incompatible with the concept of women's liberation, and the insistence of feminists on claiming Plath as their icon despite the unfeminist content of her work shows just how shallow both their politics and their understanding of Plath's poetry are. Thus, while Christina's performance of "Daddy" doesn't make her Plath-like (that is, dark, depressed, or troubled like Kat Stratford and Mallory Knox), it does provide the clue not only to her own misguidedness but also to feminism's.

"Bingo! . . . A Book of Poetry by Sylvia Plath"

The possibility that a young woman's reading habits might provide a key to her character is taken to the extreme in an episode of *Law & Order: Special Victims Unit* in which one of Plath's books becomes, literally, the clue to a criminal investigation. The episode, "The Single Life," centers on the story of thirty-two-year-old Gretchen Quinn, whose body is found on the sidewalk outside her apartment building after she has plunged from a window.[14] Unable to tell if the fall was the result of murder or suicide, the detectives on the case, Elliot Stabler and Olivia Benson, have little to go on. Even the process of finding someone who knew the deceased proves difficult—that is, until her calendar reveals the fact that Gretchen was seeing a clinical psychologist. Through their investigation, Detectives Stabler and Benson uncover several seemingly important leads in the case, from which they learn that Gretchen worked as a freelance writer who produced stories with frequent "feminist" overtones and that she had been having an affair with a prominent news personality. All the leads go nowhere, however, and Benson and Stabler remain unable to find Gretchen's next of kin. In their desperation, they decide to return to her personal items, which include a collection of her books and files, including one called "penis quotes." As the detectives leaf through the books and banter about the obvious feminist content of her files (one book, for example, *Biology of the Amazons*, discusses the candiru, a fish that can swim into a man's penis), Stabler shouts "Bingo!" and hands Benson what he describes as a "book of poetry by Sylvia Plath."

Bingo, indeed. But as it turns out, Stabler is only half right. The book is by Plath, but it's not a book of her poetry. The book, which they later learn turns out to be a long-overdue volume from the victim's high school library, is actually *The Bell Jar*, though the error is never corrected in the episode. Despite Stabler's misidentification of it, the discovery of the book, more than any other clue in the case, proves to be the key to the mystery, leading the detectives to Gretchen's real name, Susan Sodarsky, and preparing the viewer for what unfolds during the rest of the episode: the revelation that she had been sexually abused by her father as a teenager, that she had a history of "deranged lovers" and unhealthy affairs, and that she had thrown herself out the window in a desperate attempt to end her psychological torment and finally seek revenge on the men who had abused and taken advantage of her. Which is not to say that the book reveals anything new beyond the victim's real name. As Benson responds when Stabler tells her that he has found a copy of a book by Plath: "Of course."

To answer why it would be so obvious that the dead woman was a Plath reader, the show draws a number of parallels between Susan and the widely received ideas about Sylvia Plath. Most obviously, Susan is a feminist writer, and apparently a rather vengeful one, if her notes on the candiru are any indication. At one point, in fact, her career as a writer is put forward as a possible motive for her murder. In the words of Detective Munch, perhaps she was "writing a novel about how pathetic her childhood was." While it turns out that no such novel exists, Susan does write her own "obituary," which she mails to her sister, and which turns out to be the decisive piece of evidence in determining the cause of her death. In it, Susan discloses her intention to commit suicide (another obvious but important similarity between herself and Plath) and, as explanation, excoriates the men who have led her to take her own life, an act she hopes "will point an accusing finger at the men responsible" for her torment. Even before the damning mock obituary is read, however, there are plenty of signs that point to Susan's troubled past, or as one of her lovers puts it, her "dark shadows."

Nothing here, in other words, is very surprising, for the plot of the episode plays out rather straightforwardly as the detectives follow the clues to the cause of Susan's death, clues that include, most significantly, a copy of a Plath book. Indeed, while the mock obituary discloses the true nature of Susan's death, it is *The Bell Jar* (or what Stabler calls a "book of poems by Sylvia Plath") that provides the clue to her true identity, which, as it turns out, is one burdened with a sadly troubled past and a hatred for men that feeds her self-destruction. While we never see Susan read the Plath book she stole from the library as a young woman, the book is no less consequential, for it evokes a prior scene of reading that contributes to the larger narrative about Susan's depression and suicide. What matters, ultimately, is the reality that she read Sylvia Plath as a teenager (and apparently liked her enough to have kept the library book for nearly twenty years) and is now dead by her own hand.

By reducing Plath's work to a literal clue in a criminal investigation, *Law & Order: SVU* invites us, albeit inadvertently, to consider the power of the Plath reader as a sign within popular culture. When Benson responds to Stabler's discovery of the Plath book with "Of course," her words encapsulate the nature of that sign. Of course Susan Sodarsky possesses a Plath book. It's what women *like her* read. Of course Susan Sodarsky killed herself. It's what happens to young women who read books *like that* and *in that way*. And by emphasizing these points, I do mean to link Susan's reading material to her death, for I think that argument reverberates in Benson's words, which, I would suggest, implicitly construct Susan's reading as obsessive and pathological. After all, everything the detectives uncover in their investigation—from the tenor of Susan's therapy sessions to the file she kept on the candiru—point to her pathological nature. The therapy, the affairs, the abuse, the research, the writing, the reading material, the suicide: all coalesce to lead the detectives to the explanation for her fall and the viewers to a neatly coherent impression of Susan's identity. And yet even as everything comes together to form a seamless narrative, none of it need be said. That is to say, when Detective Benson replies "Of course," she has in essence shrugged off the significance of the book, for it's just too obvious a clue to be of any importance in and of itself. To return to the language I introduced at the start of this book, even as the Plath book is as good as an ID in this case, its existence among Susan's possessions is a fact that could have simply "gone without saying."

I think this last quality of Benson's comment helps explain the work that the image of the Plath reader in popular culture accomplishes. Even as it appears gratuitous, it does some heavy lifting in radically economical terms by film and television standards. In a world where coming up with thirty seconds' worth of film can sometimes require a whole day's shooting, the image of the Plath reader does an awful lot for the money. The main reason it is so economical is that it often acts as if it has merely pointed viewers to what we already knew, like a reminder about something that may have slipped our minds. Adding to its economy, it also projects the confidence of cultural consensus, in this case the cultural consensus that has been reached about the Plath reader, a projection that unfortunately leads the audience away from scrutinizing the image in any way.

Of all the images of the Plath reader I've encountered, only one stands out as a possible exception to this rule. Not surprisingly, perhaps, the image I'm speaking about comes from a television show known for its use of parody and its willingness to ridicule elements of popular culture, including itself. The show is the cartoon *Family Guy*. Titled "Fish Out of Water" (2001), the episode that features the Plath reader centers on two parallel plots. Peter, the father of the Griffin family, loses his job, buys a boat, and decides to become a fisherman; meanwhile Meg, Peter's teenage daughter, and according to her "the only one in school without plans to go on spring break," sulks about the house, arms crossed in disgust, until her mother, Lois, drags her along for a week at a spa.[15] One early scene in particular sets the stage for an episode about teen angst and ostracism, with of course a cameo appearance by *The Bell Jar*. In the scene, Peter approaches his wife and daughter as they are about to leave on their trip and tells them he will see them in a few days, to which Meg responds, "Not if I strangle myself with seaweed wraps and die." Commenting on the obvious, Peter replies in kind, "Oh, you are dark." Needless to say, mud baths do nothing to ameliorate Meg's image of herself, and the pair leave the spa earlier than planned so that Meg, as she puts it, can "go home and spend the next three days in solitary confinement where [she] belong[s]." On their way home, however, Lois spots a sign for a "Spring Break Blowout" and, while Meg sleeps, detours to the beach to surprise her pouty teenager daughter. At the blowout, it is Lois who enjoys the parties, while Meg, disgruntled as ever, struggles to fit in. After one particularly grueling night of rejection, Meg returns to her hotel room and finds solace in—what else?—*The Bell Jar*.

Because images like this might suggest that Plath need not be taken seriously as a writer, most Plath scholars would probably prefer to ignore the fact that Plath and *The Bell Jar* have become fodder even for cartoons.

Yet the image in *Family Guy* of Meg as a Plath reader should not be overlooked, for it can provide us with an interesting opportunity not only to think about why Plath and *The Bell Jar* in particular have assumed the meaning they have in literary and popular culture, but also whether that meaning can ever be transformed or resisted. While one's first inclination may be to take the image of Meg reading *The Bell Jar* at face value—that is, as a depiction meant to signal a melodramatic though no less recognizable teenage pathology—it is important to remember how much of *Family Guy* is satire, and rather sophisticated satire at that. When placed in this larger context, the image of Meg reading *The Bell Jar* becomes something more than the straightforward depictions of young adult angst, depression, or deeply dysfunctional pathology we see in films like *Natural Born Killers* and *10 Things I Hate About You*. Consider, for instance, that here we have a cartoon character who is miserable simply because she has been excluded from typical spring break festivities but who later, when given the chance to participate in the festivities, apparently finds more pleasure sitting in her hotel room reading a novel Plath had once titled "Diary of a Suicide."[16] In other words, Meg might be a mopey teenage girl, but her gloominess is hardly commensurate with Ether Greenwood's descent into deep depression. Because of this gulf in expectation, one cannot help but wonder just what the show's creators are spoofing with this image of Meg Griffin as a Plath reader. Is the object of the parody the young adult angst that presumably draws Meg to *The Bell Jar*, or is the object of the parody something more original, such as the very idea that *The Bell Jar* can function metonymically as a symbol of young women's depression? That is to say, perhaps *Family Guy* offers the comical image of Meg reading *The Bell Jar* to pose a serious question about whether it is fair to diagnose a young woman's mental state on the basis of the book she chooses to read, and therefore whether it is fair for popular culture to try to encapsulate a young woman's character simply by putting *The Bell Jar* in her hand.

Fair or not, the appearance in television and film of the young woman reader as an uncritical, even pathological consumer of Plath's writing was likely unavoidable. The migration to popular culture of the same tropes of uncritical consumption that have long defined how literary critics talk about Plath's readers shows just how ingrained the terms by which we understand Plath and her readers have become. As unavoidable as they may be, the tropes of uncritical consumption and the arguments they feed—to say nothing of the gender biases they veil—are no less pernicious. As I discussed at greater length in the introduction, attempts to draw correlations between what and how women read and the apparent pathologies they embody pervade literary history. While such correlations have always had their dangers—often resulting in prescriptive reading practices for women and even the censorship of their reading materials—their expression at the site of the Plath reader strikes me as especially destructive, not only for how they circumscribe our culture's understanding of the woman reader in question, but also for the ways they potentially feed an obsession with the reader that, in turn, restricts readings of Plath's writing and determines valuations of her body of work.

If we return to our two cinematic examples of Kat Stratford and Mallory Knox for a moment, we can see the first of these two effects at work. As I argued at the beginning of this chapter, Kat and Mallory bring to the forefront a culture's anxieties about Sylvia Plath and women readers. Because both characters are so thoroughly grounded in these anxieties, it is not at all surprising to find that by the end of both films, Kat and Mallory appear to have been put back in their proper places: Kat, an avid reader of women's writing, eventually relinquishes her books for a prom gown, while Mallory, some years after her vengeful murder spree ends, hits the road in a Winnebago with Mickey and their children. I say appears, because I think the films leave the slightest room for a second, albeit perhaps counterintuitive reading. Most notably, while Kat dons the normalizing garb of the prom gown for a night, she eventually abandons it too and returns by the film's end to her dark but artistically expressive self (one who plays guitar, draws, and plans to attend Sarah Lawrence in the fall), a return that is easily overshadowed by the final coupling of her and her once paid date in the final scene of the film. Similarly, while Mallory winds up occupying the conventional position of wife and mother at the film's close, she does so only after escaping the perversely dysfunctional domestic scene of her childhood, a scene complete with abusive and neglectful parents who parodically expose the myth of the idealized nuclear family. Perhaps, then, the characters of Kat Stratford and Mallory Knox open the door, if only slightly, to a recuperation of the figure of the woman reader I have been discussing here. I like to think so, even if it requires reading against the grain of the films, and I think other recent constructions of the Plath reader move us toward a similar recuperation.

Take, for example, the relatively recent works by cultural critic Elizabeth Wurtzel. Apparently intent on casting herself as the consummate autopathographer, Wurtzel appears to construct herself as the stereotypical (albeit real) Plath reader in her 1994 memoir *Prozac Nation* and again in her 1998 *Bitch*.[17] In the prologue to the first of the two, the twenty-something-year-old Wurtzel previews her struggles with depression and her ambivalent attitude toward the drugs that keep her from "constant-level hysteria." She writes: "I've been off lithium less than a month and I'm already perfectly batty. And I'm starting to wonder if I might not be one of those people like Anne Sexton or Sylvia Plath who are just better off dead, who may live in that bare, minimal sort of way for a certain number of years, may even marry, have kids, create an artistic legacy of sorts, may even be beautiful and enchanting at moments, as both of them supposedly were."[18] That Wurtzel should compare herself to Plath and Sexton—and in the process implicitly construct herself as someone who has read their work—is perhaps not all that surprising. Evoking the poster women of what Wurtzel calls "aching, enduring suicidal pain" underscores the extent of her illness and drives home the point of the prologue, which is after all titled "I Hate Myself and I Want to Die."[19]

At the same time, the comparison allows Wurtzel to accomplish a less obvious goal, one interwoven with her own identity as a writer. Indeed, if Wurtzel is like Plath and Sexton because she too may be better off dead, she is also like them because she shares their desire to "create an artistic legacy of sorts." As her qualifications throughout these passages indicate, Wurtzel is well aware of the constructedness of Plath's and Sexton's authorial identities, of the way they "supposedly were." Such hedging on her part also suggests she is just as aware of the constructedness of the Plath reader, especially of the way she too can construct herself as one and thus capitalize on the image of the poet herself. Her evocation of Plath and Sexton therefore serves as a kind of masterful incantation that establishes her authority not only as a reader but also as a writer with an astute awareness of her subject matter. In this way, the image of the Plath reader for Wurtzel is an image of empowerment, one that helps to explain her narrative, certainly, but also one that authorizes her identity as a reading and writing woman.

And while the focus of this book is on women readers, there's something to be said here about Plath and her influence on women writers as well. In evoking Plath in her memoir, Wurtzel calls our attention to the considerable impact Plath has had on the women writers who have come after her. Despite the rush within recent Plath criticism to downplay or deny the relationship of her work to autobiography, the influence of Plath's writing on contemporary women's literature, especially in terms of the memoir and the female coming-of-age narrative, is undeniable.[20] Pick up any number of autobiographies published in the 1990s and onward—from Wurtzel's *Prozac Nation* to Susanna Kaysen's *Girl, Interrupted* to Mary Karr's *Cherry*—and it's evident that Plath's novel, poetry, and journals prepared the way for the memoir phenomenon of these years not only by showing that there's a market for this kind of literature but also by authorizing women writers to create personal stories about their own lives and to insist on a place in literature for the subjects that matter to women.

While it's often overlooked or ridiculed in the discourse about readers, what is obvious about Plath's writing, furthermore, is that it inspires *young* women especially, and it inspires them not only to read but to write as well. To listen to these young women is to come away with a very different portrait of the young Plath reader from the one depicted in the rhetoric. In preparing to teach a class on girl culture, I came across one particularly relevant example of Plath's influence on young women. In her contribution to a collection of vignettes written by teens and published in 2003, Gwynne Garfinkle describes the summer she set out à la Esther Greenwood to write a novel, despite discouragement and criticism from her boyfriend: "That summer I learned the discipline required to become a novelist. Most weekdays I woke around nine, showered, and sat at the kitchen table with a bowl of cereal, a cup of sweetened Lipton's tea, and *The Journals of Sylvia Plath*. I'd eat and read, eating Plath's determination to be a writer, eating the books by writers she read—Virginia Woolf and D. H. Lawrence and dozens of others—her plans to study languages; her work on poems and short stories; her bitter, slangy talk. . . . Then I'd go to my room and lie on my bed with a spiral notebook and a pen."[21] Remarkable for the way it turns on its head the same trope of reading as eating that is so often used against Plath's readers, Gwynne's reflection suggests that young women readers gain something from Plath's writing that they've not been given credit for.

Returning once again to the films, I want to suggest in closing that Kat Stratford and Mallory Knox display similar potential for empowerment that comes in part at least from their reading of Plath's writings. That is, while it is true that the scenes of the two women reading *The Bell Jar* signal their pathologies, they also signal their willingness to act with authority and a sense of self-worth. In *10 Things I Hate About You*, for example, the women writers whom Kat reads serve as the only strong female role models she has, and it is through them that she often asserts her own voice. Similarly, in *Natural Born Killers*, the scene of Mallory's reading marks not just her plunge into violence but her stand against her abusive father. Kat and Mallory, in fact, could well serve as additional examples of the difficult and unruly women Wurtzel celebrates in *Bitch*, women who deserve credit because they have learned to be difficult and unruly in a society that tells them just to behave. At the very least, both serve as examples of women who attempt to take back some control over their own lives.

If either film seriously entertained the question of why the novel might appeal to its female protagonists—that is, if either film took the women seriously as readers—they would have to tell a far more complex story, one that moves beyond the iconic meaning of *The Bell Jar* to a deeper understanding of why characters like Kat and Mallory might find Esther Greenwood's narrative so interesting. What might have been examined, for example, is the similarity between Kat's and Mallory's desire to power their own lives and Esther's own preoccupation with control and self-determination. From her relationship with Buddy Willard and her mother, to her experimentation with suicide methods, to her fight to escape the bell jar, nearly all the plot episodes in *The Bell Jar* reveal Esther's struggles to gain control over her own life, to determine her own choices rather than merely accept those that society presents to her. In fact, one could argue that it is Esther's desire and search for control that threads together the many identities she struggles with, including her identity as a young woman, a patient, a daughter, a successful student, an aspiring writer, and of course a potential wife and mother.[22]

Just as the films introduce the women as readers but then fail to take their intellectual lives seriously, they also introduce the possibility of empowerment only to foreclose its achievement in the end. Even when faced with her unruliness, one cannot overlook the fact that Kat is based on the figure of the shrew in Shakespeare's play and, like her Shakespearian namesake, is destined to be tamed by a boy precisely because she is unruly and empowered. Nor can one overlook the way in which Mallory's empowerment is rendered "silly" by the film's inclusion of a laugh track and cartoon music. Not to mention the violence that transpires from Mallory's misdirected anger or the reality of her own dependence on Mickey, the man who makes her empowerment and subsequent escape from the Wilson home possible in the first place. Such realities serve to contain what is powerful about them as characters and as Plath readers. Depicting both women with *The Bell Jar*, then, appears to be simply another way for the films' creators to put them and their reading back in their place, thereby strengthening the patronizing and misogynist cultural attitudes that shape such constructions. Those reading the chapters of this book in the order in which they are laid out should recognize such cultural attitudes since they pervade the literary reception of Plath's work and have often served efforts to put her writing back in its place. Certainly their presence roughly fifty years after the poet's death expresses an entrenched unease about Sylvia Plath and her work—an unease that is only exacerbated by attempts to deny or devalue the women readers who have become synonymous with Plath's name.

CHAPTER 3

"We Did Not Wish to Give the Impression"

Plath Fandom and the Question of Representation

Bᴇᴄᴀᴜsᴇ ᴛʜᴇ ᴄᴏɴsᴛʀᴜᴄᴛɪᴏɴ ᴏғ ᴛʜᴇ ᴡᴏᴍᴀɴ ʀᴇᴀᴅᴇʀ discussed in the preceding chapters frequently assumes a relationship to Plath's actual readers, I turn in this chapter to an examination of these real or historical readers, focusing in particular on the female fan culture that has surrounded Plath since the 1970s. As part of this examination, I consider several important and, for the most part, well-known examples of this fandom, including the radical feminist activist and poet Robin Morgan, whose poem "Arraignment" has become virtually synonymous with Plath fanaticism; the women who reportedly began protesting Ted Hughes's poetry readings in the 1970s; the virtual fans who contribute to the online Plath forums that have sprung up over the past ten years or so; and finally the self-described feminists who challenged Hughes's management of Plath's literary estate in the editorial pages of the *Guardian* in 1989. Even as I use the term "fan" to describe these readers, however, I want to make it clear that I do not embrace the term unproblematically. In fact, as I discuss later in this chapter, in some cases the very groups I identify here as fans reject the application of the term to themselves, aware as they are of the pejorative judgments that often go along with the use of the term. From my perspective, the term, though a contested one, fits well insofar as it reflects not only the scope of my examination of Plath's historical readers but also the character of these readers' own con-

versations about Plath, conversations that frequently mark a significant—
some would say extreme—level of engagement with the author's work
and life. There's also the reality of public perception: while some of those
I identify as fans might want to contest the term, I think the larger public,
and certainly the mainstream media, would regard them as fans. And it is
this point—the media's frequent construction of Plath's historical readers
as fans—that I use as my starting point for this chapter.

When one turns to recent mainstream news stories about Plath (or
for that matter about Ted and Frieda Hughes), one frequently comes
across references to Plath's fans, even if the word "fan" itself doesn't get
used. Christina Patterson's piece in a 2004 issue of the *Independent*, for
example, offers a description of what she terms "the Plath effect" on readers, a phenomenon that apparently turns ordinary readers into fanatics.[1]
According to Patterson, this "afflicts not just adolescent girls, or armies
of rabid feminists united against the (male, philandering, silencing, murdering) devil, but also male literary critics of a certain age. It is, in short,
hysteria." Underscoring her fear that readerly interest has devolved into
fanaticism, Patterson adds: "It is certainly a little depressing that the online Sylvia Plath Forum offers 'in excess of one million words on Sylvia,'
and that a Google search brings up 85,200 hits. It is more than a little
depressing that a confused young woman who finally succumbed to the
siren call of suicide should be any kind of role model for anyone." While
Patterson doesn't use the word "fan" to describe the particular group of
readers she has in mind, her categorization of "the Plath effect" as "a
hysteria" and her concomitant reference to the suicidal Plath as role
model clearly point to her interest in Plath's fan culture. Furthermore,
the particular words she does choose to describe Plath's readership betray a no less unambiguous attitude toward that fan culture, one that is
unsympathetic at best. Because Patterson's attitude toward readers aligns
all too well with the one evident in the tropes of reading found in the
book reviews I discussed in chapter 1, I don't think it's necessary here to
explicate the troubling implications of her rhetoric.[2] I open this chapter
with her comments about "the Plath effect" merely to demonstrate suc-
cinctly the degree to which Plath's fan culture is well known, widely
talked about, and referred to by the mainstream media today. And yet
when one turns to examine this fan culture, as I do here, one encounters
a strange reality. While much is said about Plath fans, very little is known

about them, a reality suggested, albeit unintentionally, by Patterson her-self, who measures and characterizes the Plath fan phenomenon simply by the number of words they've posted to the Sylvia Plath Forum, rather than a concrete understanding of what they've said or who they are.

While this chapter doesn't aim to be the kind of case study of actual readers and their reading practices that would move us toward an ethno-graphic understanding of Plath's fan culture, it is meant to move us past the kind of shallow or banal understanding that has tended to define the discourse about Plath's readers.[3] To begin that process, I am interested here less in what we think we know about Plath's fans, which in some ways has been the focus of each chapter up to now, and more in what we do *not* know about them. By focusing on the latter, however, I do not mean to suggest that I aim to uncover, finally, the truth about Plath's real readers. Throughout this chapter I hope to eschew any argument that makes claims about what is or is not true about her readers, opting instead to consider that-which-goes-without-saying and, more dangerous still, that-which-never-gets-said in the discourse about them. Put another way, I want to follow the same line of inquiry that has governed the rest of this book, a line of inquiry which assumes that Plath's historical readers are as mythological, in the Barthesian sense, as the imagined one—that they too operate at the second level of signification, becoming sites of meaning that always already exists outside themselves. At the same time, a central component of this chapter is the archival research I have begun in order to try to present a more complete picture of the issues and incidents I discuss, some of which have been the subject of narratives that, though incomplete and fractured, have been allowed to circulate with little or no interrogation on the part of critics and readers. While my discussion aims to begin this interrogation, I avoid a more polemical approach to the questions I explore, hoping to avoid in turn the seeming necessity of defin-ing just what counts as a proper relationship between reader and author or, even more generally, of having to take a side in the debate over who has the better claim to Plath. In place of this kind of red herring, what interests me are the relationships among the various discourses that sur-round Plath's historical readers—including the discourses they produce and those that are produced about them—and how a more complete understanding of these relationships might help us move forward.

Before I turn to these discourses, I think it's important to acknowledge two caveats. First, the examples of the fan culture I examine here are predominantly from Plath's female, if not feminist, fan culture, a limitation that reflects not only the focus of the larger project of this book, which I explained in the introduction, but also the nature of the conversations that take place about Plath's fans, conversations that, with the exception of Christina Patterson's admission of "male literary critics of a certain age" into the fan club, tend to focus on readers' relationship to feminism. Second, when one turns to examine Plath's historical readers, one has to deal with some rather strange tensions between the imagined and real figures, tensions that complicate, I would argue, any obvious understanding of their relationship as either a mimetic or a caricatured one. Even though many of the representations of Plath's readers that have been the focus of this book up to this point, such as the one we see in *Family Guy*, are clearly intended as caricatures, they appear to owe their existence, at least on the surface, to the historical readers who are the focus of the current chapter. Indeed, the skeptical reader of my argument throughout this book will be more than a little tempted to view the figure of the Plath reader as seen in television, film, book reviews, and so on simply as a mimetic representation of real readers or fans. Certainly many of the literary reviews I discuss in chapter 1, including Anthony Thwaite's, with its memorable anecdote about the student who believed her own death was an essential part of fashioning a creative identity like Plath's, present their portraits of Plath's readers as mimetic ones. Yet as Thwaite's rhetoric also makes clear, the line between mimetic and caricatured figurations often gets blurred beyond recognition, especially in those representations of Plath's readers that, while not explicit caricature, clearly aim to exaggerate, sometimes for the sake of humor, sometimes to achieve a larger rhetorical end.

The "Rad-Fems" and Their "Holy War"

If there is one reader who could be singled out as the embodiment of the tensions between the real and the caricatured, it is the radical feminist Robin Morgan, who gained notoriety in relation to Plath in 1972 when she published her poem "Arraignment" in her first volume of poetry, *Monster*. An unapologetic attack on Ted Hughes and the literary establishment, the poem opens with what would have been to anyone outside Morgan's feminist circle a truly shocking question:

> How can
> I accuse
> Ted Hughes
> of what the entire British and American
> literary and critical establishment
> has been at great lengths to deny,
> without ever saying it in so many words, of course:
> the murder of Sylvia Plath?[4]

Carefully crafted to avoid legal reprisal on the part of Hughes, the poem responds to its initial question with a series of observations that argue Hughes's culpability in Plath's death without ever directly saying as much. That is, while Morgan paints Hughes as Plath's mental and physical "jailor" and as an abuser who has "brainwash[ed]" their children, "malappropriate[d]" her imagery, and exploited her writings for his financial gain, she does so by citing Plath's *own* accusations against Hughes in her poems and letters and by adopting language that avoids direct allegations against Hughes.[5] Moving from Plath's death to the death of Assia Wevill (the woman for whom Hughes left Plath in 1962 and who killed herself in 1969), Morgan argues that Wevill, like Plath, found the "oven's fumes less lethal than" Hughes's love but resists direct accusation once again, writing, "Only paranoiacs would assume / that such curious redundancy constitutes / a one-man gynocidal movement."[6] Morgan then turns, with ironic mockery, to blame Plath's, Wevill's, and her own insanity for any negative light her accusations might cast on Hughes.

　While the first half of the poem avoids libelous accusations, the second half shows no such compunction, directly attacking those figures from the literary establishment, including "A. Alvarez, / George Steiner, Robert Lowell, / and the legions of critical necrophiles," who have conspired against Plath by "patronizing her madness, diluting her rage, / burying her politics, and / aiding, abetting, rewarding / her perfectly legal executor."[7] Having drawn a connection between the male literary establishment and Hughes—all of whom collude in the conspiracy to deny Plath's proto-feminist politics—the poem closes with a violent fantasy of female revenge that Morgan says may or may not get enacted, a fantasy in which Morgan, now joined by other women, disguise themselves as "a covey of [Hughes's] girlish fans," find Hughes in his home, and "disarm him" of his genitalia, which they "stuff . . . into his mouth" before finally "blow[ing] out his brains."[8]

As the violent and audacious images of "Arraignment" make plain, Morgan means to vent her frustrations as a radical feminist, to grab her readers' attention, and to incite their anger. To do so, she relies largely on hyperbole, irony, and simple but deliberate language, all of which place her poem firmly within the 1970s tradition of militant feminist writing, especially that which sought to protest violence by men against women with the rhetoric of revolution, combat, and even retaliatory violence. And significantly, Morgan justifies her image of Hughes as violent abuser by citing what she calls "the testimony of [Plath's] own words—her accusations of betrayal, rape, battery, and poverty—in her last poems, letters, and journals."[9] However one feels about the poem, about Morgan, or about Hughes, one can hardly deny the force of "Arraignment," at least in terms of effect. Although it has been widely dismissed as mere feminist propaganda and hysteria, it's not a forgettable poem. Nor has it been an easy poem to dismiss or contain.

In part, the poem's ability to resist efforts to relegate it to the margins of serious literature lies outside the text itself. That is to say, if the poem still holds our attention, it's largely because of what the poem has come to represent within cultural conversations about Plath. "Arraignment," together with the figure of Morgan herself, has come to stand in for Plath fans, especially in mainstream media stories about Plath and Hughes, which often cite the poem as evidence of how feminist fans in particular beleaguered and harassed Ted Hughes. In the past couple of decades especially, references to Morgan's poem almost always lay the groundwork or offer support for a larger (and usually negative) composite of Plath's feminist fans. In a review of the 2003 film *Sylvia* for the *Washington Times*, for example, Charlotte Allen asserts:

> The rad-fems cast Mr. Hughes . . . as the ultimate masculine villain: selfish, priapic . . . , domineering, demanding, and narcissistic. Robin Morgan . . . set the gold standard for this sort of thing in a

1972 poem. . . . Other feminists periodically hacked Miss Plath's married name off her tombstone and heckled Mr. Hughes at his readings as a murderer. The oven. The children. The symbolism. Mr. Hughes had committed the ultimate male crime of forcing a poetic genius to become a housewife and mother.[10]

In the end, Allen commends the film for not following "the Robin Morgan line," which, like *Ms.* magazine, is no longer "fashionable," especially in light of the many new publications by and about Plath that "tell a more complicated tale than the martyrological sob story of the feminists."[11] Writing for the *Toronto Star* from a more sympathetic angle, Lynn Crosbie nonetheless takes a similar path from Morgan to feminist readers, pointing out the existence of several elegies that have been written about Plath, "including Robin Morgan's 'Arraignment,' which calls for the ritual castration of Hughes," before remarking on how "Hughes has been demonized by feminist critics over the years as a kind of literary Yorkshire Ripper."[12]

Other accounts in the mainstream media put forward even more direct connections between Morgan and Plath's feminist fans by pointing to the central role the poem appears to have played in the protests that were staged against Hughes begin in the early 1970s. A 1998 story in the *London Evening Standard* following the death of Ted Hughes offers one of the clearest examples of this phenomenon. Under the headline "Hate Figure for Feminist Agitators," the news story opens, "Ted Hughes was a hate figure for feminists—largely in American academe—for the way he was alleged to have treated his wife, poet Sylvia Plath."[13] It continues from there to outline feminists' accusations against Hughes, citing those "demonstrators" who picketed his readings with "placards accusing him of 'murdering' Plath," which resulted in Hughes "rarely, if ever, mak[ing] an appearance in public—and certainly not on a university campus," as well as those "feminist agitators" who repeatedly "hacked the word 'Hughes' off [Plath's] name on the headstone." A more concise example of this conflation of Morgan and feminist protesters appears in a 2002 review of Elaine Feinstein's biography of Hughes in the *Montreal Gazette*, which asserts rather confidently, "To this day, fierce feminists accuse him of murdering [Plath]."[14] Even Christina Patterson's portrait of "armies of rabid feminists" with which I began this chapter alludes to Morgan with its parenthetical paraphrase of Hughes's depiction in "Arraignment" as "(male, philandering, silencing, murdering)."

How does one poem come to speak for Plath's audience? Of course, Morgan herself opens the door to this substitution, turning by the end of the poem from a first-person speaker to a plural "we women," who together may or may not set out to destroy Hughes. Such a shift invites identification from those who share Morgan's anger; one might also argue that it invites the cooptation of the poem's tropes, which, if reports about what was written on the signs displayed by the women at the demonstrations are true, the protesters were more than happy to adopt as their own. In other words, to a certain extent one has to acknowledge that the poem and the protests are the same discourse. And yet one still has to wonder how the poem comes to represent so much, both to the protesters who adopted it and to those who feel compelled to comment on the protests.

While I do not doubt that many women identified with Morgan's powerful rhetoric when the poem appeared, I would argue that the line between the poem and the protesters is not nearly as direct as accounts like the ones I've quoted make it out to be. The line is at best a broken one, defined in large part by omissions and gaps in the narrative. This is nowhere more clear than in the story that gets told about "Arraignment" itself. Because the history of "Arraignment" has been largely, if not entirely, forgotten in the narrative, entire facets of that history are never glimpsed in mainstream media stories, facets that complicate any understanding of the poem as a feminist rallying cry directly responsible for the widespread anti-Hughes sentiment among Plath readers. One wonders, in fact, if we would still be talking about the poem today if its publication and reception history weren't as vexed as it is.

For starters, the well-known version of "Arraignment," which is also known as "Arraignment II," exists in the shape that it does solely as a product of Morgan's failed efforts to have the original poem she wrote about Plath, which would become known as "Arraignment (I)," included in *Monster*. As Morgan recounts in a 1972 essay for *Feminist Art Journal*, after returning the author's galleys to her publisher, Random House, she received a phone call from her editor explaining "that it had been decided to show 'Arraignment' to its house lawyers," who insisted that the poem was, in Morgan's words, "impossible, highly libelous, *unfair* to Ted Hughes, unsubstantiated, and endangering to Random House."

Morgan "fought back," claiming in her defense that the poem was "intensely researched" and accurate in its statements, as Plath scholars could testify, and that it was best viewed as a "descendant of a long line of honorable literary tradition in a polemical and accusative tone."[15] Furthermore, she insisted that she would take the entirety of *Monster* out of the publisher's hands before she would allow "Arraignment" to be cut from the manuscript. In the midst of these legal discussions with Random House, Morgan began to put the original poem through revisions, "aiming for something which could find sanctuary in the area of satire and irony . . . but something which would also get the facts and political message through to the readers—*and* be a moving artistic work."[16] At the end of her revision process, Morgan showed the new poem to Random House, which agreed to include it in *Monster*.

While capitulating to her publisher's demands, Morgan did not lay the original poem "Arraignment (I)" to rest. Hoping to find a larger, feminist audience for the work, she offered the poem to *Ms.* magazine, which judged it "'eminently actionable' and thus unpublishable," and then to *Feminist Art Journal*, which agreed to publish both versions of the poem, "Arraignment (I)" and "Arraignment (II)," as well as what Morgan calls her "exposé of the Random House-Hughes axis," in its fall 1972 issue.[17] But even this doesn't end the poem's unusual publication history. As Morgan explains in her 2001 memoir *Saturday's Child*, "Arraignment (II)"—the Random House–approved poem—would also be censored, in this case by the management of the Canadian Random House office, who, according to Morgan, pulled the book from all markets in the Commonwealth in response to Ted Hughes's threat to file a lawsuit. And it is at this point, significantly, that the poem begins to earn its notoriety, as feminist readers across Canada, Australia, and New Zealand started (with Morgan's permission) to "pirate" editions of *Monster* abroad, an effort fueled largely by their anger over the book's withdrawal from these markets.[18] In Australia, a "pirated" edition was published by the Melbourne Radical Feminists, and in Britain, an edition was brought out by a women's printing collective. Not incidentally, these editions frequently embodied the conflicts surrounding the book: back covers read, "Beware! Be Wary! This book has been banned!"; the first version of the poem, along with Morgan's essay on the ordeal, was added to the contents of some editions; and even Plath's photo sometimes appeared in the pages.[19] According to Robin

Morgan, the same feminists bringing out the "pirated" editions of *Monster* also began picketing Hughes's public readings, often displaying signs with lines from "Arraignment" as part of their protests. They called themselves "Arraignment Women," though Morgan herself claims never to have participated in a protest or to have orchestrated any from behind the scenes.[20]

By most accounts—including Morgan's—Hughes responded to the initial protests and the threat of continued protests by canceling public readings, both in his home country and abroad, and by generally withdrawing from the public eye. Meanwhile, Morgan became the object of another kind of protest. Widely—and according to Morgan wrongly—assumed to be the hands-on instigator of the protests, she received calls and notes from literary critics, editors, and even Doris Lessing pressuring her to "call off" the women harassing Hughes. Lessing went so far as to urge her to "withdraw *all* versions of the poem from publication *anywhere*."[21] Had Morgan acceded to such requests and removed the book after it had already appeared and gained attention, one might guess that the response from feminists would have been just as strong, perhaps even stronger, given what the book had already come to represent. Take, for example, the edition put out by the Melbourne Radical Feminists, which, according to Morgan's website, included the following statement: "*Monster* has given strength to every woman we've shown the poems to. And if not only reading the poems but publishing them becomes a revolutionary experience, then so much more power to sisterhood."[22] In any case, Morgan allowed the poem to continue to appear in published form, and in the process, I would argue, became the emblem of Plath's feminist, if not female, readership.

It's an end result that is perplexing on the one hand and seemingly inevitable on the other. I call it perplexing because as I look at what is known about the poem's publication and reception history, much of it appears to have been out of Morgan's hands. I offer this observation not because I wish to defend the poem necessarily, but rather because the poem's success and widespread circulation appear to be the result, ironically, of the very efforts made by others to keep the poem from being read.[23] Indeed, the more Random House and later Hughes or his advocates tried to keep the poem from print, the more they increased demand for it and, it is important to note, the more Hughes looked to feminists of the time exactly like the oppressive force Morgan depicts him as being.

Put another way, Morgan's portrait of Hughes in the poem as Plath's censor only gained credibility in light of the censorship of Morgan's book. One should ask, in fact, if it is more than just a coincidence that the worst anti-Hughes protests, by most accounts, took place in Australia, where the book was banned and later circulated in "pirated" editions as a book banned by Hughes. Yet it is Morgan who is generally assumed to be responsible for the poem's popularity among Plath's feminist fans, despite the role clearly played by censorship in the poem's sensational and long-lived circulation. Certainly Morgan could have denied permission to those wishing to print an edition of the book privately, and had they persisted anyway, she could have sued the parties involved for reproducing copyrighted material without permission. But wouldn't the story of Hughes and the book's censorship still read pretty much the same?

If Morgan's transformation into the sign of Plath's readership seems inevitable at the same time that it appears perplexing, it's because by writing the poem, and then later by insisting on the poem's publication, she offers those who wish to depict Plath's audience disdainfully just what they most need: discursive and therefore tangible evidence of the perceived fanatical misguidedness of Plath's readers. Anecdotes about what young women readers might be doing with Plath's writings in their homes and classrooms pale in comparison to the black and white image Morgan's poem can paint.

The ease with which critics and journalists can latch on to "Arraignment" might also explain why so much of this larger story of its publication and reception history gets omitted from discussion of the poem itself. While the poem is frequently cited as evidence of the harassment Hughes has been subjected to by Plath's feminist audience, its fuller context seldom, if ever, gets mentioned, undoubtedly because this context exists in a far less tangible, or at least less accessible, form. If in fact the feminist stranglehold on the discourse about Plath is as firm as it is made out to be, one wonders just why the poem comes to stand, in public discourse, for women's harassment of Hughes rather than for Hughes's attempts to silence certain versions of his life with Plath by either intervening in the process of publication or denying requests from scholars and biographers seeking permission to use Plath's work.[24] At the very least, it's true that the title of Morgan's *Feminist Art Journal* exposé, "Conspiracy of Silence against a Feminist Poem," turned out to be entirely prescient, given the gaps in the larger dominant narrative about the poem and the silence surrounding its rather complex publication history. While through her essay's title Morgan is obviously pointing to the efforts to silence the poem prior to its publication, it would seem that a second conspiracy has surrounded the poem since its publication, not necessarily a conscious conspiracy of silence, perhaps, but a silencing that at the very least takes the shape of historical forgetfulness. A story about Morgan's poem has already been written, and it simply doesn't allow for a full understanding of the poem's complex publication history and reception.

How does such history become lost? If Morgan had published the poem not in the early 1970s but in the late 1980s or early 1990s, at the height of the controversy surrounding Hughes's handling of the Plath estate, especially his (and his sister Olwyn's) questioned role in Anne Stevenson's biography of Plath and his refusal to work with scholars such as Linda Wagner-Martin and Jacqueline Rose who appeared to have feminist agendas, might the poem's story have resonated more fully, earning a place on our contemporary radar? Lest my questions and examination of "Arraignment" be mistaken for a defense of the poem's claims about Hughes, I want once again to clarify a key point: the question of the validity of Morgan's claims—or even the appropriateness of the poem's self-conscious hyperbole—really seems to me to be beside the point at this stage. In any case, the issue is outside the purview of this book. What interests me instead is what we know or do not know about the poem and how Morgan has been used to reify the discourse about Plath's readers, especially feminist ones. To put it another way, while there may well be grounds for conflating Morgan's poem with feminist readers more broadly, what interests me is not the validity of the conflation but what the conflation accomplishes rhetorically. That accomplishment is nothing small. The existence of Morgan's poem—and the media's ability to point to it, even if only through opaque allusion—gives credence to all the claims that follow: because the poem offers concrete evidence of just how severe the feminist attack on Hughes has been, it always already establishes evidence for claims about Hughes as the object of feminist hatred. Yet what do we know about feminists' ostensible hatred of Hughes beyond "Arraignment" and the countless allusions to it in the mainstream media? How do we get from Morgan's poem, a tangible piece of evidence of one woman's disdain for Hughes, to what in 2000 *The Times* of London calls, with much more expansive language, the "baying pack of feminists who hounded him throughout his life?"[25]

The narrative of this evolution from Morgan to packs of feminists, as it has been told, goes more or less as follows: Robin Morgan wrote "Arraignment" and subsequently orchestrated—or at the very least inspired—global public attacks on Hughes that plagued him throughout the rest of his life; these feminist attacks, which took the shape of everything from heckling at his poetry readings, to picketing his events, to chiseling the name "Hughes" from Plath's gravestone, were so intense as to cause Hughes to put an end to his public readings. As Ian Hamilton put it in a 1998 essay on Hughes, "quite often, during the 1970s, Hughes would arrive at some campus or literary festival, invited there to read from his work, only to be greeted by groups of demonstrating feminists: with banners, chants, and all."[26] In short, most accounts from journalists, memoirists, biographers, and scholars make it out to be a significant and long-lasting phenomenon.

Yet when we turn from this narrative about Hughes's feminist attackers to the historical record that might document it, we find little that illuminates the evolution of the narrative. Much like the history of the poem "Arraignment," the history of feminist attacks on Hughes appears to be largely a history of omissions, elisions, and hearsay, usually repeated by biographers and memoirists without documentation or verifiable details. To shed light on the accounts given by these biographers and memoirists, I specifically sought out news articles from mainstream papers that might have covered the harassment at the time it occurred. And to bring balance to those personal accounts of the protests that attempt to represent Hughes's perspective, I also sought out firsthand testimonials from women who may have participated in the incidents or have information about them. But I repeatedly encountered dead ends.[27] As a case study, the protests that took place at the Adelaide Arts Festival in Australia in 1976, which is the most commonly cited instance of the protests Hughes encountered, provide the richest ground for examination, in large part because firsthand accounts of the events actually do exist.

Jill Barber, who worked as press officer at the Adelaide Festival in 1976, gives one of these firsthand accounts, though it's worth noting that she didn't publish the account until 2001, and then only as part of her exposé of her four-year affair with Hughes, which began at the same Adelaide Festival. Describing Hughes's third day in Adelaide, where he was to give a reading, Barber recalls: "There was a crowd of about 200 waiting for us as we stepped out of the Hotel Australia. As soon as they spotted Ted, the mob, mostly women, held up placards and started chanting: 'You killed Sylvia.' We fled back into the hotel. We did not talk about what had happened. He only looked at me in a concerned way."[28] Unusual in its details—how large the protest was, where it took place, what was chanted—Barber's brief account allows us to imagine more fully the demonstrations Hughes faced. Nonetheless, it must be said that her credibility as witness is greatly diminished by other claims she makes in the essay, including her assertion that Hughes had revealed himself as the actual author of *The Bell Jar.*[29] Somewhat less questionable in his motives, Ian Hamilton briefly reflects on the events at Adelaide in a 1998 article on *Birthday Letters* for the *Australian*, in which he notes: "I can recall one of the banners in Adelaide when he visited the 1976 festival. It read: 'Who Killed Sylvia Plath?' and it struck me as one of the ugliest headlines I had read for a long time. Hughes, as I recall, pretended that he hadn't seen it but he surely had."[30]

A feature news story about Hughes and fellow English poet Adrian Mitchell published in the *Australian* the week after Writers' Week at the Adelaide Festival reports a similar incident at the hotel, though with much less detail than we find in Barber's account and with an apparently greater vested interest in painting Hughes as a victim of feminist vilification, rather than, say, as the target of political protest. Before even mentioning the incident itself, the reporter, Janet Hawley, goes out of her way to give context to the incident, noting the "albatross" Hughes has worn around his neck since Plath's suicide and the "certain freak sections of the Women's Liberation movement" that "prefer to see the suicide as the Devil's stigmata on Hughs' [*sic*] soul."[31] Hawley continues, "Wherever Hughes goes, he is persecuted by these feminist freaks, who hold up signs at his poetry readings . . . 'I killed Sylvia Plath—guilty.'" Turning her attention back to the Adelaide Festival, Hawley notes that "Hughes got through the first few days, managing the snipes like 'How's Sylvia?' with replies like 'she's fine,' and the comebacks, 'Don't you know she's dead, Ted?'" In the next paragraph of the story, Hawley refers briefly to a second incident when she alludes to the presence of protesters at Hughes's scheduled reading: "On Monday night, Mitchell and Hughes gave so thrilling a performance that the protestors were dumbfounded.

Hughes's reading was so intense that they were unable to force their arms to hold up those placards." Vaguely implying another incident, this one at Hughes's hotel, Hawley writes that by Thursday morning of Writers' Week "Hughes had locked himself in his room." While Hawley doesn't directly attribute Hughes's self-exile to the presence of protesters outside the hotel, she implies as much, describing an enraged Mitchell who "almost staggered out of their hotel lift" in his frustration. Though depicted as "hardly able to speak," Mitchell complains: "Why don't they charge him with murder and get it over with. . . . [I]t's an outrage, people who have never met him or Sylvia Plath playing god and judge, what kind of freaks are these who plague him?"

Although I would refrain from using Mitchell's disparaging word choice, I think his question about the nature of the "freaks" plaguing Hughes is a crucial one that seems to me at least to merit an answer. Who indeed are the women at these protests? Unfortunately, it's a question Hawley never answers beyond attaching the moniker "feminists" to the group. Furthermore, it's as though Hawley's piece has been written for an audience who already know what happened. It functions, that is, not like a news report but as editorialized comment on events already familiar to readers, a comment that makes no attempt to establish what happened at the reading or outside Hughes's hotel (in terms of either the extent or the nature of the protests) or to seek out the feminist viewpoint to provide a semblance of balanced reporting. In short, the article reads more like a gripe directed at those predisposed to sympathize with Hughes, despite its presentation as a news story in the arts section.

Unless I missed a report in my day-by-day perusal of the paper during the weeks surrounding the festival, Hawley's is the only public statement about the protests published in the *Australian*, despite the paper's full coverage of several controversies involving the festival, from the last-minute withdrawals of authors Tennessee Williams and James Baldwin to demonstrations by those protesting a Soviet author's denied exit visa and an art display that consisted of concrete statues of "Aboriginals." Equally important, Hawley's account contradicts the only official report on Hughes's departure from Adelaide I could find in the *Australian*, which, as part of the "Newsmakers" column in its main section, attributes the short duration of Hughes's visit at the festival to his need to attend to the cows on his farm in England which were about to calve.[32]

Hawley's depiction of a crowd of heckling Ted Hughes detractors is also at odds with a report by Elizabeth Riddell published about a week after Hughes's reading, following the end of Writers' Week at the festival. Riddell describes how Hughes "electrified an audience . . . which had bought tickets for [the no-show] Baldwin."[33] The local Adelaide newspaper, the *Advertiser*, contains a report the day after Hughes's reading that offers a similar portrait of the audience who attended. Describing the venue as "only about half filled," the report adds, "small though the audience may have been, it reacted enthusiastically to the readings by . . . the introspective Hughes."[34] The only sign that anything might have been amiss comes in the last sentence of the report, which describes Hughes's poems, which were "mainly drawn from his 'Crow' series, as 'more sullen'" than the poems read by the other poet on the program.[35] The *Age*, another Australian newspaper, offers a similarly bland report on the audience at Hughes and Mitchell's reading, noting, "Their public performance attracted an audience which filled almost half of Adelaide's vast baroque town hall."[36] Neither the *Advertiser* nor the *Age* offers any coverage of the Hughes protests.

How does one explain the discrepancies between Hawley's account and the others that appear concurrent with hers? If the disruption of Hughes's reading had been as terrible as it had been made out to be, it seems odd that descriptions of the audience itself in newspapers from the time would fail to take note of it. While I am not naïve enough to think that a newspaper report can offer the absolute definitive and objective evidence that is needed to illuminate everything that may have happened, I do think it's reasonable to hope for something more balanced than Hawley's contribution to the *Australian*. In any case, the apparent absence of any solid confirmation does make one wonder if Jill Barber, in describing the details of the passionate affair she and Hughes began almost immediately upon his arrival in Adelaide, doesn't provide an equally plausible reason why Hughes spent so much time in his hotel room during his six days at the Adelaide Festival. While it might sound catty to say so, I wouldn't be the first to make Barber a factor in the issue. An article in the *Times Literary Supplement* in 2007 goes so far as to blame feminists for Hughes's affair with Barber, noting that it "probably began as a counterweight to the hatred expressed by militant feminists who hounded Hughes at Adelaide, accusing him of having murdered Plath. Public vilification is hard to bear on your own."[37]

Whatever Hughes's reasons for spending so much time in his hotel room while in Adelaide, one can't deny that the few details Janet Hawley offers about the protesters in the audience at the reading itself undercut her larger narrative about the feminists. What Hawley leaves us with is an image of feminists ultimately tamed by the power of Hughes's reading: remember, according to her, the protesters were "dumbfounded" by Hughes's performance, "unable to force their arms to hold up those placards." In other words, Hawley insists we take the feminist threat seriously—for so complete is the harassment that it is ruining Hughes's life and career—yet her account of the event presents these very same feminists as mesmerized women, so silly in their complaints and so non-threatening in their politics that they are easily disarmed by the poet's charm and virility. With accounts like Hawley's, one wonders just how it was possible for the narrative of feminists as unrelenting harassers of Hughes to have become as entrenched as it has.

To explain its persistence, one has to turn to the secondhand accounts of the harassment that have circulated over the years in memoirs and biographies. Representative of the kind of overly general statements about these attacks that one tends to come across when researching the subject, Lucas Myers's memoir of Hughes and Plath tells how "for years, feminists picketed Ted's poetry readings and chanted 'Daddy' to drown out his recitation in actions reminiscent of Chinese Red Guards during Mao Zedong's Cultural Revolution."[38] Later in the same memoir, Myers describes Hughes's vilification as a three-phase transformation: phase one consisted of the repercussions of Assia Wevill's death in 1969 and A. Alvarez's article on Plath's suicide in the *Observer* in 1971; phase two was marked by the publication of Edward Butcher's biography and essay collection in 1976 and 1977, respectively; while phrase three, Myers writes, "began before the first two had completed their work of 'enablement,' reached full strength in tandem with the second phase and went on and on thereafter. This was the phase in which crowds of hecklers followed Ted like Red Guards. If they had been in a feminist one party state, they could have hauled him up before the people in 'struggle sessions (*thamzing* in Tibet).' As it was, they chanted 'Daddy' and a poem called 'Arraignment' by a woman in New York named Robin Morgan who accused Ted of the murder of Sylvia Plath."[39]

Beyond Myers's portraits in his memoir and the apparently obligatory reference in mainstream media stories to Hughes's vilification, we find slight mention of the incidents in a couple of the nearly dozen Plath and Hughes biographies written over the years, usually in the kind of overly broad, undetailed strokes used by Myers in his own portrait. Paul Alexander's biography of Plath, *Rough Magic*, offers one of the lengthier accounts, mentioning Morgan and "the radical feminists" who "conducted what they saw as a 'holy war' against Hughes" and who "harassed Hughes during his public poetry readings."[40] To support the claims, however, all Alexander can offer is that "a woman would stand up in the audience and either launch into a diatribe against him or on occasion recite 'Arraignment.'" The result, Alexander notes, was that "Hughes gave fewer and fewer readings." The few accounts that offer details more specific than these tend to refer only to Hughes's visit to Adelaide in 1976, which, as we've seen, is a case with its own set of epistemological problems. In her 2001 biography of Hughes, for example, Elaine Feinstein cites the March 1976 event as "a hideous occasion, during which placards were held up accusing him of Sylvia's murder, and women in the audience hurled angry abuse at him. It was an unusually scandalous event, which Michael Boddy, then in Australia, remembers reading about in the newspapers with horror. The transcript shows that Ted continued to give his reading, although his comments between poems are uncharacteristically stilted."[41] Additionally, Feinstein cites an incident of harassment in the 1990s, which took the form of twigs and berries left on Hughes's doorstop. As Feinstein notes, the pack of feminists suspected of leaving the twigs and berries turned out to be "a lone woman," a fact revealed through a police investigation initiated by Harold Pinter, whom the woman had targeted along with Hughes.[42] The woman, Feinstein reports, was so "susceptible to persuasion that she was committing a form of terrorism herself for which she could be in some peril" that she "ceased" the harassment.[43]

While both Feinstein and Myers count Hughes as a friend, neither can offer anything more than undetailed secondhand accounts of the harassment. Alexander, who by all reports one would not count among Hughes's friends, offers a similarly undocumented and untraceable discussion of the harassment. In none of their accounts do we find information that explains where the writer has drawn his or her information from. Still,

the three versions strike me as worth our attention, if for no other reason
than how they present the narrative of the harassment. First and perhaps
not surprisingly, the narratives, at least in the case of Myers and Alexander, rely on the same slide from Robin Morgan to feminists that one
frequently finds in mainstream media accounts of Hughes's harassment.
Here, however, it's worth noting that the harassment which begins with
one woman (Morgan), and before long is transformed into a mass effort,
returns in the end to just one woman. Recall that as Alexander describes
the moment of harassment, "*a woman* would stand up in the audience."
As examples go, this seems an odd choice if one's goal is to demonstrate
the "holy war" waged by "radical feminists." Given Alexander's less than
sympathetic view of Hughes, perhaps one might give the biographer the
benefit of the doubt and assume that Alexander himself is aware of the discrepancy between the image of an army of feminists and the lone woman
heckling Hughes from the audience. If his intention is to dispel the events
as myth, however, one would perhaps expect a better, or at least more
overt, effort to highlight the discrepancies. In Feinstein's account as well,
the claim of a mob of feminists gets juxtaposed against another account of
the harassment, one that also boils down to just one woman, this time one
with a fondness for the symbolism of twigs and berries. For readers who
notice, the slide should undercut the image of an army of feminists that
typically dominates the discourse. In addition to these discrepancies, the
resemblance between Alexander's own portrait of the feminist "holy war"
and Myers's portrait of the harassers as "Chinese Red Guards," which
recurs frequently throughout his memoir, must certainly give us pause.
Both invest, self-consciously or not, in antifeminist invective that doesn't
help to illuminate the extent or exact nature of the protests or harassment. So extreme is Myers's characterization of feminists as Mao's Red
Guard that it places any account Myers might have to offer in a dubious
light. Which is not to say that the comparison makes no sense at all. In
the dominant narrative about Hughes and feminists, the comparison fits
all too well, for not only does it paint feminists as a totalitarian regime
composed of young, student-aged members intent on punishing Hughes
through their own tribunals, and Hughes as a representative of the poets,
artists, and other culture makers persecuted and destroyed in the name
of Mao's Cultural Revolution, but also it implicitly draws a line between

Mao and Morgan, the dictator—one can even say cult figure—whose propaganda the Red Guard blindly disseminates and protects.

To put aside for a moment the problems inherent in Myers's repeated (and obviously hyperbolic) construction of feminists as Red Guard equivalents, it's worth noting that he finds the feminist persecution of Hughes a topic ripe for the "social historian" interested in undertaking the research.[44] Yet when one sets out to construct this social history, little information about it seems to exist beyond overly general and unverifiable comments like the ones Myers offers. Even Myers seems to anticipate the trouble the historian would encounter. As he puts it, "I don't know how much film of their harassment of Ted can be found, since it's probably in the canisters of the Red Guards themselves."[45] While I would not attribute the dearth of information to a feminist conspiracy as Myers does, I think he is right to highlight the larger problems one faces when trying to discuss Hughes's relationship to feminists. Without film in the canisters, those who wish to talk about the subject in any way are forced to extrapolate a larger narrative from few facts. It's no wonder, then, that when we begin to apply pressure to the dominant narrative we now operate under, cracks and curious discrepancies almost immediately appear.

One of the most curious of these discrepancies lies in accounts that actually try to go beyond Morgan to identify the other parties responsible for the protests and the continued anti-Hughes sentiment. The 1998 article in the *Evening Standard* from which I quoted earlier in this chapter is a prime example. Remember, it paints Hughes as the object of feminist hatred "largely in American academe" and then links that hatred to his reluctance to offer public performances of any kind but "certainly not on a university campus."[46] While the *Evening Standard* identifies the source of trouble as American academics and students, this account, and others like it, appear at odds with the reality of the protests: namely, that the protests and harassment, while repeatedly linked to Morgan and American scholars and students, tended to happen elsewhere, mostly in Australia and England. In other words, just as the feminist protesters and Morgan become substitutes for each other, the feminist protesters slide into American feminist scholars and students, despite the location of the actual protests themselves.[47] I find this substitution more than a bit vexing. How do we get from the protests that happened at Adelaide, Australia, in

1976, for which there is some evidence, however unsatisfying it may be, to the much broader claim that American feminists and young female university students represented a significant and continual threat to Hughes in the United States?

By most biographical accounts, Hughes traveled rather infrequently to the United States, mostly, it has been said, because of the hostility he would face here. Piecing together information from a variety of sources, including Feinstein's biography of Hughes, a timeline offered by Keith Sagar in *The Laughter of Foxes*, Diane Middlebrook's joint biography of Plath and Hughes, and Hughes's published and unpublished letters, I gather that Hughes came to the United States for poetry performances only a handful of times during and after the height of Plath's popularity among feminists in the early 1970s: in March 1971, when he toured over a dozen college campuses to promote the U.S. release of his book *Crow*;[48] in July 1977 for a tour that Sagar, Feinstein, and Middlebrook all mention but about which few details are known; in 1980 for readings and workshops outside the U.S. mainland at the Festival of the Midnight Sun in Alaska; and in September 1986, when he gave a performance at Seton Hall University.

Accounts of Hughes's reading tour of the United States during March 1971 report nothing too eventful. In his memoir *The Kick: A Life among Writers*, Richard Murphy, who joined Hughes on the tour, tracks the route of their travels, which focused for the most part on college campuses throughout the Northeast. While he doesn't go into detail about all the readings on the tour, the few stops he does mention shed light on the audiences Hughes encountered. Describing Hughes's solo reading at Amherst College at the start of the tour, Murphy reports that the room was "so crowded that people were sitting on the floor, dead quiet, hushed by awe and admiration. At the end of his reading he remained for nearly an hour, talking one by one to those who were waiting in a long line that stretched to the door. Nearly all had come from Smith College to hear him: good-looking, well-brought-up girls, like Sylvia, with long loose hair."[49] He appears to have fared only slightly less well at Colgate University the following week. While he once again faced an "overcrowded room," this time there was a whiff of trouble in the air. Nothing that Hughes couldn't dispatch, however. Murphy writes:

I sensed hostility to Ted in the audience, and only discovered the cause after he had gone. An associate professor had told his students that an English poet called Ted Hughes would be reading on the campus, and they should bear in mind that he had married an American called Sylvia Plath, who was a far better poet, and that many people thought he was responsible for her suicide. However, Ted made such a good impression that three of the girls at his reading—sophomores—joined our tour to Rochester University a few days later.[50]

While Murphy's account of the event at Colgate points to some unspoken hostility in the air (provided one sets aside the question of whether one professor could be responsible for an audience's worth of animosity), the portraits he offers of Hughes's audiences generally are far from threatening ones. In fact, Murphy's description of both the Amherst and Colgate audiences may well remind us of Janet Hawley's depiction of Hughes's Adelaide audience, the audience that has come to stand in so often for Hughes's vilification, the one so mesmerized by Hughes that even the rabid feminists in the room couldn't help but abandon their cause.

In specific accounts of performances Hughes gave outside the United States, one encounters similar portraits of the audiences Hughes encountered. The news coverage of his public appearance at the International Authors Festival in Toronto in October 1983 suggests he faced a more than amiable crowd. According to the *Globe and Mail*, Hughes and the other "luminaries" were even greeted by adoring female "literary groupies."[51] In Britain, his reception at the Cambridge Poetry Festival in 1975 appears equally warm; there, according to Elaine Feinstein, his audience listened to him with "an impassioned stillness," attention that continued at the post-performance party at Feinstein's house, where "there were many young women attracted to his side."[52] Indeed, having spent months trying to track down descriptions of Hughes's audiences at his poetry readings, I can attest that firsthand accounts of adoring—one might say seduced—young women are nearly as common as secondhand reports of harassing feminists.

Getting back to the question of the performances he offered in the United States, accounts of his 1986 appearance at Seton Hall University

in South Orange, New Jersey, shortly after his appointment as poet laureate suggest it too was uneventful.[53] Ample coverage prior to the event
in the *New York Times, Newark Star-Ledger, East Orange Record,* and
Seton Hall's student newspaper the *Setonian* suggest a strong interest in
Hughes's reading; and the only post-event coverage to be found (which
amounts to a photo of Hughes in the midst of the reading with a brief
caption) offers nothing that might suggest Hughes faced a less than welcoming audience, though all reports confirm the rarity of his appearances
in the United States between the mid-1970s and mid-1980s.[54] Nearly all
the papers note that the Seton Hall reading was his first U.S. appearance
in over ten years, which, except for a brief trip to Alaska in 1980, appears
accurate.

While it's impossible to conduct a search that would exhaust all the
possible sources that might have reported on Hughes's performances over
the years — or even to generate a comprehensive and definitive list of his
performances — the information I have uncovered can still be useful, for
at the very least it suggests a more complex narrative about what Hughes
encountered at his readings than the one that has circulated, uncorroborated yet unchallenged, for the better part of three decades. Hughes's
letters, both published and unpublished, provide further dimensions to a
revised narrative about his public performances and the feminist harassers who were ostensibly so problematic. Most helpful, perhaps, they shed
light on the reasons Hughes had for withdrawing from the public eye
beyond the threat of protests, reasons that are almost always absent from
the dominant narrative about Hughes and feminists. If Hughes's own letters to friends and colleagues are any indication, the explanations for his
retreat from public performance, especially in the United States, appear
far more varied than reports have made them out to be. In an unpublished
letter to Ben Sonnenburg in the fall of 1969, Hughes reveals that his tour
of the United States has been "undergoing modification." The reason for
this turns out to be entirely practical. According to Hughes, "Not enough
people want us at the price (not enough Treasurers, Presidents, etc—all
our encouragement comes from low down professors with no pull on
the purse strings finally).[55] In another unpublished letter to Sonnenburg
in 1986, Hughes again explains his absence from the U.S. poetry scene
during this period, this time citing his wish to avoid any reminders of the
lawsuit against him concerning the film version of *The Bell Jar.*[56] Other

comments made by Hughes cast further light on the problems with the dominant narrative, including comments he makes about his general dislike of public readings, which, it is important to note, he harbors long before Plath's stardom and the feminist harassment begin. As he remarks in a 1962 letter to his brother Gerald, "I'm off today to read poems to the assembled heads of Hull University—a doubtful exercise, this poetry-reading. I keep thinking I'll stop it."[57]

While admittedly none of this information gets us even close to the bottom of whether the dominant narrative about Morgan's poem and the feminist protests is justified, I think any attention paid to the question can only help move us nearer. And if in the end it proves insufficient to construct an alternative narrative, at the very least it helps to contextualize and therefore complicate the narrative we have, inviting, I hope, more critical reflection than we've seen so far. Nor is this need for contextualization and historicization limited to our understanding of Hughes, as we see if we turn back to the poem at the heart of the controversy and protest.

Just as it's important to avoid oversimplifying the narrative about the audiences at Hughes's public performances, it's also important not to oversimplify the complex historical moment that produces a controversial poem like "Arraignment" as well as its reception and adoption by feminist groups. Indeed, I would suggest that what everyone—protesters, journalists, and Hughes defenders alike—appears guilty of is a gross reduction of the poem itself, one that turns snippets of the poem into dehistoricized sound bites. Placing the poem back into its historical context seems to me, then, to be the first step toward a more complete narrative about the poem and its relationship to Plath's women readers.

Within the entirety of *Monster* itself, "Arraignment" represents a central moment among the poems, enacting Morgan's definition of her own poetry, which she admits, in the poem "Letter to a Sister Underground," is deliberately not the "well-wrought kind."[58] She writes "things about women, my sisters and myself / in the hope" of "ignit[ing] a fuse of righteous bitterness / in a woman (my sister or myself) / that can flash into an action no one—least of all me— / could have foreseen erupting."[59] In the title poem, "Monster," she extends the definition further, likening her poetry to "witches' incantations," "schizophrenic code," "firebombs, / poison, knives, bullets, and whatever else will invent / this freedom."[60] Within the very definition of her poetry, one can see the militant quality of Morgan's feminism, especially its call for rage and even violence in the face of social injustices against women, a call that obviously extends far beyond Plath. Moreover, to dismiss "Arraignment" for its aggressive attack on Hughes is to miss the way the poem—and other militant feminist writing—is clearly meant to work within a polemical tradition (the word "polemic," after all, derives from the Greek word for war).

Throughout the late sixties and seventies, various feminist groups frequently relied on similar tropes of war, battle, and annihilation in making their arguments, a justified response, they felt, to finding themselves locked into a system that encouraged rape and violence against women and thus made their fight one not just for equity but for survival. Feminists like Morgan saw the affirmation of women's rage as a healthy "first step toward freeing" themselves, and they viewed violence as a likely inevitable response to the "'normal,' everyday violence" directed at women.[61] Within such a worldview, fantasies of a mob of women castrating a man, as occurs in "Arraignment," were certainly not unheard of.[62] Quite simply, for Morgan's intended audience, men represented a class of people who created and perpetuated the patriarchal system keeping women down, and who generated rape, pornography, and domestic violence. It was not unusual to hear violence against this class espoused, as the slogans feminists circulated attest. Some feminists even wore buttons that unabashedly advocated violence against men, featuring sayings such as "So Many Men, So Little Ammunition" and "Stop Sucking; Start Biting," to name just two.[63] If the rhetoric sounds shocking, that's because it was meant to sound that way. As De Clarke puts it: "The very possibility of female rage and revenge is frightening and shocking to us. . . . The image of a woman killing a man . . . is blasphemy."[64] For these reasons, the image made an especially useful rhetorical tool. As a central figure of the movement, Morgan would obviously have been deeply aware of just how powerful the tool could be, not simply when it came to shocking those in the mainstream, but also when it came to inciting budding feminists to outrage about gender inequalities.

Even less radical feminists saw violence as a potential outcome of their own right to self-defense, an important tenet of second-wave feminism that made karate and other martial arts almost as popular among women as consciousness raising. While most references to "Arraignment" focus on the rhetoric of female revenge that figures strongly in the poem, few if any acknowledge the impulse toward self-defense that also underlies Morgan's poem. Before turning to her fantasy of violence against Hughes, Morgan puts forward an argument about him and his collusion with the (male) literary establishment that invites us to see the poem as an act of surrogate self-defense through which Morgan becomes Plath's protector, in this case by calling out the gender biases of the poetry world and by calling for an intervention in the posthumous handling of her work. As she puts it in one of her prose pieces in *Going Too Far*, Plath—like Woolf, Anna Wickham, and Charlotte Mew—was "driven [to suicide] by patriarchal literary indifference." For this reason, she explains, she chooses to call Plath's death a "murder," and by calling it murder, she aims to put a stop to the male critics' "desperate attempt to defuse that electric voice" by worshiping, condemning, or analyzing Plath's death over and over.[65] From its expression of rage, to its fantasy of female violence, to its protective defense of Plath's work, Morgan's poem is situated squarely within the rhetoric of the women's movement, and it seems misguided to separate the poem from this historical context, as the narratives that turn the poem into sound bites uniformly do. It's worth noting here, too, that Morgan's rejection of those who set out to worship, condemn, and analyze Plath's death is one echoed by countless scholars and book reviewers over the years, as well as by Ted Hughes himself. Such denunciations are so widespread, in fact, that one wonders if they aren't a prerequisite for publishing on Plath.

From my own perspective as a feminist critic, I feel compelled to remind readers and critics of this context and the need to explore the fuller history of the poem in part because the poem's afterlife invites feminist scrutiny, especially how it has been turned into the opportunity to vilify feminist readers, even as it has been widely read as a sign of the vilification of Hughes. This is not to say that the poem itself shouldn't be the object of scrutiny too. I personally find it difficult to understand how a poem that accuses Hughes of the murder of two "wives"[66] in order to make a point about his alleged misogyny can also justify the one literal murder that took place among the deaths depicted in the poem: the murder of baby Shura, the daughter Wevill intentionally gassed along with herself. In the dominant narrative that gets told about the poem, readers get so caught up in the imagined violence—Morgan's fantasy of a coven of women dismembering Hughes—that they forget the actual and undisputed violence that took place. I see why, in the context of her argument, Morgan goes to the extreme of depicting Wevill as the heroic Jewish mother, but why haven't her foes held the poem and Morgan accountable for the violence she condones on this front?[67] I would guess it's because this violence, like the larger context of the poem's relationship to the polemical strategies of feminism, appears to have little to do with either Hughes or Plath, the only two sides that seem to matter.

When looked at within its broader context, I think the poem's value within feminist politics comes not in its indictment of Hughes as philanderer and murderer, though I do see its place in the historical moment of 1970s feminism, but in its indictment of Hughes as a representative of the literary establishment of the time, an establishment dictating the terms of interpretation and even publication. Furthermore, as a scholar whose work has focused on the transhistorical, negative rhetoric surrounding women readers, I find the most interesting—and yet never mentioned— aspect of the poem to be how it turns the table on male readers, specifically male literary critics, and indicts them on the very same charge of misguided reading practices so often leveled at women. According to Morgan they are "necrophiles," and they fail to read Plath's poetry correctly. What Morgan does, moreover, is redefine the terms of correct reading, casting true critical reading practices here as those that are attuned to the political layers of Plath's writing, practices that do not try to diminish her anger, rage, and even madness, as the male "necrophiles" have done. Adding to this layer of the poem, Morgan seems to anticipate the rhetoric that would be hurled at her after the poem's publication, specifically the tendency among nonfeminist readers and critics to pathologize her as a Plath reader. As she notes in the poem, others are free to dismiss her own understanding of Plath as a sign that she is "patently unstable."[68]

"Don't Any of You Like Sylvia Plath?"

Morgan's invitation is one most readers outside her own feminist community seem happy to accept. So powerful is the image of Morgan as a pathological Plath fanatic that even those readers whom we might typically categorize as fans feel compelled to define themselves against her. Indeed, even as Morgan continues to stand in for Plath fans in the mainstream media and in the literary establishment's conversations about

Plath, she is almost uniformly rejected—one might say vilified—by the so-called fan community she is often said to represent. Such rejection is certainly what one finds within the most prolific online Plath community, the Sylvia Plath Forum, which includes a vast archive of the discussion posts contributors have made since the Forum's inception in 1998.[69] Entire posts—and post threads—have been dedicated to Morgan on this site, and the clear trend among these threads is the preoccupation among posters with Morgan's difference from themselves. Morgan is identified and singled out by one poster as a "fanatic," while another, especially disdainful contributor castigates her as an example of the "unbalanced feminists" and dismisses her writing as "extremist fanatical ramblings" and "juvenile venom." Concerned enough about Morgan to post another message about her a week later, this same contributor describes her as someone so silly in her pursuits that even Hughes "*must* have (at some point) laughed out loud at her sheer stupidity." Another contributor calls "her poem and her actions . . . incredibly puerile, self-justifying, and narcissistic," and in a later post calls her sense of entitlement in speaking for Plath "just weird." While one contributor makes note of the irony underlying another contributor's dismissal of Morgan as an "obsessed outsider desperately wanting to inject herself in a situation in which he/she had no basis to be included," generally speaking, contributors to the threads about Morgan are quick to depict her as a pathological, man-hating, unhappy, misguided feminist whose "wackiness" merits the "disdain" being meted out by the posters. As one frequent contributor to the Forum put it, Morgan "is a woman profoundly unhappy with her own lot in life who could seriously use some major mental health intervention." So strong is the pressure to identify against Morgan that those who start out defending her are quickly dismissed or, if they persist in their defense, are eventually brought around to accept the dominant perception of Morgan.

Given the predominance of this attitude toward Morgan, it's perhaps not surprising that the issues of feminism, fanaticism, and what is frequently labeled "Ted Hughes bashing" become subjects of often hotly contested discussion on the Forum, much of it prompted by comments about Morgan. In the case of feminism specifically, a search of the archives yields scores of posts on the question of Plath's relationship (or nonrelationship) to feminism. But while Plath is perpetually constructed by the media as the adopted priestess of the feminist movement and her

readers as Hughes-hating feminists, the posts on the Sylvia Plath Forum
paint a very different picture of her most engaged audience. More often
than not, when the issue of feminism gets raised by contributors, it's with a
tone of disparagement. This is especially so if Ted Hughes is also the subject of the post. Attacks on Hughes are simply not tolerated on the Forum.
When such comments are made, the offenders are quickly identified and
dismissed as "Hughes bashers," their comments are squelched by other
contributors (sometimes as a "typical 'feminist' type outlook"), positive
portraits of Hughes are offered to counter the negative comments, and, in
at least one case that I detected, some posts are even deleted from the archive, I assume by the Forum moderator, who, according to information
on the website, is free to edit or omit messages that are "inappropriate,
anonymous or likely to offend."

One Hughes-bashing thread that can be traced to its origins occurs in
2001. I find it a particularly worthwhile example for discussion, in part
because it encapsulates the kinds of discrepancies that have concerned so
much of this chapter but also because it functions, rather self-consciously,
as an exploration of the very definitions of Plath fanaticism. The thread
begins in June with a post announcing plans for an upcoming "Sylvia
Plath Day," to be held in Northampton, Massachusetts, in the fall. Before
long it changes directions when a contributor questions the appropriateness of such an event (exclaiming, "Sylvia Plath Day!!! come on, what's
the world coming to????") and challenges the rationale for celebrating
someone who was clearly "unhinged." Incensed by this query, one of
the members of the day's organizing committee posts a rather flaming
response that, on a tangent, calls Hughes a "scoundrel" and somehow
gives the impression that those who like Hughes or want to talk or hear
about his relationship to Plath are not welcome at the event. The backlash
is immediate and seemingly unabating. His comments are dismissed as
"just plain silly, and insulting," and one after another, community members announce their second thoughts, misgivings, and even rejection of
the event "if there is going to be an undercurrent of (or blatant) Hughes
bashing." When the contributor retorts by defending his position on the
exclusion of Hughes as a topic at the event—demanding, "Don't any of
you like Sylvia Plath? c'mon"— he is told to "curb this kind of hyperbole."
The debate, which turns to a focus on Plath and Hughes's relationship,
goes on well into the end of August

While the whole exchange will undoubtedly strike some as insignificant, it seems to me highly relevant to the issues I've been discussing in this chapter, especially insofar as it contains within itself a debate about what it means to be a Plath fan, a debate that takes place, no less, within the context of an event meant to be a celebration, as its name suggests. Implied in much of what is said throughout the exchange are questions that cut to the quick of fan discourse.[70] Can one be seriously interested in Plath's relationship to Hughes and still be a fan? Can one be critical of her or her work and still be considered a fan? What is appropriate discourse about Plath and Hughes and what is not? What does it mean to "celebrate" Plath? All together, the questions raised by the exchange over Sylvia Plath Day suggest that the very idea of fandom remains a contested one among those who participate in the Forum, for what the day's organizer seems most to want is for those on the Forum to admit to liking Plath, to having an almost visceral, uninhibited response to her and her work. What he is met with is an outright refusal on the part of some of the Forum's participants to paint themselves with such strokes.

Given the critical responses to those posts that show signs of Hughes bashing and unrestrained (in some eyes, hyperbolic) praise for Plath, it's not surprising to find that some contributors overtly resist the identity of fan, which is something that happens rather frequently on the Forum. Such resistance and rejection take many forms. One poster worries that if contributors concentrate too much "on the positive" aspects of Plath's personality, then they "leave this Forum open to the critics who think it is merely a 'fan' site and is not to be taken seriously." Similarly, when a contributor posts to invite members of the Forum to a "celebration" of Plath being planned at the site of her grave on her birthday, which is pitched as an opportunity to share her poetry and improve the "neglected state" of her grave by planting flowers there, the only responses to the invitation are critical of the idea.

Of course, none of these observations about the Forum goes so far as to debunk the myth of the Plath fan. Nor are they meant to. The Forum is simply too imperfect a case for the kind of ethnographic study that would be needed to accomplish such a task: the Forum is moderated, for one thing, and the very fact that it was formed in response to the publication of Hughes's *Birthday Letters* suggests it's likely to draw participants from among those already inclined toward an interest in both

Plath and Hughes. Still, the Forum does represent a rare opportunity to look firsthand at Plath readers (ones serious enough in their interest to join online discussions about her and her work) and to think about the complex relationship between Plath's readership and the issues that have defined discourse about it.

"Mischievous Falsehood" and "That Problem" of the Grave

Just as feminism lies at the heart of the dominant narrative about Hughes's vilification, feminism is also central to the second controversy involving historical readers I want to discuss: one played out in the editorial pages of the *Guardian* during April 1989.[71] The controversy began in early April when the *Guardian* published a letter to the editor submitted by Julia Parnaby and Rachel Wingfield. In the letter Parnaby and Wingfield, who identify themselves through their academic affiliations, relate the story of their failed attempt to locate Plath's gravesite, which, they learned on their visit to the churchyard in Heptonstall, had been left unmarked following the removal of the gravestone, the only specific sign that designated Plath's grave within the entire churchyard. As they report, the women were told that the stone had been removed after it was vandalized by "a feminist who objected to the imposition of the name Hughes as Plath's surname" on the stone.[72] In the second half of the letter, the women express their concern for what the absence of the stone must signify: that Plath's "place in the tradition of women's literature is being denied and her work devalued." As their final point, Parnaby and Wingfield make an urgent plea to "both feminists and those with a respect for the literary tradition," hoping "they will feel as upset as we are about such failure to honour [Plath's] memory."

The exchange of letters to the editor that followed traveled in several, sometimes disparate directions. The one that interests me here is the direction established by Parnaby and Wingfield's original letter when they called upon feminists to help ensure Plath's place as an important woman writer in the literary tradition lest she be forgotten. One of the first responses to take up the issue dismisses altogether "the so-called feminist aspect" of Plath's life, even as it continues to reiterate the women's call for some kind of memorial to be restored.[73] Another implies a similar critique, arguing that the issues related to Plath are "too personal" and therefore ought not "to be used and abused under the guise of support for a woman poet."[74] A later response goes so far as to dismiss the women's argument about the relationship between memorials and Plath's place as a writer in literary history as "ridiculous."[75] While one letter writer counters the dismissal of Parnaby and Wingfield's position, calling those who think Plath isn't in danger of disappearing from literary history "naïve,"[76] most of the letters that take up the issue of feminism tend to discount its relevance. All together the responses prompt a second letter from Parnaby and Wingfield, which aims to clarify the object of their original complaint. The letter opens with a significant declaration: "As feminists ourselves we did not wish to give the impression that Sylvia Plath's headstone was removed by 'enraged' 'radical feminists.' As far as we understand the situation, Mr Hughes himself had the gravestone removed." And it ends with a similar assertion that emphasizes the women's feminist politics: "We hope our original letter did not give the impression that we wished to criticise feminists."[77]

The emphatic nature of Parnaby and Wingfield's second letter becomes more than a little intriguing when one attempts to trace the trajectory from their first letter to their second. What is curious, for starters, are the apparent gaps between the presentation of their original argument in their initial letter, the arguments of those who responded to it, and the redirection of their argument in the second letter. In their original letter, Parnaby and Wingfield do not accuse feminists of either vandalizing Plath's gravestone or removing it, but they do report, as I mentioned earlier, that they "were informed that the headstone was 'vandalised' a couple of years ago by a feminist who objected to the imposition of the name Hughes as Plath's surname." Not only do Parnaby and Wingfield make clear that they are simply repeating knowledge passed on to them, but also they seem to go out of their way not to accuse feminists of the vandalism, citing specifically only one "feminist" and couching their comment in passive language and sentence structures that emphasize the information as hearsay. Moreover, the larger argument waged by them makes clear that their intent is to raise awareness among "both feminists and those with a respect for the literary tradition" about the need to honor Plath with a memorial befitting her stature as poet. When they write their second letter, in contrast, it's as if their careful articulation of their position never happened. First, they clarify that they had not claimed that feminists were responsible for the missing gravestone, or even that feminists were responsible for vandalizing the name Hughes; and second, they reassert their own feminist politics, this time in an unambiguous statement at the letter's outset. In short, Parnaby and Wingfield's second letter appears to be a very pointed reply to another text, as their quotation of the words "enraged" "radical feminists" suggests. I say appears because, if one reads through those letters in the *Guardian* that respond to the women's initial letter over the intervening weeks, one doesn't encounter a letter to which Parnaby and Wingfield seem to be directly responding, let alone quoting. It's as if the "enraged" "radical feminists" referred to by Parnaby and Wingfield in their second, corrective letter materialized out of thin air, existing literally as a quoted phrase that appears never to have been articulated in the first place. To put it another way, as with much of the discourse about Plath and her feminist fans, one tends to get lost in the gap, in what goes without saying. That is, at least, until one looks at the caption of the photo of Plath that appears above the women's original letter, which asserts: "The photograph of Sylvia Plath currently supplied by her publishers is so ghostly that it looks as if she were fading from memory. In Heptonstall churchyard her grave is now unmarked, the headstone having been removed by vandals, allegedly radical feminists enraged by the fact that it bore her husband's name."[78]

This discrepancy between the women's letter and the information contained within the staff-generated caption of the adjacent photograph encapsulates much of what I have aimed to clarify in this chapter. While the caption writer makes judicious use of the word "allegedly" and attempts to reflect the argument Parnaby and Wingfield make about the need to protect Plath's memory through its commentary on the poor quality of the photograph made accessible to the paper for reproduction, the narrative it tells, if not completely conjured from nowhere, is highly problematic. Most glaringly, it asserts that vandals had removed Plath's gravestone, something no one had alleged, as Parnaby and Wingfield make clear in their second letter. Less obviously, while Parnaby and Wingfield's first letter explains that they were informed that the vandal was "a feminist," not only does the caption transform this detail into plural form, as "a feminist" becomes a group of "feminists," but it also labels them "enraged" "radicals," words Parnaby and Wingfield never use or even suggest.

That Parnaby and Wingfield appear acutely aware of their own diction is evident not just in the correctives and clarifications they offer in their second letter but in their careful, even politicized word choice throughout all their letters. One obvious example of their attention to language is their use of scare quotes when referring to the "vandalized" grave, which signals, I gather, their distrust of the word's application in this case. Whereas most accounts of the damage to the grave opt for quite colorful diction—recall, for example, the number of reports I've already quoted which assert that the name Hughes is "hacked off"—Parnaby and Wingfield opt for words that minimize the vandalizing aspect of the act: the name comes off in an act of "deletion."[79] Additionally, the motive for the deletion is, in their words, an "object[ion] to the imposition of the name Hughes." While the two women never come out and say so, their sympathies certainly appear to lie with whoever has been responsible for the act in question. At the very least, they show a marked reluctance to accept the terms of the dominant narrative, with one exception: in explicit and implicit ways, Parnaby and Wingfield, like the authors of most other accounts, place the figure of the feminist Plath reader at the heart of the debate about Plath's grave, a fact that resonates, to varying degrees, in most of the letters that follow, especially those that take up the specific question of Plath's stature as a woman writer and the appropriate ways to honor her life.

In contrast, when Hughes himself responds to the letters about Plath's gravestone on April 20, the figure of the feminist vanishes entirely. Concerned in equal parts with Parnaby and Wingfield's letter and one submitted four days later by A. Alvarez, Ronald Hayman, and others,[80] Hughes's six-column letter fixes initially on Parnaby and Wingfield's reference to Plath and Hughes's "divorce paper" and accuses the women of perpetuating the "apocrypha" surrounding the question of whether Hughes and Plath were about to divorce (or had divorced) at the time of her death and thus whether he even had the right to determine the conditions of her burial.[81] In the last third of the letter, Hughes turns to the question of his handling of the gravesite, outlining the attention he and others have given to the matter of the stone and the appropriate memorialization of Plath. While Hughes never accuses feminists—or anyone else for that matter—of the vandalism, he nonetheless paints a revealing portrait of the culprits as he imagines them, one directly relevant, I think, to the question of feminism I've been exploring in this chapter. This portrait emerges most clearly in his suggestion that Parnaby and Wingfield have really been poor readers. While they appear to be "scholars of some kind" and thus "presumably know the basic texts," they are negligent readers who live in "some kind of Fantasia" which leaves them either out of touch with the wealth of reliable scholarly and biographical material on Plath or else duped by the "apocrypha" as if it were the "gospel." Just as important, he calls the misstatement about the divorce a "mischievous falsehood" that "can be read, to [his] mind, very like an incitement for other misguided enthusiasts to desecrate the grave afresh." In short, Hughes turns the women's letter into a dangerous, rabble-rousing act. In his scenario, Parnaby and Wingfield in fact are the ones causing damage to Plath, in this case by inviting others to vandalize the gravestone and, the argument follows, risking both Plath's memorial and her place in literary tradition by turning her grave into "one more trampled Disneyland toy in the Northern Cultural Theme Park, hawked on brochures."

On April 26 the women respond, expressing how "puzzled" they are by Hughes's interpretation of their letter, especially his reading of their argument as one intended to incite further incidents, and revealing a mild resentment that their purpose in writing could have been so misconstrued. While apologetic in many respects, the women defend themselves as readers, justifying their claim about the status of Hughes and Plath's marriage by pointing to their phrasing in the original letter (which asserted that Plath and Hughes had signed divorce papers, not that they had divorced by the time of Plath's death) and to the scholarly source of their information (Linda Wagner-Martin's biography of Plath). Not incidentally, the figure of feminism (with the exception of a reference to Wagner-Martin) is all but gone from their last letter, which recasts their initial concern that Plath will disappear from history as an argument that calls more simply for her "contribution to literature" as an author to be honored appropriately.[82]

While Parnaby and Wingfield's final letter, like the one from Hughes to which they responded, never completely conjures the specter of the feminist, the letter that ends the editorial exchange in the *Guardian* brings the debate full circle, returning to the question of the role feminist readers have to play in the Plath legacy. This final letter comes from Olwyn

Hughes, Ted's sister and, at this time, literary agent for the Plath estate, who takes the opportunity created by Parnaby and Wingfield's reference to Linda Wagner-Martin to discredit the reliability of Wagner-Martin as biographer. In Olwyn Hughes's words, Wagner-Martin had been "bent on iconising Plath for the feminists rather than writing a serious biography."[83] That it is Olwyn, rather than Ted, who draws the explicit line between the "fantasia" and the feminists is hardly surprising. As anyone familiar with her public statements on Hughes and Plath knows, Olwyn, in complete contrast to her brother, holds little back when given the chance to vent her bitter resentment of feminists in a public statement. Her criticism of Wagner-Martin here pales in comparison to what she dishes out on other occasions.

While Olwyn's letter ends the exchange in the *Guardian* over the grave, the matter appears to have been settled a week earlier, at least according to a report in the *Telegraph* on April 22, which announced that the stone had been repaired, with the name Hughes restored, and that it had been returned to its place at Plath's grave.[84] In my own research I found nothing to suggest that any further controversies or incidents over the grave have arisen since, with the exception of a story in the *Telegraph* in 2002 reporting fears among the Heptonstall locals over the possibility that the film *Sylvia* might renew interest in the grave and even revive the attacks.[85]

The *Telegraph* report in itself seems a more than fitting conclusion to the saga of the grave, embodying many of the elisions we've already seen in the discourse about Plath's feminist fans. While the report offers the perfunctory history of the grave's vandalism, noting that "the name 'Hughes' was regularly hacked off her headstone by feminists," and opens with a portrait of feminist-fearing Heptonstall locals, quotations from the locals themselves belie the portrait. Of the two women interviewed who express concern, the first does in fact voice a worry about security, but it's unclear if she thinks Plath's grave deserves special attention. In her words, "graveyards are increasingly subjected to vandalism." The second appears to be more concerned with maintenance and the overgrown graveyard generally, for according to her, "that problem [of attacks] calmed down." Moreover, what the women most want, it seems, is to secure some of the profits from the film to help out with maintenance of the grave and the management of additional visitors to the graveyard; yet what inspires the headline and opens the report is the threat of the return of the feminist grave hackers.

If the *Telegraph's* report appears to be much ado about nothing, then it serves as fitting material toward a conclusion for this chapter. Indeed, the report appears to capture the tension that defines much of the rhetoric surrounding Plath's feminist readers: it shows just how pervasive the narrative about them has been, even as it contains within itself the very evidence that belies the narrative. So persuasive is this narrative that the mainstream media continue to view all new evidence about the nature of Plath's feminist audience through the same lens, continually unaware of its possible uselessness or irrelevance. Take, as a final example, a 1998 article in *The Times* that reports on a trip to the United States made by A. Alvarez, who appeared by invitation at a symposium hosted by the Academy of American Poets. It opens: "It takes a brave man to defend Ted Hughes in America. Britain's Poet Laureate has been so reviled by American feminists for his abandonment of Sylvia Plath that one once wrote a poem accusing him of killing her. So it was quite a surprise that Al Alvarez, an old friend, dared to venture into the lionesses' den." And Alvarez himself declares, "I expected a feminist lynch mob." Yet despite being one of only two men on a panel of six "predictably stacked against him," Alvarez "won the day with a convincing vindication of Hughes," which signaled to *The Times* reporter that the "tide that flowed so strongly against Hughes in America for so many years is clearly now turning."[86] While it may be true that the publication of *Birthday Letters* prior to Alvarez's visit was changing the discourse about Hughes and Plath in 1998 (how could it not?), it seems telling to me that the lack of a feminist lynch mob at the event signals what it does to the media. Rather than suggesting that reports of the lionesses' den might have been exaggerated, the lack of hostility instead signals the victory of the Hughes camp (here represented by Alvarez in a strange moment of revisionist history) over feminists, who once again get represented as the fiercest of foes, who, ironically, prove remarkably easy to dispatch. Notice, too, the by now predictable slide between Morgan and feminists more generally ("Britain's Poet Laureate has been so reviled by *American feminists* for his abandonment of Sylvia Plath that *one* once wrote a poem accusing him of killing her").

If my comments about these two relatively recent examples smack of frustration, I admit that the story told about Plath's feminist readers does get tiresome to hear, and it's not because there's nothing new to be said about them. Of all the omissions, gaps, and elisions in the narrative that's been told about Plath's feminist readers, perhaps what's been most slighted is the large body of literary criticism produced by feminist Plath scholars over the past four decades or so. While Morgan has been singled out as the epitome of how feminists have responded to Plath and her work, she was hardly the only feminist engaged with Plath in the 1970s. To take just one example, the Routlege-produced journal *Women's Studies* featured three scholarly essays about Plath's poetry and fiction between 1973 and 1976, none of which discusses Ted Hughes, except in passing. Beyond the attention the essays pay to Plath's literary works, what one most notices about these early pieces of scholarship is the way they defend Plath against those who, like Irving Howe, accuse her of being merely a minor writer with self-indulgent tendencies, before moving on to consider her work from a feminist perspective, often centering on Plath's exploration of the struggles women face as they attempt to reconcile society's demands and their own desires. It's worth noting too that these essays avoid altogether the polemical style that is so often said to define feminist writing about Plath. And in the years since 1976, *Women's Studies* published another ten scholarly essays, two of which later became material in book-length studies by Pamela Annas and Linda Wagner-Martin. While published in the early 1980s, Lynda K. Bundtzen's much-admired study *Plath's Incarnations: Woman and the Creative Process* acknowledges its roots in early 1970s feminist thinking as well. To appreciate better the importance of what may seem a small body of criticism, consider that it was 1993 before the journal *American Literature* included its first scholarly essay on Sylvia Plath. Such contrasts ought to bring to light the important, indeed vital role feminist readers—from those professional scholars publishing in journals like *Women's Studies* to the general readers whose interest in Plath they support—have played in promoting Plath's work. To reduce the legacy of feminist writing about Plath to one poem, as so many do, evinces a misunderstanding not just of the poem itself but of the history of feminism's interest in and importance to Plath as author.

CHAPTER 4

"A Fiercely Fought Defense"

Ted Hughes and the
Plath Reader

To convey his dissatisfaction with Plath's elevation to the status of feminism's "patron saint," A. Alvarez uses the occasion of his 1976 review of *Letters Home* to consider the question of "what [Plath] would think" had she lived to experience her eventual success. While Alvarez admits that Plath's success reflected the fulfillment of "all her wildest ambitions," he ultimately concludes that the reality of that fulfillment would have "[broken] her heart all over again." As I discussed in chapter 1, Alvarez's conclusion is predicated on his perception of the undesirable nature of Plath's path to posthumous success, a path built on her unintended appeal to what he calls "young would-be writer[s] with the blues" and "dissatisfied, family-hating shrews."[1] While I think Alvarez is unfair here in his harsh judgment of Plath's readership, I do share his curiosity: What would Plath have made of her enormous popularity and success, especially with women readers?

We know that Plath prized literary success above nearly all else, and we know that she approached writing with an unflinching eye to its marketability and money-earning potential. That Plath's attitude toward authorship reflected "her American entrepreneurial spirit," as Lynda K. Bundtzen notes, is undeniable.[2] We also know that Plath did not shy away from tapping into women readers as an audience. "I hope to break into the women's slicks this summer," she writes to her mother in 1957.[3] On another occasion she vows to "slave and slave until" she does.[4] Given all this, it's hard to imagine that Plath would have lamented the success she eventually achieved. But in the end we can only speculate about her response, for Plath of course never experienced fandom in her lifetime, and so there are simply no grounds on which we might construct an answer to how she would have regarded her success or her audience.

What we do have, however, is a record of how those who inherited her literary estate and acted on her behalf since her death have perceived Plath's readers. I'm speaking here, of course, about Ted Hughes, as well as Plath and Hughes's daughter, Frieda Hughes. Together, Ted and Frieda Hughes have contributed an important dimension to the discourse about Plath's readers. In this chapter and in the conclusion I examine this contribution, which includes statements the Hugheses have made about Plath's readers in opinion pieces, personal letters, and interviews, as well as selections from their poetry that speak, often quite directly, to the question of how each has regarded Plath's audience and her posthumous success. This question is an especially important one to raise in the Hugheses' case, given the impact their perceptions of readership have had on their handling of Plath's work. At the same time, it's important to recognize that their comments about Plath's readers do not exist in some kind of Hughesian vacuum, as if divorced from the larger cultural discourse surrounding Plath and her readers. In many cases their comments engage an existing dialogue, often as personal correspondence or as direct editorial response to other people's statements and actions. Thus their comments do not simply contribute to the cultural discourse about Plath's readers; they are themselves shaped by the discourse. For this reason I aim here and in the next chapter not simply to track the tropes the Hugheses have used to depict readers and their reading practices but also to place these tropes alongside those circulating elsewhere, such as in the book reviews, popular media, and literary writings examined in the three previous chapters.

But first, a little background about the role played by Ted and Frieda Hughes in the handling of Plath's literary estate is in order. At this writing, Plath's literary estate belongs to Frieda Hughes, Plath's only living child, who together with her late brother, Nicholas, assumed control of the estate from their father in the early 1990s.[5] While separated from Hughes at the time of her death in February 1963, Plath died intestate,

and so her material possessions and all rights to her writings, published
and unpublished, fell to him, a fact that has produced no small amount
of controversy over the years, especially among the many Plath supporters
who have felt that Hughes's adulterous betrayal of Plath made him unworthy to inherit her legacy. Exacerbating this perception, Hughes, while
official literary executor of Plath's estate from 1963 to the early 1990s,
frequently turned over control of the estate to his sister Olwyn Hughes,
who shared a rather volatile relationship with Plath during her lifetime
and whose comments about Plath since her death reveal an undeniable
animosity toward the author whose work she had been chosen to represent. Olwyn, who worked as Ted Hughes's own literary agent between
1963 and the early 1990s, assisted him with many of the details involved in
overseeing Plath's estate beginning in 1964, including corresponding with
publishers, managing biographers (in one case purportedly coauthoring
a biography from behind the scenes),[6] and granting permissions for the
use of Plath's work.[7]

Given the circumstances under which Ted Hughes took charge of
Plath's estate, it's perhaps not surprising that his decisions regarding her
writing have been continually scrutinized and often publicly criticized
over the years. Several of his actions have provoked especially strong attacks, including his destruction of the journals Plath kept chronicling the
last years of her life, his rearrangement of the manuscript of poems Plath
had been working on at the time of her death (which we now know as
Ariel: The Restored Edition), and his delay in replacing Plath's vandalized
gravestone in the 1980s, all of which have been widely discussed by Plath
critics over the years. In addition to these well-known cases, throughout
the decades, but especially in the 1970s, many critics reviewing Plath's
works took the opportunity to question and criticize Hughes's decision
to publish her writing so slowly and in such small fragments. The *Times
Literary Supplement*, for instance, observes in its 1971 review of *Crossing
the Water* and *Winter Trees* that "the posthumous publication of Sylvia
Plath's poems has been an oddly ill-organized affair."[8] While the *TLS* reviewer shies away from accusation, others, including A. Alvarez, assumed
that unsavory motivations on the part of the Plath estate lay behind the
delays and odd approach. Reviewing *Crossing the Water* and *Winter Trees*
for the *Observer*, Alvarez questions the decision to publish two separate
volumes of Plath's poetry nearly simultaneously and concludes, however

tentatively, that "it may be, of course, that there are commercial reasons for bringing out two books where one would do."[9] Even those like Peter Davison who seemed willing to give Hughes the benefit of the doubt couldn't help but observe the undesirable outcome of his decisions. As Davison puts it in his review of *Crossing the Water* for the *Atlantic Monthly*, the Plath "heirs, for whatever reason, have been publishing her posthumous work à la striptease, which helps the legend on its way."[10]

While largely reticent about his relationship with Plath throughout his lifetime, Hughes did not allow the attacks on his handling of Plath's estate to go completely unanswered, opting on several occasions to respond with frank public statements in the British editorial pages or through less direct commentary in the book prefaces and short essays he composed for or about Plath's work. His first public statement about his role in the Plath estate is written in the early 1970s in response to the speculations about the estate's motives then being put forward by reviewers such as Alvarez and Davison. His last public statement comes in the form of *Birthday Letters*, the capacious volume of poems about his relationship with Plath which arrived to much acclaim in 1998, just months before Hughes's death. While only a handful of poems from the volume speak specifically about the Plath estate, those that do prove rich grounds for examining the issues at the center of this chapter. In between these two statements are a range of relevant texts written by Hughes, including additional poems, opinion pieces, and personal letters to friends and colleagues. These private letters, some of which are available in their entirety only in the archives, represent some of his most forceful statements on the topic of Plath's readers. Looked at together, these documents reveal a complex portrait of Hughes as literary executor, one defined fundamentally by his deep animosity toward Plath's reading public (both scholars and general readers alike), by the rigid relationship he imagines ought to exist between Plath's readers and her writing, and by the competing motivations that drive many of his decisions.

In the case of the opinion pieces, Hughes's statements revolve largely around conflict: they sometimes respond to conflict, they sometimes produce it, and they sometimes do both at the same time. Conflict is certainly at the heart of the three instances I look at here, the first of which marks Hughes's earliest defense of his handling of the Plath estate, though just when exactly the defense was made public remains unclear.

This essay, titled "Publishing Sylvia Plath," is presented as a response to Alvarez's October 3, 1971, *Observer* review of *Crossing the Water* and *Winter Trees*, in which, as I noted earlier, he questions the decision to publish two separate volumes of Plath's poetry instead of one larger book.[11] Despite Hughes's purported intention, however, the piece seems provoked as much by Alvarez's attempt to publish a two-part memoir about Plath in the *Observer* just a week prior as by the review itself.[12]

Whatever the actual motivations, Hughes's tone is combative from the opening. With an air of disgust, he begins by dismissing Alvarez's speculations about the "strange" publication of Plath's work, which Alvarez insinuates has been designed to capitalize on the "vast potential audience" that exists following the long-awaited publication of *The Bell Jar* in the United States—an insinuation that Hughes rather tellingly paraphrases as the "exploit[ation]" of "both the work (with the inferior audience) and the audience (with the inferior work)." Such speculation, Hughes asserts, "is nothing to what has been wafting from some corners of the Universities in the US. Possibly Mr. Alvarez doesn't know what a crazy club his article belongs to."[13]

Hughes's labeling of Plath scholarship as a "crazy club" leaves little doubt about his perception of Plath critics, just as his labeling of her general readership as "the inferior audience" in his inaccurate paraphrase of Alvarez leaves little doubt about his perception of Plath's readers. Together they provide a powerful first glimpse into Hughes's hostility toward those who read and/or publish scholarship about Plath. To understand where such hostility might originate, one would have to look at a number of factors, including the sense of persecution Hughes felt in the years following Plath's death, a persecution that would culminate in the early 1970s, when, as I discussed in chapter 3, Hughes became the object of feminist scrutiny, as well as his longtime sense that those readers and scholars who were interested in understanding Plath's death were intruding on what he felt was his right to keep his life private.

But these factors provide only a partial picture, especially when one considers that Plath's fame, and the pressures on Hughes that came along with it, was still only getting started in 1971 when Hughes made his arguments in "Publishing Sylvia Plath." To see the full picture, it is necessary to look closely at the terms by which Hughes understands Plath's readers and scholars and their collective reading practices. Although we glimpse these terms in the passages I have quoted, they are on fuller display later in the essay, when he resumes his characterization of Plath scholars and critics: "The scholars want the anatomy of the birth of the poetry; and the vast potential audience want her blood, hair, touch, smell, and a front seat in the kitchen where she died."[14] Hughes's rhetoric here, with its emphasis on vivisection, voyeurism, and even necrophilia, must certainly remind us of the discourse about readers circulating elsewhere, especially throughout the literary reviews. As I discussed at length in chapter 1, such tropes pervade Plath's literary reception, emphasizing the widespread perception among reviewers that by the late 1960s Plath had become the "priestess" of a "cult" of uncritical readers. If Hughes's own attitude differs from these perceptions, it differs only in his willingness to lump critics into the cult too. Indeed, Hughes's animosity toward Plath's audience is an equal opportunity one. For him, general readers and professional scholars are both guilty of corrupt reading practices, and thus both pose significant danger to Plath's literary legacy. One might even conclude that in Hughes's mind it is scholars—and, even more generally, acts of literary study and criticism—that pose the most pernicious threat to Plath.

As those familiar with Hughes's essay "The Burnt Fox" and the companion poem "The Thought-Fox" know, Hughes's attitude toward literary criticism is skeptical at best, disdainful at worst, the result, he suggests on several occasions, of his experiences at university trying to produce it. As he recounts in "The Burnt Fox," an essay dated 1993 and published in his 1994 prose collection *Winter Pollen*, Hughes began his studies at Cambridge in 1951 reading English, assuming that the subject would advance his own skills as a writer.[15] During the two years when he pursued this area of study, however, he began to experience an "inexplicable resistance" to the assigned critical essays he was expected to produce each week, essays presumably of literary explication. At the end of his second year, this resistance began to take on a "distressful quality, like a fiercely fought defence."[16] After a particularly laborious attempt to complete one of his last essays of the term, an attempt that went on until 2 a.m., Hughes gave up, went to bed, and dreamt. In the dream he is back again struggling to produce the essay when the door opens and a head pokes into the room. "It was a fox," he writes, whose "every inch was roasted, smoldering, black-charred, split and bleeding" and whose eyes "dazzled with the intensity of the pain." Standing beside him, the fox "spread its hand—a human hand . . . but burnt and bleeding like the rest of him—flat palm down on my blank space of the page. At the same time, it said: 'Stop this—you are destroying us,'" before revealing the bloody print it had made on the page.[17] This startling image within the dream awakens him, leading him, he implies, to the conclusion that the study of anthropology and archaeology better suited his goal to be a writer.

While this rather cryptic story offers some clues to its meaning—the fox's words and bloodied paw print being the most suggestive ones—the meaning of the epiphany Hughes recounts in "The Burnt Fox" makes more sense read within the larger aesthetic Hughes constructs for himself in his early poem "The Thought-Fox," from his 1957 collection *The Hawk in the Rain*, a poem that more completely demonstrates the symbolic meaning Hughes invests in the fox. In the poem Hughes once again sits over a blank page, this time "imagin[ing]" the "forest" in the night.[18] Out of the darkness of that forest emerges a fox who "sets neat prints into the snow," who moves "Brilliantly, concentratedly . . . // Till, with the sudden sharp hot stink of fox / It enters the dark hole of the head," and "The page is printed."

Moving with brilliance and concentration, the fox represents, for Hughes, the poet's imagination and inspiration. It produces the words of the poem and becomes the vehicle of the printed page. In short, the fox signifies both the poet and poem. In such a context the destruction of the fox, which stands in here for the literary work about which Hughes is trying to write, becomes a rather clear statement about the dangers of literary criticism, a process, Hughes argues via the words spoken by the fox itself, that destroys not only the poem but the poet too: "Stop this—you are destroying *us*," says the fox (my emphasis). Clearly, reading English at Cambridge did not provide Hughes with the experience of studying literature he had hoped for. Instead, it led him to feel alienated both from the act of criticism and from the object of the criticism. As he explains in a letter to Keith Sagar in 1979 in which he first recounts the dream about the fox:

> I connected the fox's command to my own ideas about Eng. Lit., & the effect of the Cambridge blend of pseudo-critical terminology & social rancour on creative spirit, & from that moment abandoned my efforts to adapt myself.

I might say, that I had as much talent for Leavis-style dismantling of texts as anybody else, I even had a special bent for it—nearly a sadistic streak there, —but it seemed to me not only a foolish game, but deeply destructive of myself.[19]

While Hughes goes on to say in the same letter that this mode of criticism was likely "peculiar to Cambridge at this time," his later statements suggest a much broader application of the metaphor, one that relates it to literary criticism in general. Referring to his years spent working on the pieces in his prose collection *Winter Pollen*, for example, Hughes tells Sagar in a 1998 letter that he's had it with writing *about* literature, with "5 or 6 years of nothing but prose—nothing but burning the foxes. (That fox was telling—prose is destroying you physically, literally.")[20]

Hughes's impression of literary criticism as a destructive, dismantling act is common enough. More than a few undergraduates walk away from their literature classes with just such an impression, describing criticism as a kind of dissection, and certainly there are plenty of literary critics who practice their craft with that exact aim. In the case of Hughes, the impression is worth dwelling on insofar as it provides a useful context for understanding the deeper sources of his views of Plath's critics and readers. Remember, as Hughes argues in his essay "Publishing Sylvia Plath," Plath's scholars demand the publication of her work for the sake of uncovering the "anatomy of the birth of the poetry," while her general readers demand it in the hopes of acquiring a token from Plath herself or some insight into her death. What both kinds of readers share, in other words, is an interest in Plath's writings as objects for dissection, despite the resulting destruction such processes entail. Such connections among this seemingly disparate set of texts suggest that Hughes's disparaging rhetoric about Plath's readers and scholars emerges as much from his long-standing distrust of literary criticism as from any offenses actually perpetrated by readers and scholars. One wonders, in fact, if any kind of Plath criticism would have satisfied Hughes, given that criticism already existed in his mind as a destructive act long before he was faced with dealing with Plath's vast audience.

Whatever the answer to that speculation might be, it's clear that his view of literary criticism as a destructive act infects his understanding of Plath's readers and critics and informs much of his writing on the subject. In fact, Hughes's response to Alvarez over the publication of his memoir in the *Observer* in 1971 becomes more or less a template for much of his public writing on Plath that followed. This template typically involves Hughes taking on the role of Plath's protector while constructing Plath and her work as the victims of the critics' and the general public's bad reading practices. At the heart of these practices, Hughes frequently implies, is the reader's and critic's obsession with gathering and sharing new information about Plath, an obsession that apparently renders them oblivious to their intrusions upon the Hughes family.

In 1989 the publication of Anne Stevenson's biography *Bitter Fame* and the *Observer's* reprinting of two substantial excerpts from her book seem to provoke just such a construction of Plath readers and scholars. Appearing in two parts, part one on Sunday, October 22, and part two the following Sunday, October 29, the excerpts present the portions of *Bitter Fame* that detail the disintegration of the Plath-Hughes marriage and the final, desperate days of Plath's life. Printed just below a review of *Bitter Fame* by Ian Hamilton, and appearing the same day as the second part of Stevenson's excerpts, is a letter submitted by Hughes, titled "Where Research Becomes Intrusion," motivated, apparently, by the controversy produced by Stevenson's prologue to *Bitter Fame*, in which she insinuates that the Plath estate meddled in the writing of the book. For the most part, Hughes's letter recounts his efforts over the years (which he notes have been largely unsuccessful) to prevent Plath's biographers and critics from publishing material he deemed inaccurate or damaging to Plath's loved ones. It also attempts to clarify his role in the production of Stevenson's book (which he maintains amounted to little more than providing a "few details" and asking that she distinguish between fact and opinion) and thereby refute claims that *Bitter Fame* has the estate's approval.[21] Yet even as Hughes's letter is clearly provoked by *Bitter Fame*, it's also clear that he has a long-standing grievance against Plath criticism that he wishes to air. As he says in the opening sentences of the letter: "The Plath Estate is frequently accused, sometimes in extreme terms, of attempting to suppress vital truths about Sylvia Plath. The vast literature connected with her name (over 1,000 publications), the incessant public discussions and lectures, the daily indoctrination in the English classes of schools and colleges around the world, are generally tainted with this notion."[22]

Three years later, in 1992, Hughes's difficult relationship with Plath scholars—and his fears over their access to the classroom—once again becomes the subject of a statement, this time sparked by Jacqueline Rose's study *The Haunting of Sylvia Plath*. In a lengthy letter to the editor of the *Times Literary Supplement* in April 1992 in which he responds to an earlier letter by Rose (in which she complained about the estate's treatment of her book on Plath, including the refusal to grant her permissions to quote from Plath's work), Hughes defends his previous request that Rose delete an "offending passage" from her book that speculated about the sexual themes of one of Plath's poems.[23] "I did not question her right to interpret," he argues. "But I did challenge her right to present Sylvia Plath in that fashion in a serious book that would feed its more accessible ideas straight into the educational system." Further explaining his concern for who might read Rose's book, he goes on: "For most unsophisticated readers, Professor Rose's 'fantasy' will be an attempted interpretation of the truth—therefore a 'fact.' As part of the teaching of Sylvia Plath's poetry world-wide, such a titillating 'revelation' will become, for almost everybody taught, a kind of 'fact.'" Lest his concern about readers get missed, he reiterates the argument once more toward the end, writing, "I am aware as anybody else just how teaching English in the immunity of a classroom—critically and speculatively dissecting dead writers, with total freedom of speech—makes it hard, often, to change gear when it comes to the living, the world outside."

As the Stevenson and Rose responses demonstrate, what often emerges from Hughes's arguments is an image of the critic as a dangerous force who dupes naïve, uncritical young readers, especially students, with his or her misreadings and gossip, and an image of Hughes himself as the counterforce struggling to rein in this irresponsible behavior. Within his arguments, moreover, the space of the English classroom has become an especially pernicious site. It's a place of unchecked indoctrination that encourages the dissection of literature and the destruction of living people. Even more important, it has become a space of inappropriate metacommentary, where even the issue of Hughes's handling of the Plath estate is the subject of discussion. Such arguments point us directly to the matter that most concerns Hughes: namely, the infectious nature of Plath scholarship that is made possible by the access scholars have to students, who seem especially susceptible to their ideas. Indeed, critics and scholars are dangerous mostly insofar as their ideas are received by an uncritical public, which in Hughes's mind makes readers, whether duped or not, as much the culprits as the scholars and critics themselves.

While largely concerned with the reading practices of academic circles, such constructions matter within the scope of my broader examination of Plath's general readership because they suggest the extent to which Hughes participates in, and in the process continues to give shape to, discussions of who reads Plath, how they read her, and for what reasons—regardless of where that reading takes place. Furthermore, in his disdain for Plath's young audience, we can see that Hughes has far more in common with the critical establishment he opposes than he would ever care to admit. As I have discussed in previous chapters, this establishment, which prides itself on advocating for Plath (often in direct opposition to Hughes), is as guilty as anyone else when it comes to producing disparaging rhetoric about Plath's general readers. Turning to the question of just how this disdain gets expressed, one might also notice that, even as Hughes accuses his attackers of waging their assaults in "extreme terms," he falls into a similar trap, relying largely on the sheer hyperbole of his rhetoric to make his arguments: the discussions and lectures taking place about Plath are "incessant"; the "indoctrination" of students happens "daily"; the teaching of Plath's poetry takes place "world-wide"; freedom of speech in the classroom is "total." Such hyperbolic measures and totalizing language place Hughes perfectly in line with the critical establishment he dislikes so much. At the same time, a reliance on hyperbole is clearly more than simple rhetorical strategy on Hughes's part, for he takes similar measures in private letters to friends and colleagues already sympathetic to his cause.

Indeed, as interesting as Hughes's public writings are, his private correspondence proves even richer ground for exploring his views of Plath's audience. To begin that exploration, I turn first to Hughes's private correspondence with A. Alvarez and Anne Stevenson, some of which has been made available through the publication of Hughes's letters in 2007 but much of which is still accessible only in the archives. It is important to note that this private correspondence is often contemporaneous with the public writings, sometimes composed and sent within days of the publication of the editorials. Just as the public statements do, these letters place scholars and readers in an act of perilous collusion, but they differ significantly from the editorials in their reliance on a markedly heightened or intensified rhetoric. Before turning to this escalated rhetoric, however, I want to look at the resemblances between Hughes's private and public writings in order to demonstrate more fully the extent of his preoccupation with Plath's audience.

In Hughes's private letters to Alvarez, once again one encounters his disdain for literary criticism and a distrust of the classroom as a space of literary study. Following his telegram requesting that Alvarez stop the publication of his memoir, Hughes sends him a handwritten letter asking that he "reconsider [his] writings, talks etc about Sylvia's suicide."[24] As part of his plea, Hughes insists on several occasions in the letter that Alvarez ought to have been more sensitive to how his work would be received within the classroom, arguing in one instance, "Whatever motive or intention you put upon your writing of that piece, what you have done is supplied it to classroom discussion, you know there is no other real audience for it."[25] In a second letter to Alvarez, undated but written after Alvarez's response to the first letter, Hughes directly challenges Alvarez's speculations regarding his decisions about how and when to publish Plath's works and, in the process, intensifies his rhetoric about the classroom, this time with invective aimed at American classrooms in particular:

It doesn't bother me one scrap that classes all over america get informed of the strange reasons for Sylvia's poems coming out as strangely as they have come out, not just rumours between one academic glasscased imbecile and another but notes given in class, or the other even more crazy and pointed fantasies trying to find a few facts to congeal around. All that nonsense is just rumour eating rumour. But now you have provided what seems to be substance, real fact and foundation—the story of one who was in the room. Between her writings and your article is a whole new world of hypothesis. And the commercial and career need for articles and theses and class material will make sure that world gets overpopulated, and your facts get turned into literary historic monuments. Nobody knows better than you that your article will be read with more interest that the poems ever were, and will be used by the wretched millions who have to find something to say in their papers. The only difference in the fantasies now will be that they will be ten times as confident in their outrageousness.[26]

To press his point further, Hughes goes on to frame his argument about the infectious nature of ideas in the classroom through his desire to protect the Hughes children (at this stage eleven and nine), who, instead of learning the details of their mother's death at a time of Hughes's choosing, will now learn them through the coroner's findings, which Alvarez has treacherously made available to the "Educational establishments of England and the U.S."[27]

While Hughes's rhetoric throughout his letter to Alvarez more or less reiterates the attacks he verbalizes in the published writings, a couple of points are worth noting. Perhaps most significant, one notices in this particular letter the degree of repetition and heightened rhetoric in the insults hurled at scholars and students, who are figured as "wretched" "imbecile[s]," prone to "crazy and pointed fantasies," interested more in gossip than in Plath's poetry, and driven by the need to advance their own careers and assets. Yet even with all their flaws, they wield real power and control, as evidenced in their ability to transform the facts of Alvarez's story about Plath into "literary historic monuments," primarily, we may assume on the basis of Hughes's earlier statements, because of the nature of the classroom as a space of indoctrination.[28]

Hughes's private letters to Anne Stevenson unleash a similar attack on literary criticism and its influence in the classroom. In a letter dated November 4, 1989, written to express his sympathy for the backlash emerging in the wake of Stevenson's biography, Hughes offers an explanation for why he has tended to remain silent about Plath over the years, writing:

> I preferred it, on the whole, to allowing myself to be dragged out into the bull-ring and teased and pricked and goaded into vomiting up every detail of my life with Sylvia for the higher entertainment of the hundred thousand Eng Lit Profs and graduates who—as you know—feel very little in this case beyond curiosity of quite a low order, the ordinary village kind, popular bloodsport kind, no matter how they robe their attentions in Lit Crit Theology and ethical sanctity. If they do feel anything more vigourous it is generally

something even lower: status anxiety, their professional angst on the promotion scramble.[29]

Returning to the topic again later in the letter, he continues his indictment of literary criticism, calling it a "morally destructive" enterprise that leads to a "moral imbecility," but one that gains legitimacy when it's repeated in the classroom, a "total moral vacuum" easily taken advantage of by smooth-talking scholars who are never held accountable for what they say or for how their discourse about Plath escapes into the larger public sphere. To get his point across, Hughes adopts the analogy of "slaughterhouse butchers," who

> reduce cows to cleaned out sides of beef eight minutes per cow for four hours at a stretch—coming out into the street. You know, they are so dangerous they have to go to 'cooler' before they actually are allowed into the street. By regulations they should. Classroom habits are not so obvious so they're far more persistent: in fact all kinds of rewards reinforce them so they become permanent. I'm in a good position to know something about it.[30]

Despite being written nearly twenty years after his letter to Alvarez, Hughes's letter to Stevenson figures Plath scholars through similar arguments. They are still driven by their need to advance their careers, and they are still empowered by their access to the classroom. Their ostensible preoccupation with gossip and rumor also appears in the more recent letter as well, this time through Hughes's suggestion to Stevenson that students and scholars of Plath are defined principally by their need for "higher entertainment," for "bloodsport." In addition to the typical attack on the classroom, Hughes's letter to Stevenson adds significant new dimensions to his concern. As he puts it, it would be bad enough if the discussion happened only in the classroom, but it doesn't, and therein lies its true dangerousness. The ideas, unchecked by those who ought to be accountable to Hughes, spread in a kind of contagion, and as they do, they become reified and move once and for all outside Hughes's control.[31]

While Hughes seems especially concerned with scholars and students throughout his correspondence with Alvarez and Stevenson, his perception of the classroom or academic setting as a space of indoctrination and danger is also part and parcel of his general perception of those who read

Plath. Even when not explicitly concerned with readers in the classroom,
for instance, Hughes relies on rhetoric that conveys the same general idea
about the reader. In his letters to Alvarez, Plath's audience is a "sensation-
watching and half-hysterical congregation"; they are "followers," "cretins,"
a "crazy public"; they are "that gaping note-taking public on tour of the
waxwork interior," a "greedy" "mob."[32] In his letters to Stevenson, they
are "Plath cultists,"[33] "mischievous populations," and "vast numbers" possessed of a "quasi-religious mania" who "drank [fantasy] in with their
school milkshakes."[34] And as many of these choice descriptions suggest,
they are interested in but one thing: Plath's death, an event served up all
too well, Hughes argues, by Alvarez's memoir about Plath, which Hughes
maintains is tantamount to producing her dead body to a "crowd" that
has coveted the body above all, even above the poetry.[35]

What emerges from Hughes's private letters, in short, is an image of
Plath's readers that is almost perfectly aligned with the image we see in
the wider discourse about Plath: they are morbidly obsessed consumers who exploit her for their advantage or satisfaction, with little if any
regard for how they damage Plath or Hughes, or indeed the very study of
poetry, in the process. If they are students, their obsession with Plath is
the product of the ideas they are fed; if they are scholars, their obsession
is with the reward made possible through the production of literary criticism, however morally corrupt it might be. The only quality that could
bring Hughes's portrait of the reader precisely in line with the portraits
we see in the larger cultural discourse is the designation of the reader in
question as female.

"The Incessant Interference of the Feminists"

While none of the rhetoric from Hughes's writings that I've looked at so
far genders Plath's readers, it's clear from other moments in his private
correspondence that feminist scholars and young women readers are especially bothersome to him. As early as 1966 he voices his worry about the
type of reader who seems to be most attracted to Plath's writing. To Aurelia
and Warren Plath early in 1966, he rather neutrally reports, "I hear from
friends of mine at various Universities in the States that Sylvia's poems are
already a holy text among the students."[36] Just a few months later in another letter to Aurelia, he exchanges the more neutral language for a clear

lament about the "big-scale sensation" *Ariel* had become in the United States, noting in particular "the effect the book will have on teenagers at college who set her course up as a holy example."[37] By September his portrait of the young reader comes even more sharply into focus when he voices his regret to Robert Lowell over the publication of *Ariel:* "I've wondered since if it was the sane thing to publish the book over there [in the United States]—no doubt as holy text it will push several girls over the brink."[38]

Whether one judges Hughes well or poorly for his paternalistic concern for young women here, his assessment of Plath's emerging young female audience as a body of uncritical consumers driven round the bend is hardly a flattering portrait. Yet it pales in comparison to the one he paints just a few years later after second-wave feminism had adopted Plath as icon. To Alvarez in 1971 Hughes cites "Women's Lib" as one of a collection of forces working *against* Plath at this stage in the "gladiatorial arena" where she continues to serve as "public sacrifice."[39] By the time he writes to Stevenson in November 1989, his attack is even more clearly directed at feminists. While outlining the myriad ways he has paid for Plath's words, Hughes refers to Robin Morgan's poem "Arraignment," which he deems "a death threat in immortal verse—not so much a threat as a call to the assassin—that dangles its way through US feminist anthologies without any colleague of ours, Anne, ever having lifted a word against it, so far as I'm aware." Continuing the complaint, he writes: "Generation after generation of students indoctrinated. Every poet-critic and critic-critic who hopes for a career nervously aware that two or three feminists now dominate every English Faculty Appointments Committee in the US and in Britain, and many Editorial Committees too."[40] Bringing the ostensible feminist conspiracy directly back to him, Hughes insinuates that it has contributed to the unwillingness of bookshops to stock his books and to scholars being bullied into either not writing books about his poetry or writing them in a way that accommodates the feminist view.

Two years later Hughes suggests to Stevenson that she too has fallen victim to the feminist conspiracy and offers the following explanation for the backlash against *Bitter Fame:*

When you consider that militant feminists are now in forceful control of virtually every English Faculty in the U.S. and the U.K., and

are therefore in watchful control of all appointments and promo-
tions, it's not really surprising. Literary publications, reviews etc,
are now a police state, from that point of view, and woe on the dis-
sident!! It's no joke to have 50% of readers against you on principle,
and the other fifty percent (the male of the species), frightened to
open their mouths![41]

While Hughes's belief in a feminist takeover of the university is obviously unfounded, his comments are still worth our attention, especially
given their prevalence throughout his private correspondence and their
concomitant suppression in his public writing. What we learn from his
comments about the women's movement is that in some part at least his
preoccupation with the classroom in his public writings stems from his
conviction that students are being indoctrinated into a *feminist* approach
to Plath's writing, one that has dared to concern itself, furthermore, with
his own role in Plath's life. One possible reason why he articulates this
connection in his private correspondence but not in his public writings
seems obvious enough. Such openly hostile rhetoric about feminists
would have only heightened their scrutiny of Hughes, proving him, from
their perspective at least, the misogynist they already suspected him to be.

Yet it must be said that in a rather unexpected way his identification of
the feminist scholar as a pernicious force in his private comments ame-
liorates his disparagement of readers and scholars in the public writings
insofar as it evinces the historicity of his rhetoric. That is to say, Hughes's
conviction that feminists have taken over the university and the presses—
and concomitantly his unsustainable belief that the rational white male
represents the minority at this time—places him squarely within the larger
cultural backlash then taking place against the feminist movement. No
longer simply Plath's husband assailed by persecuting Plath scholars,
Hughes becomes just another "embattled" white man of the time. Which
is not to say that I think his rhetoric ought to be excused or stands above
reproach. Rather, I mean simply to underscore once again the degree to
which Hughes's rhetoric about Plath's readers participates in the larger
literary and cultural discourse not just about women readers but about
feminist activists in particular. Indeed, not only do we find in Hughes's
writings some remarkable parallels between his own views of Plath's readers and those advanced by book reviewers, critics, and other producers

of cultural and literary texts, but we find the broader discourse of the feminist backlash repeated as well. As I discussed in chapter 1, the cultural discourse surrounding the women's movement of the 1970s frequently depicts two types of feminists: the older ones who have no compunctions when it comes to spreading their feminist ideology and the younger ones who take in those ideas with no awareness of their own susceptibility to manipulation and indoctrination. This same type of construction is certainly evident in Hughes's own rhetoric, which seems inordinately concerned with what students will take away from their classes, students who in Hughes's view remain empty vessels to be filled by irresponsible scholars, especially feminist ones.

To understand why feminists in particular could have such an impact on Hughes, one has to face the difficult subjects of not only the reality of how Hughes has been viewed and treated by feminists over the years but also Hughes's broader attitude toward women. While a close and in-depth examination of these two undoubtedly related topics is beyond the scope of this project, some context does seem necessary for my own argument here. To begin, one has to acknowledge the phenomenon of feminist activism in the 1970s and the protests and public scorn it unleashed on Hughes in particular. While accounts have likely been exaggerated, as my discussion in chapter 3 makes clear, it's safe to say that a few feminists have been less than kind to Hughes. It's also safe to say that, however exaggerated reports of feminist attacks have been, Hughes felt persecuted by feminists, so much so that he convinced himself of the need to retreat from the public eye in order to avoid inciting the group any further.

Given his feeling of persecution, it's perhaps not surprising that women begin to emerge as especially niggling if not outright destructive figures in his poetry during this time. In those poems published in the 1970s and after, women often represent danger and pain: they are vengeful seductresses, gossips, and betrayers. In the thirteenth poem of the sequence "Prometheus on His Crag" from 1973, for example, they are "wombs" into which men are "being fed,"[42] and thus they are Prometheus's regretted invention. In the small collection of poems about Plath titled *Howls & Whispers*, which Hughes published as an expensive limited edition in 1998, Plath too becomes imperiled by other women. In poems like "The Laburnum" and "Howls & Whispers," Hughes even goes so far as to attribute Plath's suicide to the women in her life, including her mother,

Aurelia Plath, her former analyst Ruth Beuscher, and an unnamed female friend, presumably Suzette Macedo. According to the poem, these three women "killed" her through their gossip about Hughes and the letters they sent to Plath pushing her to seek a divorce.[43] Or as he puts it in "The Laburnum," "They almost laughed / To show you your grave."[44] It's a sentiment he echoes in the poem "Night-Ride on Ariel" from *Birthday Letters*, where once again he accuses the women in Plath's life of pushing her to self-destruction.

On the one hand, one might read Hughes's antagonism toward women as a simple act of deflection. A poem like "Howls & Whispers" at least seems a clear attempt to redirect responsibility for Plath's suicide onto anyone but Hughes himself, who assumes no culpability in the poem whatsoever. On the other hand, it's clear that Hughes also lashes out in the poem on his own behalf, an expression, perhaps sublimated, of his resentment of his own persecution by women. That is, while Hughes indicts women for their role in Plath's death, he is just as interested in cataloging their persecution of him, particularly their behind-the-scenes efforts to facilitate the dissolution of the couple's marriage. Underscoring this image of Hughes as the object of a covert investigation, the women in "Howls & Whispers" serve as Plath's "Intelligence Corps" and "spy" in what appears to be a collaborative effort to expose his crimes and try him at the same time.[45] While used here in an entirely different context, such metaphors reverberate with Hughes's favored rhetoric in regard to feminists. Consider again, for example, his letter to Anne Stevenson in 1989, where he casts the feminist-controlled university as a "police state," a representation given even more depth later in the letter when he refers to them as Plath's "K.G.B."[46]

In painting feminist scholars and the ordinary women in Plath's life with such strokes, Hughes evokes, incidentally, much of the rhetoric that has defined feminist writings about him, most obviously perhaps Morgan's poem demanding the prosecution of Hughes for the crime of murdering Plath. Indeed, if Morgan's poem sets out to try Hughes for killing Plath—for which, we should remember, her book was banned in the United Kingdom and elsewhere—Hughes's poem "Howls & Whispers" sets out to try women for the same crime. Through this unstated dialogue, Hughes not only turns the tables on women but also wages a defense against his prosecution by feminists without ever having to bring them up directly, much as his public writings attack scholars in the classroom without actually having to identify the culprits as feminists.

Despite the suppression of overt attacks on feminists in his public writings, it's clear that in writing the poems that would eventually make up *Howls & Whispers*, Hughes felt empowered enough to unleash his animosity toward those women who he felt had imperiled Plath, including scholars, friends, and family alike. In personal letters to Nicholas Hughes and Keith Sagar in 1998, Hughes describes *Birthday Letters*, the companion collection to *Howls & Whispers*, as a similar kind of unleashing, one that had long been prevented, he tells both men, by feminists. Describing his struggles to write after 1969, Hughes explains to Nicholas: "All I was aware of, all that time, was the desperate need to break the glass door, and blow up the log jam, but I *didn't dare* because it was — the business of your mother and me. The incessant interference of the feminists and everything to do with your mother's public fame made it impossible for me — it seems — to deal with it naturally, and express it indirectly, obliquely, through other symbols, because everything I did was examined so minutely for signs of it."[47] Explaining to Sagar why it took him so long to figure out how to write about Plath as he does in *Birthday Letters*, Hughes describes how he once sought distance from her death in order to write about it only to find that he "was pulled inescapably back . . . by the huge outcry that flushed me from my thicket in 1970–71–72 when Sylvia's poems & novel hit the first militant wave of Feminism as a divine revelation from their Patron Saint."[48]

"The Dogs Are Eating Your Mother"

Given the inextricable connections in Hughes's mind between the composition of *Birthday Letters* and his animosity toward feminists, one should not be too surprised to find traces of his resentment toward critics and readers in the poems that make up the collection. His preoccupation with how readers and critics have destroyed Plath — as well as the Hughes family — drives what is arguably the most memorable poem of *Birthday Letters*, "The Dogs Are Eating Your Mother." First published in 1994 in his *New Selected Poems*, it appears again as the penultimate poem in *Birthday Letters*.[49] As the title makes clear, the addressees of the poem are the Hughes's children as they look upon the horrific scene of their dead mother's body, which, as the poem opens, is being pulled apart by what "seem to be dogs" beneath the children's window (from which Plath has jumped). But they are not dogs exactly; what they are, Hughes implies, are two-legged creatures who "drop on all fours" only as they descend on Plath's body, "pulling her remains, with their lips / Lifted like dog's lips." Later in the poem, "a kind / Of hyena" comes on the scene, one whose desire for Plath leads it to dig her from her grave once more. With the body unearthed, the hyena appears to merge with the pack, and together "they batten / On the cornucopia / Of her body"; they even greedily eat bits of "gravestone," "grave ornaments," and dirt.[50]

Hardly subtle in its presentation, Hughes's imagery does not require a vast knowledge of his poetry to understand the significance of the extended metaphor he employs. Depicted as devouring, even scavenging beasts, Plath's readers "batten" on Plath, presumably, as the word suggests, fastening upon her and fattening themselves on the bounty of her work, even thriving from the very destruction they cause to her or her children. In their haste, they fail to discern the difference between Plath's body—which at this point in the poem can certainly be seen as a trope for her body of work—and what might best be called Plath artifacts or memorabilia: her gravestone, grave ornaments, even the very soil she is buried under. Hughes's construction of Plath's readers here, in other words, is very much reminiscent of the one circulating throughout his prose writings. The reference to Plath's vandalized gravestone even points to the feminist reader insofar as it evokes those occasions when Hughes's name has been chiseled from Plath's gravestone by what he and others have widely assumed to be angry feminists. And here, too, Hughes is concerned with literary critics. In fact, he makes no distinction between the dogs who vandalize Plath's gravestone and the dogs who "vomit / Over their symposia."[51] Which is not to say that the tropes Hughes relies on in "The Dogs Are Eating Your Mother" are simple reproductions of those we've already seen. Indeed, his depiction of readers as "dogs" has an originality to it that emphasizes the personal meaning of the image, a meaning, he implies, that will help his children more fully understand the danger readers pose.

With a typically parental tone, he evokes this private meaning when he interjects into the narrative of the dogs' destruction of Plath's body a simple but no less resonant question for the children: "Remember the lean hound" who paraded about with "The dangling raw windpipe and lungs / Of a fox?"[52] It's a question that draws its power both from the startling imagery of the fox as it has been reduced to but a few leftover organs and the significance of the fox as a symbolic animal within Hughes's poetic and biographical mythology. Generally a symbol of the creative enterprise for Hughes, as we saw earlier, here the fox stands in for Plath herself, or more precisely what is left of her, which turns out to be an important distinction in the poem since, according to Hughes, she has been so ripped to pieces that it is no longer possible "To salvage what she was." Significantly, this capitulation comes just as the poem turns toward fable. The lesson Hughes wishes to impart to the children takes the form of a warning as he cautions them against defending her lest they become victims themselves. For their own protection, therefore, they should let her go and "Let her be their spoils." In her place, he encourages them to find comfort in the geographical refuges they found as adults, Nicholas in the Brooks Range of Alaska and Frieda in the Nullabor Plains of Australia, and to imagine her "Spread with holy care on a high grid / For vultures / To take back into the sun."[53]

While it is presented as a better and wished-for alternative to dogs pulling Plath apart, the image of the vultures feeding on her body at first seems an unlikely way to close the poem since it appears to evoke the very same concepts as the image of the dogs themselves: animals scavenging on Plath. But Hughes makes clear that the vultures perform a function wholly different from that of the dogs. The vultures and beetles work as part of the cycle of death and life, he suggests. Their work is organic and regenerative: the vulture, whose innate role is to consume carcasses, provides food to the dung beetles in the process.[54] This understanding of the vulture's role is further supported by Hughes's allusion to the Tibetan practice of sky burial in the final stanza of the poem, a death ritual during which the deceased is dissected by monks or *rogyapas* (body cutters) and spread on a flat altar-like rock for consumption by vultures.[55] It's a ritual of, in Hughes's words, "holy care," undertaken primarily for the benefit of the vultures. In other words, it is understood as an act of charity, whereby the survivors of the dead provide sustenance to the vultures through their offering of the deceased's body.

Significantly, sky burial is also a deeply guarded ritual. Non-Tibetans are generally not permitted to view the ceremony; thus, even as it is performed in public to demonstrate the return of the body to the earth,[56] it's very much a family affair, an element that certainly fits in with the poem's previous reference to the private graveside rituals once undertaken by Hughes and the children. In an uncharacteristically poignant moment in the poem, Hughes remembers the children as they "played" graveside and "arranged / Sea-shells" to leave behind. But the affecting, and private, scene is undermined, Hughes insists, by the hyena and dogs who "Gulp down" the gifts left by the children.[57] Against such a backdrop, sky burial takes on added significance as an affair that secures their privacy as the surviving family of the deceased. Just as important, sky burial once and for all protects Plath's body from those who would exhume it by effectively reducing that body to nothing. The poem's final allusion, then, brings the poem's overall purpose into clear focus, much as the earlier fable elements do. It paints Hughes as the protector of Plath's legacy, in terms of both her writing and her children, even as it suggests that this role for the Hughes family has been reduced to mere fantasy. The sky burial remains something they can only "imagine," lest they risk their own destruction by the dogs.

Of course, Hughes's attitude toward readers in "The Dogs Are Eating Your Mother" serves the ethos he had constructed for himself as the beleaguered protector of Plath's vulnerable legacy in his previous writings on Plath. In one of his letters to Anne Stevenson that I cited earlier, Hughes in fact compares Plath to a fox in need of his protection. In contrast to "The Dogs Are Eating Your Mother," in the letter to Stevenson, Hughes uses the trope of the hound to describe not readers but his own allies, who, in acts of misguided protectiveness, attack Plath in order to defend him. Protecting Plath from her "fierce" detractors such as Dido Merwin, he writes, was "like trying to protect a fox from my own hounds while the fox bit me."[58] While concerned with his own defenders, the analogy nonetheless fits squarely with the images he settles on in "The Dogs Are Eating Your Mother," with its use of the fox and dog to signify, respectively, Plath and those who would threaten her.

In the image of the fox and hound, Hughes clearly found a powerful vehicle to express what he felt were the dangers posed to Plath's legacy by the range of people speaking for her and her work, from readers and critics to friends and colleagues. But the seemingly simple analogies or allegories one finds in a poem like "The Dogs Are Eating Your Mother" convey only part of the picture. As Hughes scholars have argued in other contexts,[59] the fox, while bound to Hughes's imagination, is a multivalent totem in his poetic mythology, one laden with Hughes's own complicated relationship to the animal itself. Understanding the complexities of this relationship provides additional insight into Hughes's often confounding comments about Plath's body of work and readers' relationship to it.

Given that Hughes's early years were very much defined by the avid interest in hunting he shared with his older brother, I admit I find it more than a bit puzzling that he settles on the fox as the vehicle for writing not only about Plath but also about the interior life of the poet and the creative enterprise. How do we reconcile, for example, that just a year before publishing "The Dogs Are Eating Your Mother" in *Birthday Letters*, Hughes published a feature piece in the *Guardian* arguing, though with careful nuance, *against* a ban on deer hunting and traditional foxhunting, a practice that animal welfare activists have deemed an unusually cruel form of blood sport?[60] Isn't it hypocritical of him to rely on the animal's imagery to such sympathetic effect in his poetry while advocating for the fox's literal destruction? Isn't it strange that he would align Plath with an animal he would see torn to pieces by hounds?

The simple answers to these questions lie, of course, in the distinctions we make every day between literality and metaphor: the fox is able to exist as metaphor on the one hand and as literal animal on the other. But such a simple understanding would fail to account for the way Hughes blurs the distinction between the two by regarding the literal fox itself as already a totem. And it's this blurred distinction—this turning the live animal into totem—that is central to his argument in favor of foxhunting. According to Hughes in the *Guardian* opinion piece, deer hunting and foxhunting by hound are paradoxically the best ways to protect and preserve red deer and foxes, for without the ritual of the hunt, both animals would lose their revered positions and find themselves slaughtered in greater numbers, either for direct financial gain (for their meat and pelts) or, in the case of the fox, because they destroy other sources of income, such as sheep. The logic is strange (at least to a non-hunter like myself), but what emerges clearly from it is Hughes's desire to protect the fox and deer not necessarily as living creatures with innate value but as what he calls "totems of a special way of life." In short, the implication of Hughes's argument is that the fox, despite its "symbolic meaning," can only exist either as the object of the hound hunt or as a pelt for trade on the market. In Hughes's mind, the former preserves its true value, while the latter diminishes it. Just as important, the fox's value depends largely on whether it maintains its "spell" as a "totem" over "country people" in particular, those most likely to reduce the fox to its mere market value should it be redefined as just an ordinary animal. Thus the fox comes to embody the tension between the exploitation of a commodity and the value of a revered totem. And while Hughes doesn't say as much, several assumptions seem to be important to how he arrives at his argument: first, the hound itself is simply a means to an end, one whose contribution to the hunt benefits those who wish to see their way of life protected; second, in subjecting the fox to the hunt, hunters are merely fulfilling a duty to the fox by protecting it in a larger sense; and, finally, while the fox will be consumed in the end, it is by a method of consumption that is inherently superior to others, for foxhunting by hound emphasizes the fox's totemic value over its value as commodity.

To wrap up my discussion of Hughes, I want to argue that his advocacy of foxhunting points us toward thinking about how the same tensions that shape Hughes's relationship to the fox also shape his rather vexed relationship to Plath's literary estate. Indeed, if anything can be gleaned from Hughes's often puzzling actions as the inheritor of Plath's writings, it is the confounding tensions that underlie those actions. These tensions bring us back, I think, to my examination of Hughes's construction of Plath's audience in the prose writings with which this chapter began. In several important ways, the issues that emerge out of Hughes's argument in favor of foxhunting evoke the ideas he first lays out in his early prose piece on his handling of the Plath estate, "Publishing Sylvia Plath," in which he refutes Alvarez's accusations regarding the motives behind his publishing decisions. Following his dismissal of Alvarez as part of that "crazy club" of people writing about Plath, Hughes goes on to answer Alvarez's complaint about his handling of the Plath estate by explaining his motivations, what he calls his "obligation," as executor:

> They are, first, towards her family, second, towards her best work. Just like hers, in fact—a point to be considered, since I feel a general first and last obligation to her.
>   For her family, I follow her principle and try to manage the writing in ways that will earn as much income as possible. For her

work, I have tried to publish it in ways that would help the best of it make its proper impact and take its proper place, uncompromised by weaker material. And that has not been such a simple business as her admirers might think.[61]

As argumentative strategies go, Hughes's approach to the insinuation, one that forcefully evokes Plath's own wishes, gains him immediate ground. After all, it is difficult to argue against his obligation to Plath and to their children. But what muddles his intentions is the emphasis he places on another kind of obligation, one that defines his and the reader's relationship to Plath's work through terms related to the conditions of duty—duty both to financial gain and to some "higher" literary ideal.[62] In this particular essay, it is the financial obligations that seem the most obviously pressing to Hughes. At the very least, it is the issue that he returns to throughout the essay, citing paragraphs later Plath's own desire to sell "every line she wrote,"[63] and closing with his admission that he does in fact hope that the very calculation Alvarez implicitly accuses him of—in publishing *Crossing the Water* and *Winter Trees* as two separate volumes—will "coax along" that "vast potential audience" and thus "earn more income" for the estate. He puts it plainly: "What has persuaded me to publish this other material now is sure enough her fame. . . . I did waken to the commercial opportunities of this situation just in time."[64] All of which is to say, what seems to drive Hughes's decisions about publishing Plath's work is a financial obligation to the children, which means turning Plath's work into the most profitable commodity it can be.

Even in the wake of feminists' (to Hughes, unwelcome) elevation of Plath to icon and their concomitant "persecution" of his role in her estate, this correlation between Hughes's publishing and editorial decisions and his desire to capitalize on Plath's body of work doesn't change. If anything changes, it's his awareness that some methods of consumption are a better means to the end than others—that with publishing, as with foxhunting, some methods protect the work's value not simply as commodity but as totem. As he tells Craig Raines in 1984 during an exchange about the prospect of publishing a selected edition of Plath's poetry: "One of my concerns—which you might feel unjustified—was to keep the actual number of poems low enough, or at least to that critically low number at which the reader feels it is being given only a taste of the real feast, well below the number that seems enough of a meal. Obviously we don't want a book that though it omits a good deal of ARIEL nevertheless manages to displace it as a necessary purchase."[65] Beyond Hughes's obvious concern with manipulating Plath's reading audience here, what one ought to notice about this passage is its reliance on the very tropes of consumption Hughes uses elsewhere to condemn readers. Not unlike the dogs who devour Plath's body in "The Dogs Are Eating Your Mother," readers here are implicitly troped as consumers of Plath's work. What one should also notice, however, is that Plath's work is *positively* imagined in the letter to Raines as a feast, one to be shared with or withheld from readers in accordance with what would be most profitable for the Plath estate. In other words, if measured by his own rhetoric, Hughes's strategy as Plath's literary executor was to create a mass audience of readers hungry for every small bit of Plath he could produce, the very pack of dogs he professes to hate.

With such tensions in mind, I suggest that the appearance of the rhetoric of obligation and debt throughout Hughes's earliest writings speaks to the larger conflicts that often inhabit his public statements about Plath's writing, conflicts intricately tied up with the question of the value of Plath's work as commodity (as something consumed by readers) and Hughes's desire to protect not Plath herself necessarily but her work's value as totem. It's puzzling, for example, that after admitting that one of his two principal obligations is to earn as much money as possible from the publication of Plath's work, he also feels the need to claim that he has no sense of obligation to the audiences who make such earnings possible, whether they be the general book buyers shelling out money for Plath's books or the literary critics who, in the wake of Hughes's silence, were largely responsible for promoting Plath's work in newspaper and journal tributes after her death. While one might wish to argue that Hughes, or Plath for that matter, owes readers nothing, it strikes me as an odd way of viewing readers and scholars. Note, in particular, that Hughes's explanation of the obligations he doesn't feel results in a rather strange contortion whereby readers become the ones with a debt to fulfill to Plath. In any case, we have to wonder, what explains the tensions inherent in Hughes's understanding of his obligations?

Perhaps such tensions can be explained by the unfortunate position Hughes finds himself in, a position of essentially having to protect two

Plath legacies: her literary one and her familial one. For Hughes, these positions are ultimately at cross-purposes. As Hughes makes clear in "Publishing Sylvia Plath," to fulfill the familial obligation is to take advantage of Plath's market value, to reduce her to commodity. Despite being upfront about his efforts to keep Plath's work profitable, Hughes never seems entirely comfortable with the project of commodifying Plath's work, for his financial obligations compete, often directly, with what he sees as his obligation to the work itself, specifically Plath's "best work," which appears to Hughes much in need of his protection lest its aesthetic merits become overshadowed by the weaknesses of her larger body of work. Indeed, Hughes wishes to publish as much as possible to make as much money as possible, but he fears that overpublishing will diminish Plath's reputation—endangering her "proper place"—by revealing her to be a writer unworthy of critical admiration. It's as if he's been forced to hawk a product he doesn't quite believe in.

For Hughes, turning Plath into commodity jeopardizes the literary legacy in another way as well, for publishing her work comes with an unfortunate consequence: it makes it available to scholars, and the masses of readers those scholars feed, whose very acts of reading diminish the work's value—not its monetary value of course, but its pure literary value.[66] In other words, to enable Plath to fulfill her obligation to her family is necessarily to toss the fox to the hounds, who in their act of undiscriminating consumption serve only to jeopardize all facets of the estate, literary and familial alike. Furthermore, to reduce her to commodity places the very object being commodified outside Hughes's control, subjecting it to interpretations beyond his own.

These dilemmas, however, don't fully explain the tensions underlying Hughes's interest in what is or isn't owed to or by the Plath estate. For a more complete explanation, one has to account for the appearance of the fox in his other poems about Plath. In particular, I think Hughes's concern with Plath's work as commodity and totem and its resonance with his argument in favor of foxhunting lead us to look twice at the role the fox plays in its less allegorical presentations within Hughes's poetry. One poem that uses the fox in this way is "Epiphany," another selection from *Birthday Letters* that on first appearance has little in common with "The Dogs Are Eating Your Mother" beyond its reliance on the appearance of a fox. In "Epiphany," Hughes encounters a man on the street with a fox cub peeking from the neck of his jacket. Hughes inquires about the cub and is met with an offer: "You can have him for a pound." Overcome with his surprise at encountering a fox, Hughes asks, "Where did you find it? What will you do with it?" to which the man responds, "Oh, somebody will buy him. Cheap enough / At a pound." Despite being enamored of it, Hughes doesn't buy the cub. What appears to stop him from doing so is a realization that the fox would hardly fit in with the couple's life, "into our crate of a space," and his uncertainty of what Plath herself would think of its "smell / And mannerless energy." That realization and uncertainty do not stop him from pondering the fox further, however. Looking it over, he notices, "the eyes still small, / Round, orphaned-looking, woebegone," as well as its vulnerability, which prompts the response: "My thoughts felt like big, ignorant hounds / Circling and sniffing around him." In the end, he walks away, "As if out of my own life," only to wonder in the present moment of the poem's composition what would have been "if [he] had paid that pound . . . if [he] had grasped that whatever comes with a fox / Is what tests a marriage and proves it a marriage."[67]

Within the sequence of *Birthday Letters*, "Epiphany" reads as a rather straightforward poem about the struggles of married life, a life recently impacted by the addition of the couple's first child. In particular, the closing stanza, in which Hughes wonders about the missed opportunity the fox presented, combined with allusions to the wildness and independence of the fox, has, on the one hand, led some critics to assume that Hughes identifies some part of himself with the fox, the part that marriage to Plath and the addition of a child had forced him to suppress.[68] Olwyn Hughes, on the other hand, has argued for a different reading of the poem, one she spells out in a personal letter to Hughes's biographer Elaine Feinstein. As she puts it, the fox's "woebegone eyes" are Plath's.[69] Diane Middlebrook offers yet another approach, one that recalls Hughes's earlier use of the fox to signal the process of the poetic imagination. For her, the fox represents Hughes's belief in the "necessity of protecting the inner wilderness" in himself and in Plath as married poets.[70]

While all are similar in their focus on the poem as a statement about the couple's marriage, this range of responses invites us to read against the grain of the poem, so to speak, to consider the ways in which the poem resists easy allegorization, resists attaching the fox's image to either Plath or Hughes. The explanation for why it does so lies, I want to suggest, in the fox's existence within the poem as explicit commodity, which is initially introduced in the poem by the fox's owner and then nearly repressed by Hughes himself. Indeed, when the man offers Hughes the fox for a pound, Hughes steps over the offer, asking in the moment of excitement, "What will you do with it?" as if oblivious to the fact that the man has already revealed his intention to sell it.[71] While such clumsiness on Hughes's part signals his excitement on seeing the fox, it also calls attention to the fox's presence as commodity and to Hughes's unease with the idea that the fox could be reduced to a price, that someone, if not Hughes, will buy the fox for a pound. Furthermore, as Hughes contemplates the fox and what it would mean to bring it home to Plath, it becomes clear that one of the motives driving his interest in the fox is its vulnerability and his own desire to protect it. What is left unspoken in the poem, however, is the simple fact that Hughes can protect the fox only if he first supports its exploitation as commodity by taking the man up on his offer to sell it.

Such tensions resist easy resolution in the poem, especially if one is looking to attach the fox to either Plath or Hughes. Compounding the hermeneutic difficulties is the poem's use of the hound image. As if inviting comparisons to "The Dogs Are Eating Your Mother"—where Plath plainly figures as fox—Hughes pairs the fox with a hound in "Epiphany" once again. Yet if the fox in "Epiphany" is Plath or some part of her, then it is Hughes, not Plath's scholars and readers, who poses the threat to the vulnerable fox this time (remember, as he considers the fox before him, his "thoughts felt like big ignorant hounds / Circling and sniffing" the vulnerable cub). It's no wonder that the poem resists, if not suppresses, the very allegorization it at other times appears to invite. While he does it with ease elsewhere in *Birthday Letters* where the fox is physically consumed by readers but significantly never commodified by Hughes, in "Epiphany" Hughes simply cannot cast Plath (or poetry) as the fox because here the animal embodies the very complexities shaping his view of the fox as both totem and commodity.

If we bring this argument back to Plath's literary estate, the significance of Hughes's resistance to the idea of a totem's commodification is considerable. For starters, while Hughes reveals himself in his letters to be well aware of the value of Plath's work as commodity, he cannot admit that his own investment in it as commodity has implications for its status as totem beyond those he imagines when he considers all the ways that publishing Plath's work is not a "simple business." Among those implications: the very readers and scholars Hughes scorns do not merely provide the income that fulfills Plath's obligation to her family; they are *key* to maintaining the status of her work as totem, the very quality that protects her "true value." What we see, in a manner of speaking, is Hughes's desire to maintain the fox's status as totem without having to rely on the *hounds*. It's an unattainable desire, of course, because Plath's ability to exist as totem, like her ability to exist as commodity, depends on readers in the end. The fox survives as totem only by virtue of the hounds that make the foxhunt possible. This is a reality Hughes cannot bring himself to allow fully, for it would mean recognizing that Plath's work might have value as totem for someone besides himself. That is to say, while Hughes thinks of Plath's work as a totem whose consumption can be manipulated for his (and his family's) own benefit, the reality is that it is readers' adoption of Plath as *their* totem that ultimately protects her and that allows Hughes to fulfill his obligations. Acknowledging this implication would mean acknowledging the possibility that it might be Hughes who is indebted to readers after all.

For this reason, perhaps, Hughes depicts the publication of Plath's works elsewhere in *Birthday Letters* as a process beyond his control, desires, or responsibilities. In the poem "Costly Speech," *The Bell Jar* appears in the United States through the "spooky chemistry / Of opportunity,"[72] while in the poem "Freedom of Speech" everyone *but* Plath and Hughes (author and editor, respectively) celebrate the existence of *Ariel*. Such abrogation of responsibility changes nothing for Hughes, of course, which might explain why, in "Epiphany," he passes on protecting the fox, suggesting a moment of fantasy on his part where he walks away from Plath's work entirely, leaving it to fend for itself, where it might have done just as well without him. Or alternatively, it can explain the final fantasy that closes "The Dogs Are Eating Your Mother," the fantasy in which Plath, at last wholly consumed by vultures, leaves no trace of herself or her work behind, thereby releasing Hughes entirely from his obligation to her.

"I Don't Mean Any Harm"

Frieda Hughes, Plath Readers,
and the Question of Resistance

I F HER PUBLIC STATEMENTS ARE ANY INDICATION, FRIEDA
Hughes inherited from her father, Ted Hughes, not only the rights to
Plath's literary estate but also his rather enigmatic attitude toward readers
and their relationship to Plath's writing. Although her time as literary
executor has been relatively short so far, her statements seem even more
pertinent than her father's in light of what appears to be her eagerness
(in contrast to her father) to participate in the public discourse about
her mother's readers, a reality brought to many people's attention by the
controversy that swirled around the 2003 film *Sylvia*. Frieda,[1] as news
stories in a range of periodicals reported around the time of the film's
production, denied the filmmakers' request to use Plath's poetry at any
length in the film. Supplying fuel to the controversy, Frieda published a
poem called "My Mother" in the March 2003 issue of the British magazine *Tatler*, in which she rails against the filmmakers for digging up her
mother for "repeat performances" of her suicide, all for the entertainment
of the "peanut eaters." Despite the poem's title, Frieda challenges the
filmmakers' right to make the film less from the position of daughter than
from that of literary executor, one now possessed of authority and control
over her mother's writing. As she puts it, it is she who could "give them
[her] mother's words" but refuses.[2]

But even before most people were aware that she had acquired this control, Frieda spoke with particular authority not simply about Plath but about Plath's readers. One of the public's earliest glimpses of Frieda as a poet, in fact, comes in the form of a poem about Plath's audience titled "Readers," which she published in the *Guardian* on November 8, 1997, and republished in 1998 in her first volume of poetry, *Wooroloo*, with the deletion of the two original final lines of the poem. In "Readers," Frieda evokes images from her father's poem "The Dogs Are Eating Your Mother" and borrows many of the same tropes that define her father's attitude toward Plath's audience. Of the many similarities, perhaps the most striking is her allusion to Plath's gravesite and the grave ornaments once lovingly left by the children but now dug up along with Plath's body itself. Continuing the parallels to her father's poem, Frieda figures Plath's readers through tropes of consumption. At various points in the poem, readers are cast as scavengers or cannibals who consume Plath in order to possess her, though not always with metaphoric consistency. For example, even as Frieda describes how readers treat Plath "like meat" on a spit, the subsequent line suggests that the end goal of this process is not consumption at all but rather investigation. Readers do it to find Plath's "secrets."[3]

Despite the slippage in metaphors, the end result is more or less the same. The destruction of Plath's body is undertaken so that readers can inhabit her eyes and voice. In other words, Frieda's imagined reader wants to be Plath, to possess her, not simply to consume her, for it is through the act of possession that they can take on her knowledge and then speak for her. Implicating scholars in particular, rather than general readers, the lines that follow suggest that scholars' desire to speak for Plath results from a kind of competitiveness: though they consume her flesh and organs, they do not feed on the same things, and the result is that each one claims privileged knowledge, to have discovered the "right recipe." Regardless of their differing approaches to Plath, the result appears to be the same: all have "gutted, peeled // And garnished her." All felt she was "theirs."[4]

In the original version of the poem published in the *Guardian*, the theme of possession evident in the final line of the *Wooroloo* version ("They called her theirs") is carried further with two additional lines, which significantly pivot on a claim of ownership, as Frieda reveals that she had thought her mother "belonged" to her "most."[5] While I can imagine a number of reasons for the deletion of the two lines, one reason perhaps is their ill fit within the poem. For one thing, the word "most" grants the reader at least some right to possession, some degree of authority belied by the rest of the poem. The very final line also undercuts the speaker's mature voice prior to this moment. Or to put it another way, the deleted lines make Frieda sound like a child, which simply doesn't work within a poem in which she is otherwise trying to muster authority as one who had recently taken on literary executorship of Plath's estate.

But even as Frieda revises the poem to achieve the level of authority so often assumed by Ted Hughes in his own writing, she departs from the template he uses in "The Dogs Are Eating Your Mother" in two important ways. Most significant perhaps is her willingness to attack feminist readers in particular. Whereas Hughes kept his rants about feminists to his private letters, Frieda opens her poem with an image that indicts women directly for "collect[ing]" Plath's "words" and "dream" in order "to breathe life into their own dead babies."[6] The image not only introduces the trope of consumption and possession that dominates the poem but also suggests that Plath's readers are failed mothers/creators who, in their desperation, live parasitically off Plath.[7] They are also undiscriminating and oblivious to how they jeopardize Plath insofar as they want every word she wrote published. Having stripped Plath in this way, they then attempt to refeather her, to re-dress Plath for their own purposes. While much of the poem's imagery is straightforward, it is not without some puzzling details, including the refeathered "vulture" whose "bloody head" is "inside its own belly."[8] Given that Frieda echoes her father's work elsewhere, one might expect the vulture image to evoke Hughes's own use of the bird in "The Dogs Are Eating Your Mother." But the vulture here conveys none of the Tibetan or spiritual allusions found in Hughes's poem. It appears here along more secular lines, as a trope more clearly suited to our common understanding of the bird as a scavenger. Just what Frieda is attaching the trope to, however, is not clear. On the one hand, its association with scavenging might point to the idea of the reader as uncritical consumer, one so confused that it has its head up its own behind. On the other hand, the introduction of the vulture immediately after the line that figures Plath as a refeathered bird, combined with its singular rather than plural noun form, suggests that Plath is the vulture. If we follow this line of thinking, then the poem suggests that readers have re-dressed Plath, the bird, apparently in the form of a vulture which they make out to be self-absorbed with "its own death." In either case, readers come off badly, either as plainly uncritical consumers of Plath's work or as overly invested in Plath as suicidal martyr.

With her 2002 collection *Waxworks*, which creatively retells myths, legends, and the lives of a variety of figures from history, Frieda appears to back away from such overt attacks on readers in favor of more allegorically disguised criticism.[9] Despite the heavy dressing, however, the primary tropes by which she presents readers and their reading practices remain much the same. Echoes of her rhetoric in "Readers" can be found, for instance, in the poem "Burke and Hare," which recounts the atrocities committed by the historical figures William Burke and William Hare, two men who in the late 1820s lured victims to their boardinghouse, murdered them, and sold their corpses to anatomists. Burke, whose transgressions began with simple grave-robbing, is depicted as usurping the bodies of the dead, "who could not talk," so that he could take over the telling of their stories:

> He could dig up each ended life
> And render it with meaning.
>
> He could write out its diaries
> And dismember its intention. . . .
>
> He could sell it then, as newly anointed
> For vivisection.[10]

While the lines never point to Plath and her readers directly, the emphasis on how the victims' words are co-opted, interpreted, and even dismembered is certainly reminiscent of the images in "Readers," where Plath is gutted, peeled, garnished, and consumed by her audience. And of course, one cannot help but find significance in Frieda's choice to retell the story of Burke in particular, a grave-robber out to make a buck. Not only does his story reverberate with the trope utilized in both Frieda's and Hughes's poems about Plath's readers, but also it calls to mind the comments Frieda has made in interviews in which she likens public interest in her mother to grave-digging. As she is quoted as saying in a 2004 piece in the *Independent*, aptly headlined "Stop Digging Up Mother's Troubled Past, Says Plath's Daughter," "When things are quiet for a while, I get a sense of the earth settling over her and a sense of peace. And then it is dug up again."[11]

Adding to the richness of the Burke story as an opportunity for Frieda to wage a veiled attack on Plath's readers, the bodies Burke dug up were utilized, of course, for vivisection. As my previous chapter demonstrates, vivisection as trope provides much of the rhetoric Ted Hughes relies on in his descriptions of literary criticism. The resonances between "Burke and Hare" and those poems more directly about Plath's readers also suggest that it is the trope of choosing for Frieda as well when it comes to depicting misguided and, in their effect, dangerous reading practices. Her use of the trope in her foreword to *Ariel: The Restored Edition* in 2000 makes its meaning quite clear. She explains there, "I saw poems such as 'Lady Lazarus' and 'Daddy' dissected over and over, the moment that my mother wrote them being applied to her whole life, to her whole person, as if they were the total sum of her experience."[12] The act of dissection, furthermore, appears to go hand and hand with what inspires readers' spurious interest in her mother: their desire to "possess" and "reshape" her "anguish," to make versions of Plath that "reflect only the inventors," especially their desire to vilify Ted Hughes.[13] As she writes in the foreword, "The collection of *Ariel* poems became symbolic to me of this possession of my mother and of the wider vilification of my father."[14]

The implication of Frieda's shift from readers who want to possess Plath to those who want to vilify Hughes is clear enough, I think. The readers who most trouble Frieda are feminist readers. While nothing in her poems about Plath's readers refers incontrovertibly to feminists, Frieda's comments elsewhere certainly point in that direction. In the article "One Hundred Per Cent Me" that accompanied the publication of "Readers" in the *Guardian*, for example, Frieda plainly characterizes readers as women misguidedly invested in Plath's death. In it the reporter describes Frieda as "suitably scornful of the casting of her mother as a prototype feminist martyr" and then quotes Frieda directly as saying: "Most martyrs do not choose their fate. And the feminists tend to forget that my mother wanted to be a wife and mother as well as a poet. She chose both roles."[15] In similar fashion, Frieda turns the foreword to *Ariel: The Restored Edition* into another opportunity to complain about feminists. In it she retells the controversy surrounding the commemorative blue plaque awarded to Plath by the English Heritage in 2000. Although it was originally proposed for Fitzroy Road, where Plath moved following her separation from Hughes and where she later committed suicide, the

Hughes family argued for the plaque to be placed at 3 Chalcot Square, Plath and Hughes's first London home together in 1960–61. According to Frieda, the conflict—and her perception that the general public saw Fitzroy Road as Plath's most significant address—only solidified her conviction that feminists had elevated Plath and *Ariel* to icons solely because of her suicide and the book's proximity to it.

I have emphasized Frieda's *perception* of public sentiment here because, in actuality, I could find very little evidence that any kind of significant conflict existed around the blue plaque. On January 22, 1998, the *Evening Standard* includes a very brief mention announcing that English Heritage planned to erect a plaque in honor of Plath at 23 Fitzroy Road and notes the unusualness of having two blue plaques on the same house (the first being, of course, the one honoring Yeats which inspired Plath to rent the house).[16] A year and a half later the *Evening Standard* once again includes a brief mention of the plaque, this time noting that it was to be placed on the house at Chalcot Square in accordance with the family's wishes.[17] The next mention of the blue plaque appears on July 21, 2000, in the *Evening Standard*, which simply offers a brief statement about the impending unveiling.[18] It is followed a week later by a second announcement, on July 28, the day of the plaque's unveiling on the house at Chalcot Square, which mentions that the "event has been dogged by controversy" and then reports that "friends" were "angry" that the plaque was not being placed at Plath's final home.[19] Given the lack of any news items or editorials between 1998 and 2000, it's unclear just what shape this "controversy" took. The only evidence of angry friends appears in the *Times* coverage of the unveiling the following day, which quotes A. Alvarez as saying: "It's in the wrong place. The [other] house already has a blue plaque because W. B. Yeats lived there. That was one of the reasons Sylvia was so excited by living there. What on earth are they doing?"[20] Following the *Times* report, Frieda publishes two pieces about the plaque in the next two months. The first, a letter to the editor, corrects several errors in the *Times* report, including its description of the house on Fitzroy Road as the place where Plath wrote *The Bell Jar* and finished *Ariel*.[21] The second, substantially longer piece appeared on September 30, 2000, and recounts in detail the day of the unveiling, including an incident involving a man who said to Frieda after the ceremony, "The plaque's on the wrong house!"[22] The only other evidence of conflict appears in Frieda's second recounting of the incident for the foreword to *Ariel: The Restored Edition* in 2004. In this version of her encounter with the angered spectator, Frieda includes several additional details, noting, for example, that "the newspapers echoed" the man's cry and that she interrogated the journalists until she got them to "confess" that they too wanted the plaque placed on the house on Fitzroy Road "because that's where she died."[23]

While there certainly could be more to the incident than I have been able to uncover in my research, I do not think it would change the most interesting facet of the blue plaque "controversy": namely, that Frieda cites the conflict over the plaque as further evidence of how Plath's death was "really the reason for her elevation to feminist icon,"[24] despite the fact that the only expressions of anger mentioned in any of these accounts are identified as coming from "newspapers" or from men, one of whom, Alvarez, rests his case solely on the significance of Plath's excitement about living where Yeats once did. Such moments of extrapolation are interesting, not for their problems with logic but for what they suggest about the specter of the feminist that haunts Frieda's perceptions of Plath's audience. For Frieda, feminists are synonymous with constructions of Plath as martyr; any rhetoric interpreted as constructing Plath along similar lines must be, if not a direct product, then a byproduct, of feminists' abuse of Plath as icon. Yet if we return again to the case of Robin Morgan—the figure who has come to stand in for feminists in discussions of Plath's work—we uncover yet another peculiarity in the dominant narrative about Plath's readers: one of the reasons Morgan calls Plath's death a *murder* is that she wishes to end the male literary establishment's fixation with Plath's death as *suicide*. In short, Morgan and Frieda have much more in common than either would probably be willing to admit.

While puzzling within the context of the blue plaque controversy, Frieda's identification of the construction of Plath as martyr as a particularly feminist one is not really surprising. As chapters 1 and 3 make clear, within the mass media and the larger public, feminism is still largely associated with constructions of Plath as suicidal martyr. And as Frieda's own writings on the subject make plain, feminism is still synonymous with what has been widely called the "vilification" of Ted Hughes.[25] That such attitudes persist despite decades of feminist criticism that has brilliantly illuminated everything from Plath's thematic treatment of motherhood, to her use of poetry as a tool for revising female identity, to her place as a woman poet in the (male) lyric tradition, to the influence of 1950s culture and gender expectations on her writing, is puzzling. Indeed, when Frieda seizes the opportunity in the foreword to *Ariel: The Restored Edition* to disparage and dismiss feminist readers, one can't help but question the appropriateness of doing so, given the role that feminist scholars have played in bringing such an edition about. That is to say, the very group Frieda so scornfully dismisses are those who have called repeatedly over the years for the restoration of Plath's voice and in effect created the very audience for a restored *Ariel* that has made it so successful. While it's certainly possible that the new edition might well have emerged on its own, solely through the initiative of David Semanki at HarperCollins, who Frieda says "first suggested that my mother's original arrangement of poems might make a good book,"[26] it seems unlikely that anyone would have arrived at the idea without the scholars and book reviewers who, in their "public scrutiny" of Hughes's editorial decisions, demonstrated so powerfully not simply an interest in but a need for a restored edition. To give credit to Semanki is to ignore—indeed elide—the work of feminist critics such as Marjorie Perloff, who, back in 1984, first made clear why the differences between the two versions of *Ariel* matter, and Lynda K. Bundtzen, whose 2001 book-length study *The Other "Ariel"* presented new ways of thinking about the restored *Ariel* even before its publication, to say nothing of the many scholars writing about the editing of *Ariel* in between Perloff and Bundtzen.[27]

While such an observation may appear a harsh criticism of Frieda, its intention is less to criticize than it is to point out, once again, just how powerfully entrenched the discourse about women readers has become in the cultural narrative about feminists which persists despite a lack of evidence to support it or even in spite of abundant evidence to the contrary. The conversation simply cannot untether itself from the narrative, perhaps because the investment in it by now is so great.

But as entrenched as Frieda's rhetoric is in the larger discourse about women readers, it's important to notice that her depiction of Plath's audience is not always straightforward or simple. While much of her rhetoric depicts readers as overly invested in her mother's suicide—so overidentified with Plath that they want to be her—she also depicts them as fickle voyeurs who don't comprehend the gravity of the situation. Take again, for example, "My Mother," with which I began my discussion of Frieda's writings. Originally directed at the filmmakers behind *Sylvia*, the poem shifts its focus in the second, third, and fourth stanzas to the audience for whom the film is ostensibly made, namely, "anyone lacking the ability / To imagine the body, head in the oven," and "the peanut eaters" who, "entertained" by the view of Plath's death, will buy the video as a "souvenir" so they can watch, rewind, and rewatch the film, pausing as needed "to boil a kettle" while Plath "holds her breath on screen / To finish dying after tea."[28] Of course, the fact that Frieda paints readers as so uncaring that they pause their viewing of Plath's death for a tea break makes little difference in her larger portrait of Plath's audience. Readers, whether they are overly invested in Plath or mere voyeurs looking for a spectacle, are at bottom uncaring and self-absorbed and therefore always a danger to Plath. Just as important, they still remain removed from the real death, which, according to Frieda, can only be experienced by—and therefore should be of concern only to—the family itself.

Such overall seamlessness does not mean, however, that there aren't inconsistencies in Frieda's larger narrative about readers. One such inconsistency emerges without the need for much scrutiny. That is, even as Frieda protests the public's interest in her mother, her actions produce, if not court, that very same interest. I am certainly not the first person to make the observation. Her complaints about the constant unearthing of her mother by readers in the November 2004 article in the *Independent* rather conspicuously coincide with the U.S. release of *Ariel: The Restored Edition* that same week, a fact even the reporter feels compelled to comment upon. And before that, the publication of the poem "My Mother," which likewise lambastes the dredging up of her mother's death, becomes a publicity generator not only for Frieda but for the film as well, calling more attention to *Sylvia* and to Plath than either would otherwise have garnered. "Readers" and "My Mother" in fact spurred at least a dozen stories in newspapers in the United Kingdom and abroad about the publication of the poems themselves; "My Mother" alone received coverage by media as wide ranging as CNN and the *Montreal Gazette*. But perhaps the example a truly cynical mind might most easily notice is the curious coincidence in timing between the publication of *The Journals of Sylvia Plath, 1950–1962* in the United Kingdom in March 2000 and *The Unabridged Journals* in the United States in October 2000 and the overstated "controversy" over the blue plaque just a couple of months prior. Indeed, Frieda's account in September 2000 of why she was determined to see the plaque installed at Chalcot Square closes with what is essentially an advertisement: "The Journals of Sylvia Plath *are published by Faber and Faber*, £30."[29]

This list of observations, I want to emphasize, is intended not to attack Frieda Hughes for her handling of the Plath estate or her desire to earn money from her mother's legacy. Undoubtedly, some of what seems like opportunism is simply what happens with the release of books: the media take an interest in the book, and those associated with it get asked for interviews, comments, and so on. What my observations aim to do, rather, is to provide a larger context for understanding Frieda's perceptions of Plath's readers and her own willingness to perpetrate their disparagement. Publications like "My Mother" garner publicity not only because they are written by Frieda Hughes (daughter of two of the most important poets of the twentieth century) but also because they provocatively disparage readers. Such publicity cannot but fuel sales of Plath's books. Thus, disparaging Plath's book buyers appears not merely fashionable but, ironically, quite profitable. Saying so does not preclude the likelihood that Frieda may also have an emotional investment in seeing readers as her family's true enemy. Nor is it meant to accuse Frieda of self-conscious exploitation. Rather, it is meant as an observation of the outcome: whether publicity and profit are Frieda's intention or not, they are undeniably the results of her public statements about her mother's readers.

Besides gaining publicity and profit, each time Frieda speaks out about her mother in public, she also generates more of the same scrutiny that she wishes to avoid. Within the media her statements are picked up, widely distributed, and commented on. And within reader circles the same effect occurs, as her statements are picked up, repeated, and analyzed, often by the very same readers disparaged in the statements. In debates that have taken place on Plath's online fan sites, Frieda in fact proves as much a lightning rod as a subject as Ted Hughes himself, though for different reasons. While her remarks engender sympathy from readers who try to imagine what it would be like to be Frieda, just as often they also engender confusion. Readers see themselves implicated in her rhetoric, and they fail to understand the reason for it. As one online poster puts it:

Frieda Hughes does not have to be so territorial re: Plath. Plath WAS, as someone in this group mentioned, a confessional poet—her life, her depression, and suicide were all centerpieces of her poetry. How can anyone not be interested in the poet after reading the poems? I know I was. After I read Ariel and the Colossus, I read the Bell Jar, then I bought her journals, and then I bought "Rough Magic" (a biography). It's natural, I think; it is human curiosity. I don't mean any harm, nor do any of Plath's other readers/fans.[30]

Not only does this post highlight the power (one might even say the addictive power) of Plath's writing, especially the way one book serves as gateway to another and another and another, but it brings us full circle as well, evoking my own narrative of reading with which I began this book.

As was the case with my narrative, this reader's perspective ought to remind us of a simple reality: the ways in which we talk about readers and their reading practices matter a great deal, and because they do, our discourse deserves self-reflection, if not critical scrutiny. Being more mindful of our rhetoric is one way we can raise awareness about the stakes involved in our conversations, particularly about what is lost or gained, elided or privileged, when we choose to value one way of reading over another. And as this post and others like it demonstrate, whatever Frieda's intentions, her comments only serve to inflame the debate about Plath's readers rather than put it to rest. There will always be ways of reading that strike us as uncritical or unschooled, as naïve or uninformed, even as unfair or unkind, and Plath is hardly alone in attracting such modes of interpretation. Furthermore, women readers, from young novices to feminist scholars, are not going to stop reading Plath anytime soon; nor are they likely to read her in ways that differ profoundly from how they already have read her. And why should they? It seems hardly worth saying, and yet the whole history of the discourse I've been tracking throughout this book demonstrates that it hasn't been said enough: Plath's readers are not a liability to her. They are trying, as all readers do, to make Plath's words and, yes, her life reverberate with meaning, and in doing so, they keep her work alive for future generations of readers to discover.

If it sounds as though I think there's a lesson to be learned here, it's because I do. And the lesson begins with Frieda's own words. In her inaugural column for The Times in 2006 Frieda writes: "I believe there is poetry for everyone. . . . Some people just haven't fallen over a poem that they identify with. . . . In this column I want to write about the poems I love, what they mean to me, and what makes them relevant on a personal level."[31] These words echo an earlier piece she published in the *Guardian* in 2001, in which she declares: "Poetry is for everyone; the trouble is that everyone doesn't know it yet. We should tell them."[32]

I could not agree with these sentiments more. Plath's poetry and her larger body of writing are indeed for everyone, including young women readers, feminist critics, and anyone who can make her writing resonate with meaning on any level, whether it be personal, political, or literary. The trouble is, not everyone gives readers the benefit of the doubt or seeks to understand reading practices that are different from their own or different from what they expect. It's time we all did.

NOTES

Preface

1. Quoted in Ian Thomson, "Under the Bell Jar," *Independent* (London), March 12, 1988, 21.

Introduction

1. Janet Badia, "The 'Priestess' and Her 'Cult': Plath's Confessional Poetics and the Mythology of Women Readers," in *The Unraveling Archive: Essays on Sylvia Plath*, ed. Anita Helle (Ann Arbor: University of Michigan Press, 2007), 159–81.
2. *10 Things I Hate About You*, directed by Gil Junger (Burbank: Touchstone Pictures, 1999), DVD.
3. Badia, "The 'Priestess' and Her 'Cult,'" 160.
4. Sandra Gilbert, "'A Fine, White Flying Myth': Confessions of a Plath Addict," *Massachusetts Review* 14, no. 3 (Autumn 1978): 585–603.
5. Kate Flint, *The Woman Reader, 1937–1914* (Oxford: Clarendon Press, 1993).
6. Ibid., 73.
7. Ibid., 13.
8. Ibid., 22.
9. Jacqueline Pearson, *Women's Reading in Britain, 1750–1835: A Dangerous Recreation* (Cambridge: Cambridge University Press, 1999), 83.
10. Suzanne Ashworth, "Susan Warner's *The Wide, Wide World*, Conduct Literature, and Protocols of Female Reading in Mid-Nineteenth-Century America," *Legacy* 17, no. 2 (2000): 145.
11. Ibid., 143.
12. Catherine Golden, *Images of the Woman Reader in Victorian British and American Fiction* (Gainesville: University Press of Florida, 2003), 3.
13. Flint, *Woman Reader*, 58.
14. Just take, for example, the seemingly endless pool of paintings reproduced as part of the Pomegranate line of "Reading Women" calendars, note cards, and journals. For more on the "Reading Women" line and the image of

the woman reader as cultural icon, see Jennifer Phegley and Janet Badia, "Introduction: Women Readers as Literary Figures and Cultural Icons," in *Reading Women: Literary Figures and Cultural Icons from the Victorian Age to the Present*, ed. Janet Badia and Jennifer Phegley (Toronto: University of Toronto Press, 2005), 3–26.

15. Flint, *Woman Reader*, 50.

16. Golden, *Images of the Woman Reader*, 98.

17. Flint, *Woman Reader*, 75.

18. Quoted in Golden, *Images of the Woman Reader*, 99.

19. Stephen Schindler, "The Critic as Pornographer: Male Fantasies of Female Reading in Eighteenth-Century Germany," *Eighteenth-Century Life* 20 (November 1996): 74. According to Jacqueline Pearson, it's hardly a coincidence that those prescribing the cures were often literary magazines, which, like today's deodorant manufacturers, created the very anxieties that led to the need for the remedy (in this case the magazines themselves) in the first place. Jacqueline Pearson, " 'Books, My Greatest Joy': Constructing the Female Reader in *The Lady's Magazine*," *Women's Writing* 3, no. 1 (1996): 8.

20. Susan Wood, review of *Words for Dr. Y: Uncollected Poems by Anne Sexton*, *Washington Post Book World*, October 15, 1978, E3.

21. Susan Wood, "Anne Sexton's Letters: 'Poetry Has Saved My Life,' " review of *Anne Sexton: A Self-Portrait in Letters*, *Washington Post Book World*, November 20, 1977, E3. All additional quotes are from this page.

22. See chapter 1 for a discussion of how these same tropes of cult and priestess get applied to Kate Millett's *Sexual Politics* at around this same time, a phenomenon that demonstrates the extent to which the reception of women's writing generally became caught up in the backlash against the women's movement.

23. See Janet Badia, "Viewing Poems as 'Bloodstains': Sylvia Plath's Confessional Poetics and the Autobiographical Reader," *a/b: Auto/Biography Studies* 17, no. 2 (Winter 2002): 180–203.

24. Judith Kroll, *Chapters in a Mythology: The Poetry of Sylvia Plath* (New York: Harper and Row, 1976), 1–2.

25. Ibid., 1.

26. Ibid.

27. Gary Lane, *Sylvia Plath: New Views on the Poetry* (Baltimore: Johns Hopkins University Press, 1979), jacket copy.

28. Jon Rosenblatt, *Sylvia Plath: The Poetry of Imitation* (Chapel Hill: University of North Carolina Press, 1979), jacket copy.

29. Mary Lynn Broe, *Protean Poetic: The Poetry of Sylvia Plath* (Columbia: University of Missouri Press, 1980), jacket copy.

30. Harold Bloom, ed., *Modern Critical Views: Sylvia Plath* (New York: Chelsea House, 1989), jacket copy.

31. Tracy Brain, *The Other Sylvia Plath* (Harlow, England: Longman, 2001). I would add that, despite taking issue with Brain's concern with readers, I think the admiration is deserved. I especially appreciate what I would call her "textual studies" approach to Plath's writing, including her examination of the manuscripts and their editing, and the way she combines it with an analysis of the historical contexts of the works. I do not regard her approach as being inherently incompatible with the autobiographical approaches she criticizes, however.

32. Ibid., 6.

33. Ibid., 15.

34. Ibid., 3.

35. Ibid., 15.

36. Amy Rea, "Reclaiming Plath," *Readerville Journal*, January–February 2003, 39, 40.

37. Ibid., 40.

38. Ibid., 43.

39. Tony Bennett, "Texts in History: The Determinations of Readings and Their Texts," *Journal of the Midwest Modern Language Association* 18, no. 1 (Spring 1985): 12.

40. Tony Bennett, *Critical Trajectories: Culture, Society, Intellectuals* (Malden, Mass.: Blackwell, 2007), 51.

41. Bennett, "Texts in History," 12.

42. Christina Britzolakis, *Sylvia Plath and the Theatre of Mourning* (Oxford: Clarendon Press), 7.

43. Meg Wolitzer, *Sleepwalking* (New York: Random House, 1982), 3. Subsequent references will be given parenthetically in the text.

44. Jeffrey Berman indirectly takes up this question in his exploration of student responses to *The Bell Jar*. His own experiences with teaching *The Bell Jar* suggest that the novel (and other texts like it) can, in fact, have an infectious effect on readers, leading to symptoms not unlike those suffered by the young women in *Sleepwalking*. As he puts it, "a reader's identification with a fantasy, fear, or conflict in a text may be so powerful and disturbing that it threatens to overwhelm his or her defenses." On the basis of his teaching experiences, he suggests that female students are especially prone to the effect. Jeffrey Berman, "Syllabuses of Risk," *Chronicle of Higher Education* 48, no. 23 (February 15, 2002): B9. It seems important to note that in over sixteen years of college teaching I've never had experiences with students that resemble the ones Berman describes, despite having taught several seminars solely on Plath's writing. I would suggest that the context in which he teaches *The Bell Jar*, a course called "Historical/Hysterical Imagination," which he notes focuses on the "cultural and psychological implications of mental illness" (B7), explains the effect in large part at least.

45. Roland Barthes, *Mythologies*, trans. Annette Lavers (1957; New York: Farrar, Straus, and Giroux, 1994), 115.
46. Ibid., 117.
47. Ibid., 11.
48. It's well worth noting that for Tony Bennett, whose work I cited earlier in this introduction, acknowledging the specious nature of claims to the text itself doesn't mean that distinctions in value among different readings can't be made. He writes: "It is merely to argue that the differences between them cannot be resolved epistemologically by claiming for a particular reading the warrant of a relationship to the 'text itself' such that all other readings are thereby automatically disqualified in its favor. Rather, readings can only be assessed politically in terms of a calculation of their consequences in and for the present." Bennett, "Texts in History," 12. One might argue that the bullying of readers I identify in Plath criticism constitutes just such an act of political assessment, one in which the critics voice their concern over the consequences to Plath's reputation that certain modes of reading might pose. But I think such an application of Bennett's argument would first have to rest on the assumption of an equal distribution of power between critics and the readers being disparaged, which is clearly not the case.

1. "Dissatisfied, Family-Hating Shrews"

1. See Paul Alexander, *Rough Magic: A Biography of Sylvia Plath* (New York: Penguin, 1992), 251–78 passim and 334–64; and Linda W. Wagner, introduction to *Critical Essays on Sylvia Plath*, ed. Linda W. Wagner (New York: G. K. Hall, 1984), 1–24, especially 6–15.
2. Anxieties about women readers are not the only anxieties shaping Plath's reception, though I would argue that they are the predominant ones. Jacqueline Rose identifies a confluence of anxieties within early Plath criticism revolving around female sexuality, femininity and feminism, and the supposed "degeneracy" of culture as they center on Plath herself. See especially Jacqueline Rose, *The Haunting of Sylvia Plath* (Cambridge: Harvard University Press, 1992), 11–28.
3. Catherine X, "Sylvia Plath—Transitional Poems from the Gut," review of *Crossing the Water*, by Sylvia Plath, *Los Angeles Free Press*, March 24, 1972, sec. 2, 13.
4. Saul Maloff, "The Poet as Cult Goddess," review of *Letters Home: Correspondence, 1950–1963*, by Sylvia Plath, *Commonweal*, June 4, 1976, 374.
5. A. Alvarez, "Inside the Bell Jar," review of *Letters Home*, *Observer* (Manchester), April 18, 1976, 23.
6. Steven Mailloux, *Reception Histories: Rhetoric, Pragmatism, and American Cultural Politics* (Ithaca: Cornell University Press, 1998), ix.

7. Ibid., 75.

8. Ibid., 50–51.

9. Ibid., 50.

10. Ibid., 34–35.

11. Once again I have in mind Mailloux, specifically his interest in turning "reception history into rhetorical hermeneutics, focusing not only on the rhetoric of literary texts but on the rhetoric of their historical interpretations and the diachronic and synchronic dimensions of the cultural conversations in which those interpretations participate." Ibid., 122–23.

12. In a letter to her mother, Plath reports that Heinemann hadn't "bothered to advertise" *The Colossus* and attributes the neglect to the book's lack of prizes and failure to find an American publisher. Sylvia Plath, *Letters Home: Correspondence, 1950–1963*, ed. Aurelia Schober Plath (New York: Harper-Perennial, 1992), 399.

13. For these periodicals, see the following reviews of *The Colossus*: A. E. Dyson in *Critical Quarterly* 3 (Summer 1961): 181–84; Dom Moraes, "Poems from Many Parts," *Time and Tide*, November 19, 1960, 1413; Roy Fuller in *London Magazine* 8 (March 1961): 69–70; A. Alvarez, "The Poet and the Poetess," *Observer*, December 18, 1960, 12.

14. Alvarez, "The Poet and the Poetess," 12.

15. As small as it may have been, the initial response to *The Bell Jar* represents an important moment in the reception of Plath's work, especially given the relative vacuum in which the novel is first published and reviewed. As Robert Taubman in the *New Statesman* makes clear, the novel's identity in 1963 is that of a first novel by a literary newcomer. In stark contrast, when it's released under Plath's name in the United Kingdom in 1965 and, even more so, when it's published for the first time in the United States in 1971, the novel has a very different identity: it exists as the only novel by a literary icon known widely and equally for both her writing and her suicide. Robert Taubman, "Anti-Heroes," review of *The Bell Jar*, by Victoria Lucas, *New Statesman* 65 (January 25, 1963): 128.

16. Ibid.

17. Laurence Lerner, "Transatlantic Englishmen," review of *The Bell Jar*, *Listener* 69 (January 31, 1963): 215.

18. Simon Raven, "The Trouble with Phaedra," review of *The Bell Jar*, *Spectator* 217 (February 15, 1963): 203.

19. See Alexander, *Rough Magic*, especially 338–39, for a discussion of the tributes and anthologies that appeared in leading literary magazines and journals after Plath's death, including the tributes published in *Encounter* and *The Review* in October 1963 (the month of what would have been Plath's thirty-first birthday).

20. While Plath's early success and the increased attention paid to posthumous

works such as *Ariel* and *The Bell Jar* have been conventionally explained as an effect of her suicide—particularly the public's fascination with tragedies of this kind—such explanations, I would argue, oversimplify the other forces propelling Plath into the literary spotlight during this time, including the championing and expert promotion of her work by a handful of young but no less influential critics and poets, including Robert Lowell, who provided the foreword to *Ariel*.

21. "Russian Roulette," review of *Ariel*, by Sylvia Plath, *Newsweek*, June 20, 1966, 110–11; "The Blood Jet Is Poetry," review of *Ariel*, *Time*, June 10, 1966, 118–20.

22. Compare, for example, the language of the reviews with this oft-quoted passage from Lowell's foreword: "These poems are playing Russian roulette with six cartridges in the cylinder." Or a less infamous passage: "The truth is that this *Ariel* is the author's horse. Dangerous, more powerful than man, machinelike from hard training, she herself is a little like a racehorse, galloping relentlessly with risked, outstretched neck, death hurdle after death hurdle topped." Robert Lowell, foreword to *Ariel* (New York: Harper and Row, 1966), viii, vii.

23. "Blood Jet," 118.

24. "Russian Roulette," 110.

25. Alan Ross, review of *Ariel*, *London Magazine* 5 (May 1965): 101.

26. Marius Bewley, review of *Ariel*, *Hudson Review* 19 (Autumn 1966): 491.

27. Dan Jaffe, "An All-American Muse," review of *Ariel*, *Saturday Review*, October 15, 1966, 29.

28. Robert L. Stilwell, "The Multiplying of Entities: D. H. Lawrence and Five Other Poets," review of *Ariel*, *Sewanee Review* 76 (Summer 1968): 533.

29. "Blood Jet," 118.

30. Alexander, *Rough Magic*, 343–44.

31. Frances McCullough, foreword to the Twenty-fifth Anniversary Edition of *The Bell Jar*, by Sylvia Plath (New York: Harper & Row, 1996), xiii.

32. According to Paul Alexander, "*The Bell Jar* became so popular that, when Bantam Books brought out an initial paperback edition in April 1972—a run of 375,000 copies—it sold out that printing, plus a second and a third, in one month. In the mid-eighties, more than a decade and a half later, *The Bell Jar* paperback edition was selling some fifty thousand copies a year." Alexander, *Rough Magic*, 348.

33. Lucy Rosenthal, review of *Ariel*, *Saturday Review*, April 24, 1971, 42.

34. Robert Taylor, "Bright Journey into Night," review of *The Bell Jar*, *Boston Globe*, April 16, 1971, 17.

35. Linda Ray Pratt, "The Spirit of Blackness Is in Us . . . ," review of *Ariel*, *Crossing the Water*, and *Winter Trees* by Sylvia Plath, *Prairie Schooner* 47 (Spring 1973): 87.

36. Clarence Peterson, review of *Ariel, Washington Post Book World*, April 30, 1972, 8.

37. In his essay "Sylvia Plath: A Partial Disagreement," Irving Howe refers to Plath ironically as the "authentic priestess," while Webster Schott calls her "the high priestess of the confessional poem" in his review "The Cult of Plath," to name just two examples. Irving Howe, "Sylvia Plath: A Partial Disagreement," *Harper's*, January 1972, 88; Webster Schott, "The Cult of Plath," review of *Winter Trees, Washington Post Book World*, October 1, 1973, 3.

38. Alexander, *Rough Magic*, 352.

39. Sylvia Plath, "Three Women: A Poem for Three Voices," *Ms.*, Spring 1972, 85–88.

40. Sylvia Plath, *The Journals of Sylvia Plath*, ed. Ted Hughes and Frances McCullough (New York: Ballantine, 1983), 126.

41. Harriet Rosenstein, "Reconsidering Sylvia Plath," *Ms.*, September 1972, 44–51.

42. While I'm obviously concerned with the historical relationship between Plath's reception and the women's movement, the question of Plath's relationship (or the relationship of her writing) to feminism is not one I take up at any length in this book. Which is not to say that the question isn't deserving of attention; it's just better suited to a project with an overall different purpose than mine, one more focused on making an argument about her writing than about its reception. Having said that, I agree with Jacqueline Rose's assessment of how feminism figures in the reception itself. Within the discourse of literary criticism, "the irrelevance of feminism to an understanding of Plath" seems to be the only point that unifies Plath's supporters and detractors—this despite the long, rich history of feminist Plath criticism itself, which has surely proven that Plath had plenty to say that is relevant to feminism. Rose, *Haunting of Sylvia Plath*, 99.

43. McCullough, foreword, xiv.

44. In identifying the Plath reader here as "implicitly white," I mean to call attention to the way the discourse seldom, if ever, identifies the Plath reader's race and thereby implies her white identity. As my discussion of visual images in the next chapter makes clear, the implication is obviously there. To explain why the Plath reader is assumed to be white, not to mention young, female, and middle class, one would have to account for several factors. The one most relevant to my discussion thus far is the Plath reader's association with the women's movement of the 1970s, which has been widely critiqued for a myopic attention to the problems of white, middle-class women and its assumption that the category "woman" could account for the diversity of all women. And as I discuss later on in this chapter, the rhetoric of Plath's reception frequently constructs the reader's interest in Plath as self-absorption and

narcissism. What Plath's readers most want, according to this narrative, is to create themselves in Plath's image. Not surprisingly, then, the Plath reader becomes the mirror image of Plath in the critic's mind: she's young, white, middle class, female, and sick. Adding yet another layer to the explanation, there's the practical side of Plath's targeted demographic: Plath frequently crafted her writing for publication in women's magazines such as *Ladies' Home Journal,* whose implied audience in the 1950s and 1960s (if not still today) was clearly a white, middle-class woman. Whether any of these assumptions about Plath's readers is accurate is a question that would require an ethnographic study of audience that is beyond the scope of my project here.

45. Alvarez, "Inside the Bell Jar," 23. All quotes are from this page.
46. Rosalyn Baxandall and Linda Gordon, introduction to *Dear Sisters: Dispatches from the Women's Liberation Movement,* ed. Rosalyn Baxandall and Linda Gordon (New York: Basic Books, 2000), 15.
47. Ruth Rosen, *The World Split Open: How the Modern Women's Movement Changed America* (New York: Viking, 2000), 302.
48. Susan J. Douglas, *Where the Girls Are: Growing Up Female with the Mass Media* (New York: Three Rivers, 1994), 7.
49. [Ruth Brine], "The New Feminists: Revolt against 'Sexism,'" *Time,* November 21, 1969, 53.
50. Ibid.
51. Ibid., 54.
52. "Women's Lib: The War on 'Sexism,'" *Newsweek,* March 23, 1970, 74.
53. Sandie North, "Reporting the Movement," *Atlantic,* March 1970, 105.
54. "Other Voices: How Social Scientists See Women's Lib," *Newsweek,* March 23, 1970, 75.
55. Quoted in "Women's Lib: A Second Look," *Time,* December 14, 1970, 50.
56. Irving Howe, "The Middle-Class Mind of Kate Millet," review of *Sexual Politics,* by Kate Millett, *Harper's,* December 1970, 129, 123, 110.
57. Ibid., 118, 126.
58. Ibid., 121.
59. Ibid., 110.
60. Frank Prial, "Feminist Philosopher: Katharine Murray Millet," *New York Times,* August 27, 1970, 30.
61. "Women's Lib: A Second Look," 50.
62. Seldon Rodman, "Petrified by Gorgon Egos," review of *Delusions, Etc.,* by John Berryman, *Braving the Elements* by James Merrill, *The Book of Folly* by Anne Sexton, and other books, *New Leader,* January 22, 1973, 20.
63. Howard Sergeant, review of *Crossing the Water,* by Sylvia Plath, *Walking to Sleep,* by Richard Wilbur, and other books, *English* 20 (Autumn 1971): 106.

64. Pearl Bell, "Poets of Our Time," review of *The Awful Rowing toward God*, by Anne Sexton, *Diving into the Wreck*, by Adrienne Rich, and *Self-Portrait in a Convex Mirror*, by John Ashbery, *New Leader* (Spring Book Issue), May 26, 1975, 3.

65. To appreciate fully the significance of Bell's rhetoric about the common reader and serious art, one can also situate her comments—and in fact much of the discourse about women readers that concerns me in this book—within broader efforts to feminize and thereby denigrate mass culture and the popular. For more on this, see Andreas Huyseen, "Mass Culture as Woman: Modernism's Other," in *Studies in.Entertainment: Critical Approaches to Mass Culture*, ed. Tania Modleski (Bloomington: Indiana University Press 1986), 188–207.

66. Alan Williamson, "Confession and Tragedy," review of *The Collected Poems*, by Sylvia Plath, *Poetry* 142 (June 1983): 173.

67. Howe, "Sylvia Plath," 88.

68. Ibid.

69. Ibid., 91; emphasis added.

70. In his concern with reading practices, Howe seems to want to indict both the general and the professional reader. That is to say, Howe directs his attack as much toward Plath critics and scholars as to her general audience. For the purposes of this book, I do not emphasize the distinction, for most of the critics I discuss here, including Howe, suggest that Plath scholars and readers are all more or less cut from the same cloth; they are all guilty of uncritical reading habits. In Howe's essay, for example, if Plath's "young readers" uncritically consume her "vibrations of despair," scholars, in a similar fashion, pile heaps "of adoring criticism" around her in a "semi-mimetic frenzy." Ibid., 88.

71. Ibid., 90.

72. Ibid., 88.

73. Susan B. Rosenbaum, *Professing Sincerity: Modern Lyric Poetry, Commercial Culture, and the Crisis in Reading* (Charlottesville: University of Virginia Press, 2007), 133. While not concerned with Plath's relationship to feminism, Rosenbaum goes on to show how Plath negotiated the complexities of her dual interests in achieving commercial success (largely by writing prose for magazines) and literary reputation (by "modernizing the poetess, fashioning a poetic persona that accommodated a conventional emphasis on death, loss, and suffering by embracing the stoicism and violence prevalent in the writing of the male modernists") Ibid., 137.

74. Rose, *Haunting of Sylvia Plath*, 167.

75. Ibid., 168–69.

76. Melvin Maddocks, "Sylvia Plath: The Cult and the Poems," review of *Ariel*, *Christian Science Monitor*, June 30, 1966, 13.

77. Gene Baro, "Varied Quintet," review of *Ariel*, *New York Times Book Review*, June 26, 1966, 10.

78. Stephen Philbrick, "The Life, Work and World of Sylvia Plath," review of *Crossing the Water*, *Providence Sunday Journal* (Leisure Weekly) October 31, 1971, H6.

79. Paul West, "Fido Littlesoul, the Bowel's Familiar," review of *Crossing the Water*, *Washington Post Book World*, January 9, 1972, 8.

80. Marjorie Perloff, "On the Road to *Ariel*: The 'Transitional' Poetry of Sylvia Plath," review of *Crossing the Water*, *Iowa Review* 4, no. 2 (Spring 1973): 94.

81. West, "Fido Littlesoul," 8.

82. Richard Locke, "The Last Word: Beside the Bell Jar," review of *The Bell Jar*, *New York Times Book Review*, June 20, 1971, 47.

83. Helen Dudar, "From Book to Cult," review of *The Bell Jar*, *New York Post*, September 2, 1971, 38.

84. Maurice Duke, "Sylvia Plath's 'Winter Trees' Will Not Change Readers' Views," review of *Winter Trees*, *Richmond Times-Dispatch*, October 1, 1972, F5.

85. Catherine X, "Sylvia Plath," 15.

86. Philbrick, "Life, Work and World," H6.

87. Schott, "The Cult of Plath," 3.

88. Catherine X, "Sylvia Plath," 13.

89. Schott, "The Cult of Plath," 3.

90. Jill Baumgaertner, "Four Poets: Blood Type New," review of *Winter Trees*, *Cresset* 36 (April 1973): 17.

91. Jan Gordon, "Saint Sylvia," review of *Winter Trees*, *Modern Poetry Studies* 2, no. 6 (1972): 286.

92. Robin Skelton, review of *Crossing the Water*, *Malahat Review* 20 (October 1971): 138.

93. Schott, "The Cult of Plath," 3.

94. Sylvia Plath, "Lady Lazarus," in *Ariel* (New York: Harper and Row, 1966), 6–9.

95. A. Alvarez, "Publish and Be Damned," review of *Crossing the Water* and *Winter Trees*, *Observer*, October 3, 1971, 36.

96. James Finn Cotter, "Women Poets: Malign Neglect?" review of *Winter Trees*, *America*, February 17, 1973, 140.

97. Gordon, "Saint Sylvia," 285–86.

98. Melvin Maddocks, "A Vacuum Abhorred," *Christian Science Monitor*, April 15, 1977, 11.

99. Dudar, "From Book to Cult," 3.

100. Ibid., 38.

101. Ibid.

102. Ibid.

103. Ibid.

104. Review of *Letters Home*, *Booklist*, October 15, 1975, 273.

105. Nancy Gail Reed, "Still Those Ellipses. . . ," review of *Letters Home*, *Christian Science Monitor*, January 7, 1976, 23.

106. Doris Eder, "Portrait of the Artist as a Young Woman: (1) Sylvia Plath," review of *Letters Home*, *Book Forum* 2 (Spring 1976): 242.

107. Maloff, "The Poet as Cult Goddess," 374.

108. Harriet Rosenstein, "Pure Gold Baby," review of *Letters Home*, by Sylvia Plath, *New Review* 3 (May 1976): 53.

109. Carol Bere, review of *Letters Home*, *Ariel: Review of International English Literature* 8 (October 1977): 99.

110. Karl Miller, "Sylvia Plath's Apotheosis," review of *Letters Home*, *New York Review*, June 24, 1976, 3.

111. Bere, review of *Letters Home*, 99.

112. Anthony Thwaite, "'I Have Never Been So Happy in My Life': On Sylvia Plath," review of *Letters Home*, *Encounter* 46 (June 1976): 66.

113. Jill Neville, "The Sylvia Plath Industry," review of *Letters Home*, *Sydney Morning Herald*, April 3, 1976, 18.

114. Joyce Carol Oates, "One for Life, One for Death," review of *Winter Trees*, *New York Times Book Review*, November 19, 1972, 7.

115. Susan Fromberg Schaeffer, "Sylvia Plath: The Artist Possessed," review of *The Journals of Sylvia Plath*, ed. Frances McCullough, *Chicago Sun-Times*, April 11, 1982, 22.

116. Eder, "Portrait of the Artist," 244.

117. Geoffrey Wolff, "Genius and Gee Whizzery," review of *Letters Home*, *New Times*, December 26, 1975, 64.

118. Erica Jong, "Letters Focus Exquisite Rage of Sylvia Plath," review of *Letters Home*, *Los Angeles Times Book Review*, November 23, 1975, 1.

119. Maureen Howard, "The Girl Who Tried to Be Good," review of *Letters Home*, *New York Times Book Review*, December 14, 1975, 1.

120. Stephen Trombley, review of *Letters Home*, *Critical Quarterly* 19, no. 2 (Summer 1977): 93–94.

121. Rosenstein, "Pure Gold Baby," 53.

122. Thwaite, "I Have Never Been," 65.

123. The publication history of *Letters Home* is far more interesting and complex than the reviews of the book suggest. As has been widely discussed within Plath and Hughes scholarship, *Letters Home* results from some kind of agreement reached between Ted Hughes and Plath's mother, Aurelia. Hughes, it would seem, did not want the letters to be published, but Aurelia Plath thought her daughter's letters to her were needed to balance the publication of *The Bell Jar* in the United States. It remains unclear, however, just how formal the agreement could have been, given the inevitability of *The Bell Jar's*

publication no matter Aurelia Plath's objections. For a helpful summary of the issue, see Sarah Churchwell, "Secrets and Lies: Privacy, Publication and Ted Hughes's *Birthday Letters*," *Contemporary Literature* 42, no. 1 (Spring 2001): 102–48.

124. Bere, review of *Letters Home*, 103. See also Hugh Haughton, "In Her Mother's Kingdom," review of *Letters Home*, *Times Higher Education Supplement*, July 16, 1976, 15.

125. Larry McMurty, "Letters and a Superb Autobiography," review of *Letters Home*, *Washington Post Book World*, November 24, 1975, B14.

126. Eder, "Portrait of the Artist," 242.

127. Ibid., 254.

128. Susan R. Bordo, "The Body and the Reproduction of Femininity," in *Gender/Body/Knowledge: Feminist Reconstructions of Being and Knowing*, ed. Alison M. Jaggar and Susan R. Bordo (New Brunswick: Rutgers University Press, 1989), 18.

129. Ted Hughes, introduction to *Johnny Panic and the Bible of Dreams and Other Prose Writing*, by Sylvia Plath (New York: Harper and Row, 1979), 7.

130. To be fair, it should be noted that even Plath had asked, "Who would want to read them?" when considering her ability to get some of her short stories published. Quoted in ibid., 4.

131. Kay Dick, review of *Johnny Panic and the Bible of Dreams*, *Times* (London), December 1, 1977, 9.

132. Ibid.

133. Carol Bere, review of *Johnny Panic and the Bible of Dreams*, *Southern Humanities Review* 13 (Fall 1979): 358.

134. Simon Blow, "Sylvia Plath's Prose," review of *Johnny Panic and the Bible of Dreams*, *Books and Bookmen* 23 (June 1978): 42.

135. Douglas Hill, "Living and Dying," review of *Johnny Panic and the Bible of Dreams*, *Canadian Forum* 58 (June–July 1978): 32.

136. Katha Pollitt, "Aesthetic Suicide," review of *Johnny Panic and the Bible of Dreams*, *Harper's*, February 1979, 83.

137. Christopher Reid, "The 'I' and the Ear," review of *The Collected Poems*, *Observer*, November 1, 1981, 33.

138. Susan Fromberg Schaeffer, "Plath's Poems Resurrect Her from Shadows of Myth," review of *The Collected Poems*, *Chicago Tribune*, December 20, 1981, sec. 7, 1.

139. Dave Smith, "Some Recent American Poetry: Come All Ye Fair and Tender Ladies," review of *The Collected Poems*, *American Poetry Review*, January–February 1982, 43.

140. Tom Clark, "Raw Nerves at the Cabaret of Despair," review of *The Collected Poems*, *San Francisco Chronicle Review*, October 11, 1981, 4.

141. Ibid.

142. Denis Donoghue, "You Could Say She Had a Calling for Death," review of *The Collected Poems, New York Times Book Review,* November 22, 1981, 30.

143. Helen Vendler, "An Intractable Metal," review of *The Collected Poems, New Yorker,* February 15, 1982, 124.

144. William Pritchard, "An Interesting Minor Poet?" review of *The Collected Poems, New Republic,* December 30, 1981, 33.

145. Steven Ratiner, "New Collections Reveal Literary Development of Poets Plath and Sexton," review of *The Collected Poems,* by Sylvia Plath, and *The Complete Poems,* by Anne Sexton, *Christian Science Monitor,* January 27, 1982, 15.

146. Review of *The Collected Poems, Virginia Quarterly Review* 58, no. 2 (Spring 1982): 58.

147. Michael Hulse, "Formal Bleeding," review of *The Collected Poems, Spectator,* November 14, 1981, 20.

148. Helen Chasin, "What Have You Done? What Have You Done?" review of *The Collected Poems,* and *The Journals of Sylvia Plath,* ed. Frances McCullough, *Yale Review* 72 (Spring 1983): 427.

149. Ibid., 438.

150. Ibid.

151. Ibid., 429.

152. Paul Stuewe, "Cloying Robots . . . Plathian Jottings . . . Twainian Tales . . . ," review of *The Journals of Sylvia Plath,* ed. Ted Hughes and Frances McCullough, *Quill and Quire,* July 1982, 69.

153. Phoebe Pettingell, "The Voices of Sylvia Plath," review of *The Journals of Sylvia Plath,* ed. Ted Hughes and Frances McCullough, *New Leader,* May 17, 1982, 10.

154. Ibid., 11.

155. Kathy Field Stephen, "Plath Journals Offer New Insights," review of *The Journals of Sylvia Plath,* ed. Ted Hughes and Frances McCullough, *Christian Science Monitor,* September 7, 1982, 17.

156. Joyce Carol Oates, "Raising Lady Lazarus," review of *The Unabridged Journals of Sylvia Plath, 1950–1962,* ed. Karen V. Kukil, *New York Times Book Review,* November 5, 2000, 11, 10.

157. Cynthia Ozick, "Smoke and Fire," review of *The Unabridged Journals of Sylvia Plath, Yale Review,* October 2001, 99, 100.

158. Ibid., 100.

159. Ibid.

160. Christina Britzolakis, "Very Raw Writer's Materials," review of *The Unabridged Journals of Sylvia Plath, Times Higher Education Supplement,* November 17, 2000, 44.

161. Carol A. McAllister, review of *The Unabridged Journals of Sylvia Plath, Library Journal,* September 15, 2000, 76.

162. Barbara Hoffert, "Plath as She Was," review of *Ariel: The Restored Edition,* by Sylvia Plath, *Library Journal,* November 1, 2004, 84.
163. Anthony Cuda, "Among These Silk Screens," review of *Ariel: The Restored Edition, American Book Review,* September–October 2005, 19.
164. Hoffert, "Plath as She Was," 84.
165. Lee Upton, "'I / Have a self to recover': The Restored *Ariel*," *Literary Review* 48, no. 4 (Summer 2005): 261.
166 Zoë Heller, "Ariel's Appetite," review of *The Unabridged Journals of Sylvia Plath, New Republic,* December 18, 2000, 33.

2. *"Oh, You Are Dark"*

1. *10 Things I Hate About You,* directed by Gil Junger (Burbank: Touchstone Pictures, 1999), DVD. Throughout this chapter all quotations from visual media are from the cited DVD versions.
2. Of course, Mr. Morgan's own position as a black man complicates any straightforward reading of his character as a symbol of patriarchy. On the one hand, it is clear that his primary role in the film is that of the male authority figure who keeps Kat in line. On the other hand, the fact of his race would suggest that his character is also meant to underscore Kat's privileged position and thus undercut her later claims to oppression. In either case, Kat usually comes off badly in the scenes in which she interacts with Mr. Morgan.
3. *Annie Hall,* directed by Woody Allen (Los Angeles: MGM Pictures, 1977), DVD.
4. I'm interested here in Alvy's reference to college girls more than in the fact that Annie herself appears to be a Plath reader too. It's her copy of *Ariel,* after all, that Alvy waves in the air. Just how engaged a Plath reader she is remains difficult to judge, for when confronted with Alvy's complaint, Annie responds in typically clumsy fashion, "Well, I don't know, I mean, uh, some of her poems seem—neat, you know."
5. Meg Wolitzer, *Sleepwalking* (New York: Random House, 1982), 3.
6. According to the film, Kat and Bianca's mother "left" them all some three years prior, essentially, it would appear, vanishing from the girls' lives.
7. Some plot summary may be helpful here. Because the girls' father has forbidden Bianca to date until Kat does (a new rule he imposes because he thinks it will prevent both girls from dating, since Kat has renounced boys altogether), one of Bianca's devotees, Cameron James, develops a scheme to get Kat to date so he can then take out Bianca. As part of the scheme, he offers to broker a date between Bianca and Joey Donner, another boy who is also interested in Bianca, though for less innocent reasons, and who has loads of money to offer Patrick in exchange for taking out Kat. Once Kat begins dating Patrick, Cameron is able to ask Bianca to the prom.

8. *Natural Born Killers*, directed by Oliver Stone (Burbank: Warner Bros., 1994), DVD.

9. Carol Anshaw, *Seven Moves* (New York: Houghton Mifflin, 1996). I am indebted to Susan Van Dyne for referring me to Anshaw's depiction of a Plath reader.

10. Ibid., 69.

11. Ibid., 132.

12. In the director's commentary on the DVD of *Natural Born Killers*, Oliver Stone describes how he self-consciously "staged" the fight as a "silly sort of Tom and Jerry cartoon."

13. "Def Poet's Society," *The Fresh Prince of Bel Air*, season 1, episode 7, directed by Jeff Melman, aired October 22, 1990 (Burbank: Warner Home Video, 1990), DVD.

14. "A Single Life," *Law & Order: Special Victims Unit*, season 1, episode 2, directed by Lesli Linka Glatter, aired September 22, 1999 (Universal City: Universal Studies Home Entertainment, 1999), DVD.

15. "Fish Out of Water," *Family Guy*, season 3, episode 10, directed by Bert Ring, aired September 19, 2001 (Century City: 20th Century Fox, 2001), DVD.

16. Robin Peel, *Writing Back: Sylvia Plath and Cold War Politics* (Cranbury, N.J.: Fairleigh Dickinson University Press, 2002), 66.

17. Elizabeth Wurtzel, *Prozac Nation: Young and Depressed in America* (New York: Riverhead Books, 1994), 8. See also Wurtzel's *Bitch: In Praise of Difficult Women* (New York: Doubleday, 1998).

18. Wurtzel, *Prozac Nation*, 8.

19. Ibid., 8, 1.

20. For a more detailed discussion of the relationship of *The Bell Jar* to autobiography, see Mary Evans, "Extending Autobiography: A Discussion of Sylvia Plath's *The Bell Jar*," in *Feminism and Autobiography: Texts, Theories, Methods*, ed. Tess Cosslett, Celia Lury, and Penny Summerfield (New York: Routlege, 2000), 76–88.

21. Gwynne Garfinkle, "Putting All My Eggs in One Basket," in *No Body's Perfect: Stories by Teens about Body Image, Self-Acceptance, and the Search for Identity*, ed. Kimberly Kirberger (New York: Scholastic, 2003), 25–26.

22. For a more detailed discussion of the novel's treatment of the themes of control and self-determination, see Janet Badia, "*The Bell Jar* and Other Prose," in *The Cambridge Companion to Sylvia Plath*, ed. Jo Gill (Cambridge: Cambridge University Press, 2006), 124–38.

3. "We Did Not Wish to Give the Impression"

1. Christina Patterson, "In Search of the Poet," *Independent* (London), February 6, 2004, 2. All quotations are from this page.

2. Another piece by Patterson illustrates how her rhetoric perfectly fits with the rhetoric I describe in chapter 1. Elsewhere in the *Independent*, she briefly discusses *The Bell Jar*, which she says "remains one of the most powerful portrayals of madness in fiction. It doesn't, however, make [Plath] the patron saint of terminally depressed teenage girls. Sadly, they don't know that." Christina Patterson, "The Bell Jar," *Independent*, April 29, 2005, 5.

3. A rare example of a study that aims to take Plath's readers seriously in the vein of the ethnography is Judith Higgins, "Sylvia Plath's Growing Popularity with College Students," *University: A Princeton Quarterly* 58 (Fall 1973): 4–8, 28–33.

4. Robin Morgan, "Arraignment," in *Monster* (New York: Random House, 1972), 76.

5. Ibid.

6. Ibid., 77.

7. Ibid., 78.

8. Ibid.

9. Robin Morgan, *Saturday's Child: A Memoir* (New York: Norton, 2001), 309.

10. Charlotte Allen, "Sylvia: No Poetic Justice in Biopic of Plath," *Washington Times*, October 24, 2003, D01.

11. Ibid.

12. Lynne Crosbie, "And a Rebirth of the Sun," review of *Birthday Letters*, by Ted Hughes, *Toronto Star*, February 21, 1998, N14.

13. Peter Bradshaw, "Hate Figure for Feminist Agitators," *Evening Standard* (London), October 29, 1998, 17. All quotes are from this page.

14. Elizabeth Abbott, "Ted Hughes: Neither Saint Nor Demon," review of *Ted Hughes: The Life of a Poet*, by Elaine Feinstein, *Montreal Gazette*, Books and Visual Arts Section, January 5, 2002, 11.

15. Robin Morgan, "Conspiracy of Silence against a Feminist Poem," *Feminist Art Journal* 1, no. 2 (Fall 1972): 4.

16. Ibid., 21.

17. Ibid.

18. Morgan, *Saturday's Child*, 312–13. I use scare quotes around the word "pirate" following Morgan's own use of the word. Since Morgan gave permission for the printing of the texts, "pirate" seems a potentially misleading or at least oversimplifying term, which I assume is the idea behind her own use of the scare quotes. Booksellers, by contrast, frequently list the various privately printed editions as simply pirated editions.

19. My descriptions of the various editions of *Monster* are drawn from Morgan's in her memoir, as well as bookseller descriptions of the rare editions at AbeBooks.com. Ibid., 312.

20. Ibid., 313. On her website, Morgan puts forth a slightly different version of the harassment: "Women all over the Commonwealth carried it further.

They made it impossible for Hughes to give public poetry readings in his own country: English feminists picketed the venue with signs quoting lines from "Arraignment." His reading tours in Canada, Australia, New Zealand, and the United States were canceled because of *threatened* mass protests by what came to be called "Arraignment Women," who also repeatedly chiseled Hughes' name off Plath's grave marker." In addition to suggesting that the harassment was widespread (at least as a threat), Morgan also attributes the vandalizing of Plath's grave to the Arraignment Women, which, I would emphasize, is the only specific instance I have found that identifies the vandals as the so-called Arraignment Women. Morgan, via her assistant, denied my e-mail request to answer questions about Hughes and the feminist protesters, citing an upcoming book deadline and pointing me to *Saturday's Child* for her knowledge of the history. Robin Morgan, *Monster*, "Robin Morgan's Website" 2006, accessed July 8, 2008, www.robinmorgan .us/robin_morgan_bookDetails.asp?ProductID=21; emphasis added.

21. Morgan, *Saturday's Child*, 313.

22. Morgan, *Monster*, "Robin Morgan's Website."

23. It's worth noting, too, that Morgan claims to have offered to remove the poem from *Monster*, provided she could publish the book with "a blank, black-bordered page where the poem *would* have run, stamped simply CENSORED," but Random House refused. Morgan, *Saturday's Child*, 309.

24. I'm thinking here of Linda Wagner-Martin and Jacqueline Rose, both of whom ran into significant opposition when they sought permission to quote from Plath's work. To those familiar with Janet Malcolm's book *The Silent Woman*, the details of these cases will be well known. For discussion from the authors themselves, see Jacqueline Rose, preface to *The Haunting of Sylvia Plath* (Cambridge: Harvard University Press, 1992), ix–xii; Jacqueline Rose, "Ted Hughes and the Plath Estate," *Times Literary Supplement*, April 10, 1992, 15; Linda Wagner-Martin, preface to *Sylvia Plath: A Biography* (New York: St. Martin's, 1988), 11–14. For Hughes's views on Wagner-Martin and Rose, see, respectively, Ted Hughes, "Where Research Becomes Intrusion," *Observer* (Manchester), October 29, 1989, 47; and "Ted Hughes and the Plath Estate," *Times Literary Supplement*, April 24, 1992, 15. I also have in mind Hughes's successful intervention in the publication of excerpts from A. Alvarez, *The Savage God: A Study of Suicide* (New York: Random House, 1971), which were to appear in two parts in the *Observer* during November 1971. After the publication of the first part, Hughes appealed to the paper and was able to have the second installment withdrawn from publication. Malcolm rehearses the details of this case as well. For Hughes's and Alvarez's perspectives, see Ted Hughes, letter to the editor, *Times Literary Supplement*, November 19, 1971, 1448; A. Alvarez, letter to the editor, *Times Literary Supplement*, November 26, 1971, 1478. Such roadblocks have remained even

after Hughes's death in 1998, as Lynda K. Bundtzen discusses in her preface to her 2001 book on Plath, *The Other "Ariel."* Acting on behalf of the Hughes estate, Faber and Faber refused to grant Bundtzen permission for the material she requested use of, initially without even an explanation for their denial. Lynda K. Bundtzen, preface to *The Other "Ariel"* (Amherst: University of Massachusetts Press, 2001), ix–xiii. See the preface to this book for a discussion of my own difficulties.

25. "The Jarring Bell," editorial, *Times* (London), April 10, 2000, 17.

26. Ian Hamilton, "The Last Post," *Australian*, April 8, 1998, B06–B07.

27. My e-mail inquiries to key feminist figures of the 1970s and current feminist online discussion boards turned up no firsthand or even secondhand knowledge of the harassment and protests.

28. Jill Barber, "Ted Hughes, My Secret Lover," *Mail on Sunday* (London), May 13, 2001, 50.

29. Ibid., 52.

30. Hamilton, "The Last Post," B07.

31. Janet Hawley, "The Tale of Two Poets," *Australian*, March 17, 1976, Arts, 10. All quotes are from this page.

32. "Good Omen Turns into a Bad Break for Mathis," *Australian*, March 11, 1976, 2. The column reports Hughes as saying, "I've some beautiful cows about to drop calves and there's no one on my farm to handle it." Lest one conclude that the writers of the "Newsmakers" section deemed mobs of women too trivial to report on, consider that just a couple of days later a report in this section of the paper noted an incident in which another writer at the Adelaide Festival had been mobbed by women, these ones adoring fans. "Girls Find a Goon in the Store," *Australian*, March 15, 1976, 2.

33. Elizabeth Riddell, "That Was the Writers' Week that Was," *Australian*, March 15, 1976, 8.

34. John Doherty, "Poets in Contrast," *Advertiser* (Adelaide), March 9, 1976, 6.

35. Ibid.

36. Stuart Sayers, "Excellent Cake beneath Poetic Icing," *Age* (Melbourne), March 13, 1976, 21.

37. Craig Raine, "Pursued by Bears," review of *Letters of Ted Hughes*, ed. Christopher Reid, *Times Literary Supplement*, November 23, 2007, 5.

38. Lucas Myers, *Crow Steered Berg Appeared: A Memoir of Ted Hughes and Sylvia Plath* (Sewanee, Tenn.: Proctor's Hall Press, 2001), 100.

39. Ibid., 137.

40. Paul Alexander, *Rough Magic: A Biography of Sylvia Plath* (1991; reprint, New York: Penguin, 1992), 358. All quotes are from this page.

41. Elaine Feinstein, *Ted Hughes: The Life of a Poet* (New York: Norton, 2001), 197. Given the absence of any report beyond Hawley's, I assume Feinstein's reference to a newspaper article about the harassment is to Hawley's article,

though I cannot be completely certain of this, since Feinstein does not identify the report Michael Boddy remembers reading. Adding another layer
of curiosity to the events at Adelaide, Ann Skea, who transcribed the performance, reports to me that the audio recording from which she took the
transcription reveals no audible heckling. She does note, however, that "Ted
told [her] that women at the Adelaide festival held up signs saying 'Murderer'
at his reading," and reports that "the feminist antagonism to Ted in Australia
has only started to diminish very recently and is still quite widespread." Ann
Skea, e-mail to author, April 8, 2008.

42. Feinstein, *Ted Hughes*, 236; see also 256, n. 5. I am not certain, but I would
guess that the incident Feinstein describes is somehow connected to reports
that circulated in British newspapers in the early to mid-nineties about the
Daughters of Eve, a group that a reporter for the *Independent* describes as
"a misogyny-monitoring sorority from UCLA" who indicted Hughes, Pinter,
and John Osborne for causing "fatal damage" to their wives (though it should
be noted that other reports identify the women as being from the University
of Southern California). At least it's true that the details of the reported cases
overlap: in both cases the threats were made to the same three men, and
both purported to involve witchcraft-like curses. Paul Taylor, "Strindberg and
the Zuni Curse," *Independent*, January 11, 1995, 25. See also John Dugdale,
"Daughters of Eve vs Ted Hughes," *Sunday Times* (London), July 24, 1994,
25; "Sisters of Vengeance Line Up Their Targets," *Independent*, February 21,
1993, 23; Lynn Barber, "Poetic Justice?" *Sunday Times*, November 21, 1993, 2.

43. Feinstein, *Ted Hughes*, 236.

44. Myers, *Crow Steered*, 151.

45. Ibid., 152.

46. Ean Higgins follows a similar progression in his review of *Birthday Letters*:
"Feminists hounded Hughes out of Australia during the 1976 Adelaide
Festival as 'the man who murdered a genius,' confronting him with placards
reading 'I killed Sylvia Plath—Guilty.' He has faced campus protests in
the United States, where generations of students have been brought up on
Plath's poems, diaries, letters, and autobiographical novel, The Bell Jar." Ean
Higgins, review of *Birthday Letters*, by Ted Hughes, *Australian*, January 24,
1998, 19.

47. I gather from the larger context of the comments that those who refer to
American feminists as the troublemakers have in mind figures such as Linda
Wagner-Martin, Lynda K. Bundtzen, and Susan R. Van Dyne, three prominent American Plath scholars who have openly acknowledged their feminist
approaches to Plath's work. See note 24 for more on feminists' difficult relationship to Hughes and the Plath estate.

48. According to Richard Murphy, this visit was Hughes's first trip to the United
States since he'd lived here with Plath during the first years of their marriage

in the late 1950s. Richard Murphy, *The Kick: A Life among Writers* (London: Granta, 2002), 295.

49. Ibid., 295–96.

50. Ibid., 296.

51. Carole Corbeil, "Eager to Shower Men of the Pen with Adoration," *Globe and Mail* (Toronto), October 20, 1983, 14.

52. Feinstein, *Ted Hughes*, 189.

53. According to one news report, Hughes's reading at Seton Hall was one of two he was to give during his two-day visit to the States. I've not been able to identify where, or even whether, the second performance took place. "Poet Laureate to Give Reading," *Jersey Journal* (Hudson County, N.J.), September 19, 1986.

54. "English Poet to Visit SHU," *Setonian*, September 11, 1986, 12; Frank Emblem, "New Jersey Guide," *New York Times*, September 14, 1986, New Jersey section, 18; Bette Spero, "British Poet Laureate Dabbles as Playwright," *Newark-Star Ledger*, September 9, 1986; "England's Poet Laureate at Seton Hall for Readings," *East Orange Record*, September 9, 1986.

55. Ted Hughes to Ben Sonnenburg, November 13, 1969, Ted Hughes Collection, Manuscripts, Archives, and Rare Book Library, Emory University, Atlanta (hereafter cited as MARBL).

56. Ted Hughes to Ben Sonnenburg, March 6, 1986, Ted Hughes Collection, MARBL.

57. Ted Hughes to Gerald Hughes, December 1962, in *Letters of Ted Hughes*, ed. Christopher Reid (London: Faber and Faber, 2007), 209–10.

58. Robin Morgan, "Letter to a Sister Underground," in *Monster*, 58.

59. Ibid.

60. Robin Morgan, "Monster," in *Monster*, 85.

61. Robin Morgan, "On Violence and Feminist Basic Training," in *Going Too Far: The Personal Chronicle of a Feminist* (New York: Vintage, 1978), 139.

62. See, for example, Tara Baxter and Nikki Craft, "There Are Better Ways of Taking Care of Bret Easton Ellis Than Just Censoring Him . . . ," in *Making Violence Sexy: Feminist Views on Pornography*, ed. Diana E. H. Russell (New York: Teachers College Press, 1993), 245–53. In this essay Baxter shares her fantasy of seeing Bret Easton Ellis, author of the ultraviolent novel *American Psycho*, tortured and castrated.

63. Quoted in Diana E. H. Russell, "From Witches to Bitches: Sexual Terrorism Begets Thelma and Louise," in *Making Violence Sexy*, 267.

64. De Clarke, preface to Baxter and Craft, "There Are Better Ways of Taking Care of Bret Easton Ellis," in Russell, *Making Violence Sexy*, 246.

65. Robin Morgan, "International Feminism: A Call for Support of the Three Marias," in *Going Too Far*, 206.

66. Morgan refers in the poem to Hughes's relationship with Wevill as his second

marriage but also points out that they were not in fact married. Morgan, "Arraignment," 76–77.

67. I assume that this depiction of Wevill alludes to the story of the Jewish rebels at Masada during the first century A.D. who, according to some accounts, chose mass suicide rather than be killed or enslaved by the Roman army. This seems to fit with Morgan's assertion that Wevill killed Shura to spare her rather than leave her behind for Hughes to raise. Morgan, "Arraignment," 77.

68. Ibid.

69. All online postings are from the Sylvia Plath Forum, www.sylviaplathforum .com/archives/57.html. This forum was administered by the apparently undaunted Elaine Connell, author of *Sylvia Plath: Killing the Angel in the House* (Hebden Bridge, West Yorkshire: Pennine Pens, 1993). Following her death in October 2007, the forum was maintained on the Web but without accepting new messages to the discussion.

70. Adding to the provocative nature of the exchange, the debates about these questions are staged largely—even predominantly—by men, suggesting the need to rethink our understanding of Plath's audience even more.

71. While I don't discuss it here, a parallel conversation about Plath takes place in the editorial pages of the *Independent* during this same time. Prompted by a letter from Ronald Hayman that attempts to flesh out more fully the history of the problems with the gravesite as he understands them, the exchange of letters circles mostly around perceptions of Hayman's credentials and interest in the matter. Feminism is an implied concern in only one of the letters, written by Jill Tweedie, who argues that the answer to the problem of the vandalism is for Hughes simply to return the gravestone absent the name Hughes, which for Tweedie represents a fuller understanding of the importance of names as markers of self-possession. This exchange, like the one initiated by Julia Parnaby and Rachel Wingfield, prompts a lengthy response from Hughes that covers some of the same ground as his letter to the *Guardian*, both of which I discuss in this chapter. Ted Hughes, "Sylvia Plath: The Facts of Her Life and the Desecration of Her Grave," letter, *Independent*, April 22, 1989, 19; Jill Tweedie, "The Power of the Namer over the Named," letter, *Independent*, April 24, 1989, 21; Ronald Hayman, "The Poet and the Unquiet Grave," letter, *Independent*, April 19, 1989, 19.

72. Julia Parnaby and Rachel Wingfield, "In Memory of Sylvia Plath," letter, *Guardian* (Manchester), April 7, 1989, 39. All quotes are from this page.

73. A. B. Ewen, letter, *Guardian*, April 12, 1989, 22.

74. William Park, letter, *Guardian*, April 12, 1989, 22.

75. Margaret Drabble, letter, *Guardian*, April 13, 1989, 22.

76. Rhea Vigert, letter, *Guardian*, April 15, 1989, 22.

77. Julia Parnaby and Rachel Wingfield, letter, *Guardian*, April 13, 1989, 22.

78. *Guardian*, April 7, 1989, 39.

79. Parnaby and Wingfield, April 13 letter, 22.

80. As angry as Hughes is toward Parnaby and Wingfield and what they appear to represent (i.e., feminism), he seems even more incensed by the letter signed by A. Alvarez, Joseph Brodsky, Helga Graham, Ronald Hayman, Jill Neville, Peter Orr, Peter Porter, and John Carey, which seconds Parnaby and Wingfield's concerns and asks for clarification as to whether the stone had been removed by vandals or by Hughes following its defacement. One gathers that Hughes felt betrayed by the letter and the lack of any defense on his behalf. Indeed, the opening of his letter makes clear that one real cause of his anger is that Parnaby and Wingfield's letter did "not receive the response that might have been expected." According to Jacqueline Rose, Ronald Hayman authored and circulated the letter; Joseph Brodsky soon after disavowed it. Rose, *The Haunting of Sylvia Plath*, 246, n. 1; A. Alvarez et al., "Problems Strewn on the Path of Sylvia Plath's Grave," letter, *Guardian*, April 11, 1989, 18.

81. Ted Hughes, "The Place Where Sylvia Plath Should Rest in Peace," letter, *Guardian*, April 20, 1989, 22. All quotes are from this page.

82. Julia Parnaby and Rachel Wingfield, "Plath's Place in Literary History," letter, *Guardian*, April 26, 1989, 22.

83. Olwyn Hughes, "Debatable Points from Sylvia Plath's Biography," letter, *Guardian*, April 29, 1989, 22.

84. Nigel Reynolds, "Poet's Headstone Is Returned to Her Unquiet Grave," *Telegraph*, April 22, 1989, P1.

85. Sarah Womack, "Locals Fear Sylvia Plath Film Will Revive Attacks on Grave," *Telegraph*, July 29, 2002, 8. All quotes are from this page.

86. James Bone, "Feminist Tide of Hostility to Hughes Is Turning," *Times* (London), March 7, 1998, 13.

4. *"A Fiercely Fought Defense"*

1. A. Alvarez, "Inside the Bell Jar," review of *Letters Home: Correspondence, 1950–1963*, by Sylvia Plath, *Observer* (Manchester), April 18, 1976, 23.

2. Lynda K. Bundtzen, *The Other "Ariel"* (Amherst: University of Massachusetts Press, 2001), 9.

3. Sylvia Plath, *Letters Home: Correspondence, 1950–1963*, ed. Aurelia Schober Plath (New York: Harper and Row, 1975), 312.

4. Ibid., 290.

5. According to Olwyn Hughes, Ted Hughes gave ownership of copyright to Frieda and Nicholas in the early 1990s. While Frieda and Nicholas shared rights to Plath's estate from this time until Nicholas's death in March 2009, Frieda has acted as the public face and deciding agent for the estate for much of the period since the transfer of copyright. Olwyn Hughes, Olwyn Hughes Papers, 1951–1997, MARBL.

6. The controversy surrounding Anne Stevenson's *Bitter Fame* is well known, so I will not rehearse it here in any detail. What's worth noting is the disclaimer in the author's note to the book in which Stevenson insinuates that Olwyn's editorial oversight of the manuscript was so heavy-handed that she nearly deserves coauthorship credit. For more on the controversy, see Janet Malcolm, *Silent Woman: Sylvia Plath and Ted Hughes* (New York: Knopf, 1994).

7. This description of Olwyn's role is gathered from a note written by Olwyn that accompanies Ted Hughes's papers at Emory University. According to Olwyn, her role in managing Plath's estate began as early as 1964 during Hughes's negotiations with Faber and Faber over the publication of the manuscript for *Ariel* and ended when she withdrew as agent following Ted's transfer of ownership to the children, at which time Faber assumed responsibility for reviewing and granting permission requests. Olwyn Hughes Papers.

8. "A World in Disintegration," review of *Crossing the Water* and *Winter Trees*, by Sylvia Plath, *Times Literary Supplement*, December 24, 1971, 1602.

9. A. Alvarez, "Publish and Be Damned," review of *Crossing the Water* and *Winter Trees*, *Observer*, October 3, 1971, 36.

10. Peter Davison, "Three Visionary Poets," review of *Crossing the Water*, *Atlantic Monthly*, February 1972, 105.

11. Ted Hughes, "Publishing Sylvia Plath," in *Winter Pollen: Occasional Prose*, ed. William Scammell (New York: Picador, 1995), 163–69. The editor of *Winter Pollen*, among other sources, cites this essay as having been originally published in the *Observer* on November 21, 1971. But as far as I can tell, this is an error; a letter from Hughes does appear in the paper on that date, but it is definitely not this one. Whether this essay was in fact published prior to *Winter Pollen* remains to be seen. My own research could turn up nothing definitive. Because it was obviously written in the early 1970s as an opinion piece, and since it was published in Hughes's lifetime in *Winter Pollen*, I have chosen to treat it as a public document rather than as a private letter.

12. For those unfamiliar with the controversies surrounding Hughes's handling of the Plath estate, some context is in order. In early November 1971 Alvarez published the first of what was to be two installments of a memoir about Plath's final days, to be published in his forthcoming book *The Savage God*. The second installment was halted, however, following Hughes's intervention. Alvarez's papers at the British Library include the original telegram sent on November 15 from Hughes to Alvarez, in which Hughes asks him to please stop the publication of any additional installments.

13. Hughes, "Publishing Sylvia Plath," 163.

14. Ibid., 164.

15. Ted Hughes, "The Burnt Fox," in *Winter Pollen*, 8.

16. Ibid.

17. Ibid., 9.

18. Ted Hughes, "The Thought Fox," in *Collected Poems*, ed. Paul Keegan (New York: Farrar, Straus and Giroux, 2003), 21. All quotes are from this page.

19. Ted Hughes to Keith Sagar, July 16, 1979, in *Letters of Ted Hughes*, ed. Christopher Reid (London: Faber and Faber, 2007), 423.

20. Ted Hughes to Keith Sagar, July 18, 1998, ibid., 719–20.

21. Ted Hughes, "Where Research Becomes Intrusion," *Observer*, October 29, 1989, 47.

22. Ibid. Just weeks later, Ronald Hayman's review of *Bitter Fame* on November 10 for the *Independent* provided Hughes with an invitation to reiterate the sentiment of this complaint. Responding to Hayman's selective quotation of a comment Hughes had made about *Bitter Fame* a week earlier, Hughes provides the full context of the quote Hayman had only excerpted: "I dissociate myself from the distorting and often damaging fantasies contained in the thousand publications and the endless teaching and lecturing and debating about her by those who never knew her at all or, as in some cases, met her only for a few hours." He goes on, "We can ignore the idol of the sentimental cultists, whose attempt to use her gallant happiness to smother the bleak truth of these poems is sustained by a simple inability to understand what the poems say." Ted Hughes, letter to the editor, *Independent* (London), December 7, 1989, 26.

23. Ted Hughes, "Ted Hughes and the Plath Estate," letter to the editor, *Times Literary Supplement*, April 24, 1992, 15. All quotes are from this page.

24. Ted Hughes to A. Alvarez, November 1971, in *Letters of Ted Hughes*, 321.

25. Ibid.

26. Ted Hughes to A. Alvarez, n.d, Alvarez Papers, British Library, London.

27. Ibid.

28. Ibid.

29. Ted Hughes to Anne Stevenson, November 4, 1989, Stevenson Papers, Cambridge University Library, Cambridge.

30. Ibid.

31. An unpublished letter excerpted in Janet Malcolm's *Silent Woman*, 46–47, makes clear that Hughes repeated similar attacks to Jacqueline Rose. In the letter he bemoans, for example, how literary critics stand in their classrooms, say whatever they please, and in turn inspire students to do the same. My own attempt to examine this letter in the correspondence housed with Hughes's papers at Emory turned up only an early handwritten draft, which, when decipherable, appears to echo some of those concerns found in Hughes's letters to Alvarez and Stevenson, including a preoccupation with how Rose's interpretations will be uncritically received by young audiences who can't help but be under a professor's power.

32. Hughes to Alvarez, n.d.

33. Ted Hughes to Anne Stevenson, autumn 1986, in *Letters of Ted Hughes*, 516.

34. Ted Hughes to Anne Stevenson, March 16, 1988, Stevenson Papers.

35. Hughes to Alvarez, n.d.

36. Ted Hughes to Aurelia and Warren Plath, March 1966, in *Letters of Ted Hughes*, 253.

37. Ted Hughes to Aurelia Plath, July 13, 1966, ibid., 259.

38. Ted Hughes to Robert Lowell, September 14, 1966, ibid., 260.

39. Hughes to Alvarez, n.d.

40. Hughes to Anne Stevenson, November 4, 1989. In particular, Hughes seems especially bothered by feminists such as Helen Vendler, Marjorie Perloff, and Linda Wagner-Martin.

41. Ted Hughes to Anne Stevenson, January 25, 1991, Anne Stevenson Papers.

42. Ted Hughes, "Prometheus on His Crag," in *Collected Poems*, 291.

43. Ted Hughes, "Howls & Whispers," in *Collected Poems*, 1179.

44. Ted Hughes, "The Laburnum," in *Collected Poems*, 1177.

45. Hughes, "Howls & Whispers," 1178, 1179.

46. Hughes to Stevenson, January 25, 1991.

47. Ted Hughes to Nicholas Hughes, February 20, 1998, in *Letters of Ted Hughes*, 712. Earlier in the letter he explains the significance of the year 1969, citing the "death of Assia and my mother and the general struggles to solve how I could look after Frieda and you" that marked the year. Ibid., 711.

48. Ted Hughes to Keith Sagar, July 19, 1998, in *Letters of Ted Hughes*, 719.

49. In between these two publications, the poem also appeared in *Asylum: The Magazine for Democratic Psychiatry* 9, no. 3 (Spring 1996): 10.

50. Ted Hughes, "The Dogs Are Eating Your Mother," in *Birthday Letters* (New York: Farrar, Straus and Giroux, 1998), 195.

51. Ibid., 196. In his poem "Foxhunt," dated December 27, 1975, Hughes depicts the hound of the hunt with imagery relevant to "The Dogs Are Eating Your Mother." The hound pursuing the fox is described as "A machine with only two products: / Dog-shit and dead foxes." Ted Hughes, "Foxhunt," in *Collected Poems*, 507.

52. Hughes, "The Dogs Are Eating Your Mother," 195.

53. Ibid., 196.

54. In this way, the image of the vulture in "The Dogs Are Eating Your Mother" reflects its image in other Hughes poems, most notably the Prometheus sequence, in which, as Keith Sagar explains, the vulture functions "as the midwife attending [Prometheus's] own necessarily painful rebirth." Keith Sagar, *The Laughter of Foxes: A Study of Ted Hughes* (Liverpool: Liverpool University Press, 2000), 132.

55. John Powers, *Introduction to Tibetan Buddhism* (Boulder: Snow Lion, 2007), 350.

56. Ibid., 351.

57. Hughes, "The Dogs Are Eating Your Mother," 195.

58. Hughes to Stevenson, November 4, 1989. Dido Merwin, a friend of Plath and Hughes during their marriage, wrote a scathing memoir of Plath that, to Hughes's disappointment, paints Plath's destruction of some of his papers in 1962 as an act he refused to forgive or forget. In the letter to Anne Stevenson, Hughes offers Merwin's conclusion as an example of the kind of animosity toward Plath that came from his defenders. Ibid.

59. See, for example, Sagar, *The Laughter of Foxes,* especially 146–51.

60. Ted Hughes, "The Hart of the Mystery," *Guardian* (Manchester), July 5, 1997, 21.

61. Hughes, "Publishing Sylvia Plath," 163–64.

62. In her essay "Secrets and Lies: Plath, Privacy, Publication and Ted Hughes's *Birthday Letters," Contemporary Literature* 42, no. 1 (Spring 2001): 102–48, Sarah Churchwell offers a compelling explanation for Hughes's concern with debts owed. See especially 114–15.

63. Hughes, "Publishing Sylvia Plath," 165.

64. Ibid., 168.

65. Ted Hughes to Craig Raines, November 3, 1984, in *Letters of Ted Hughes,* 489.

66. In her reflection on Hughes's unease with her literary interpretation of Plath's work, Jacqueline Rose offers this helpful insight: for Hughes, "interpretation transmutes itself back into facts. No question. It is the inevitability of this process, its unstoppable nature that Hughes insists on, as if all readings were powerless against the drift. In this world, all statements are proposition, all poems bear the scars of vulgar (mis)understanding almost before they have been read." Jacqueline Rose, "Sylvia Plath—Again," in *On Not Being Able to Sleep: Psychoanalysis and the Modern World* (Princeton: Princeton University Press, 2003), 59.

67. Ted Hughes, "Epiphany," in *Birthday Letters,* 113–115.

68. See, for example, Elaine Feinstein, *Ted Hughes: The Life of a Poet* (New York: Norton, 2001), 106; Erica Wagner, *Ariel's Gift: Ted Hughes, Sylvia Plath, and the Story of "Birthday Letters"* (New York: W. W. Norton, 2001), 182–83.

69. Quoted in Feinstein, *Ted Hughes,* 106. While Hughes uses the image of the fox elsewhere to stand in for Plath, Olwyn's projection of the fox's "woebegone eyes" onto Plath—and the implication that the "loud-mouth, flashing temperament" of the fox represents Plath as well—likely says more about Olwyn's troubled relationship with Plath and her perception of Hughes as her altruistic protector than anything else. For more on Olwyn's relationship with Plath, see Malcolm, *Silent Woman,* especially 47–52 and 189–93.

70. Diane Middlebrook, *Her Husband: Hughes and Plath—A Marriage* (New York: Viking, 2003), 102.

71. Hughes, "Epiphany," 115.

72. Ted Hughes, "Costly Speech," in *Birthday Letters,* 171.

Conclusion

1. To avoid confusion, I refer to Frieda Hughes as Frieda and Ted Hughes as Hughes throughout this chapter.

2. Frieda Hughes, "My Mother," *Tatler*, March 2003, 125. Reprinted in the appendix to Sylvia Plath and Frieda Hughes, *Ariel: The Restored Edition* (New York: HarperCollins, 2004), 13–14; and in Frieda Hughes, *The Book of Mirrors* (Northumberland: Bloodaxe Books, 2009), 32–33.

3. Frieda Hughes, "Readers," in *Wooroloo* (New York: HarperPerennial, 1998), 61.

4. Ibid., 62.

5. Frieda Hughes, "Readers," *Guardian* (Manchester), November 8, 1997, 6.

6. Hughes, "Readers," in *Wooroloo*, 61.

7. The opening line also calls to mind, knowingly or not, Plath's own poems, including "Stillborn," "Barren Women," and "Childless Women." Having said that, I should also point out that Frieda has claimed, rather persistently, not to have read any of her mother's poetry until fairly recently. In her speech on the first public reading of *Ariel: The Restored Edition*, she says that she first picked up her mother's poetry in 1995, only after she had completed her first collection, *Wooroloo*, in which "Readers" appears. Frieda Hughes, "Frieda Hughes's Speech for the First Public Reading of *Ariel: The Restored Edition*" ("P.S. Insights, Interviews, and More"), in *Ariel: The Restored Edition* (New York: HarperCollins, 2004), 11.

8. Ibid.

9. In her 2006 work *Forty-five*, Frieda accounts for these autobiographical traces, describing her poems in *Waxworks* as a collection that "disguised [her] truth in poetry / Of waxwork effigies" in order to avoid "The gawping stares, the gazes" that would "poke and pry" if she were to write more straight-forwardly about "what's happened." Frieda Hughes, *Forty-five: Poems* (New York: HarperCollins, 2006), 95. While many of the poems seem to be about her strained relationship with Carol Hughes, her stepmother, she describes the effigies as "The mothers, fathers, brothers / Born of me." Ibid., 100. In a feature in *The Times* in 2006, which inaugurated her new column on poetry, she similarly explains how several of the poems in *Waxworks* have "two lives: the life of the name in the title of each poem and the 'other' life, often illus-trating an aspect or relationship in my own life." Frieda Hughes, "There Is Poetry for Everyone," *The Times* (London), September 4, 2006, 4.

10. Frieda Hughes, "Burke and Hare," in *Waxworks* (New York: HarperCollins, 2003), 10.

11. Frieda Hughes, "Stop Digging Up Mother's Troubled Past, Says Plath's Daughter," *Independent* (London), November 30, 2004, 15.

12. Frieda Hughes, foreword to *Ariel: The Restored Edition*, xvii.

13. Ibid.

14. Ibid.

15. Frieda Hughes, "One Hundred Per Cent Me," *Guardian*, November 8 1997, 6. It's important to note that Frieda herself rejects feminism, though I would suggest her rejection is tantamount to the common refrain "I'm not a feminist, but . . ." Later in the same article the reporter quotes her as saying: "I'm not a feminist myself. I would describe my position as 'equalitarian'—I believe it's both possible and desirable for men and women to balance each other."

16. "Plath Plaque," *Evening Standard*, January 22, 1998, 10.

17. *Evening Standard*, July 23, 1999, 12.

18. "Blue Plaque for Sylvia Plath," *Evening Standard*, July 21, 2000, 24.

19. "Stir over Plath Plaque," *Evening Standard*, July 28, 2000, 7.

20. Alex O'Connell, "Plath's Blue Plaque Angers Her Friends," *The Times*, July 29, 2000, 8.

21. Frieda Hughes, "Plath's Blue Plaque," letter, *The Times*, August 4, 2000, 19.

22. Frieda Hughes, "A Matter of Life and Death," *The Times Magazine*, September 30, 2000, 21.

23. Hughes, foreword, xix.

24. Ibid., xviii.

25. Frieda uses the phrase in her foreword to *Ariel: The Restored Edition*, as well as in a letter printed on January 14, 2004, in *The Times*, in which she likens the allegations made about Prince Charles's involvement in Diana's death to the treatment her father received, citing specifically how her father was "vilified by feminists . . . who subjected [him] to endless misery . . . right up until his death." But it should be noted that the idea of Hughes's vilification circulates widely, not only in the 1970s and 1980s but even more so in the reception of *Birthday Letters*. Frieda Hughes, "Charles, Ted Hughes, and Conspiracy," letter, *The Times*, January 14, 2004, 21.

26. Hughes, "Frieda Hughes's Speech," 10.

27. Marjorie Perloff, "The Two *Ariels*: The (Re)Making of the Sylvia Plath Canon," *American Poetry Review* 13 (November–December 1984): 10–17; Lynda K. Bundtzen, *The Other "Ariel"* (Amherst: University of Massachusetts Press, 2001).

28. Hughes, "My Mother," 125.

29. Hughes, "A Matter of Life and Death," 21.

30. Sylvia Plath Mailing List, March 1, 2006, http://groups.yahoo.com/group /sylviaplath/message/6231?var=1, accessed July 15, 2008.

31. Hughes, "There Is Poetry for Everyone," 4.

32. Frieda Hughes, "The Family Business," *Guardian*, October 3, 2001, Features 6.

INDEX